THE NATIONAL
WWII
MUSEUM

When
BASEBALL
Went to
WAR

Edited by
TODD ANTON & BILL NOWLIN

TRIUMPH
BOOKS

This book is available in quantity at special discounts for your group or organization. For further information, contact:

Triumph Books
542 South Dearborn Street
Suite 750
Chicago, Illinois 60605
(312) 939-3330
Fax (312) 663-3557

Printed in U.S.A.

ISBN: 978–1–60078–126-1

Photos courtesy the National Baseball Hall of Fame and Library unless otherwise indicated.

Editing, Design, and Page Production: Red Line Editorial

Dedicated to the brave men and women
of the United States Armed Forces.

Table of Contents

More Than a Game

Many would think that winning three World Series while playing professional baseball is the pinnacle of my career. As an athlete, it's what I've trained myself to do. For me, the determination to win is something I demand of myself. It feels natural. And naturally I am proud of what my teammates and I have accomplished.

But when you look at the men and women who have put their lives on the line for people in faraway places that they never knew or met, it's not comparable. I can't put my career and their sacrifice in the same stratosphere. I am in awe of the men and women of the "Greatest Generation" and those even today who answer the call to defend liberty and freedom.

I was raised by a man who proudly served 20 years in the United States Army and during those years, Dad instilled in me a profound sense of appreciation and respect for men and women whose core values are centered on service to others. I have spent my life in deep respect for those who believe in service to others as their ultimate calling. In my mind, no act better embodies that ideal than making the commitment to serve in the armed forces of the United States. These people are the real heroes.

When your dad is your hero, he is and will always remain larger than life. As a kid I went through his footlocker, putting on his uniforms, imagining faraway battles and all the glory that comes with it—a child's fantasy. The reality is something different. Men die—and for what? Is it solely for liberty, freedom, and the right for us to determine our own destiny? To make our own free choices and not have political or economic institutions imposed on us by anyone or by another nation?

Perhaps.

The veterans who fought and those who died sacrificed not just for America, but fought and died for the buddy in the very next foxhole who would have gladly died for them. That spirit embodies a deep and passionate love that we can never fully grasp. In professional sports, we experience a faint shadow of this teamwork, one that exists to achieve the goal of winning in a given season. In sports, the goal is victory, but to the average GI, the primary goal can simply be to survive. Victory in warfare is an abstraction. It sometimes has no real meaning. You just want to make it through another day, another mile. That is the victory. The men and women who won World War II never cease to amaze me and they still are all around us living their lives in quiet dignity, not asking for attention. To them, any personal attention almost tends to dishonor those who paid the supreme sacrifice. All they will say about "The War" is that they were "proud to be part of a team of some 16 million men and women who all did their duty." It is as simple as that.

I respect that. Many veterans in the major leagues set aside their careers to change from one uniform to another. Men such as Bob Feller, Jerry Coleman, Johnny Pesky, Ted Williams, Lou Brissie, Yogi Berra, and scores of others all sacrificed some prime playing years, and still they say nothing about themselves. They prefer to talk about others who they saw do more, or pay the ultimate price. The more I get to know them and listen to their stories, the more I am in awe of the character and integrity that is the backbone of the great and noble experiment that is America and the game of baseball.

I was recently asked to become a member of the National World War II Museum's Board of Trustees. As an avid historian in my own right, this was indeed a high honor. But being on a board of trustees is meaningless unless you are doing something to further its cause. So combining with baseball/WWII historian Todd Anton, a fellow Board of Trustees member, author Bill Nowlin, and Dr. Nick Mueller, president and CEO of the Museum, we envisioned a conference that could honor the men of baseball still among us who served both the nation and the game itself by preserving victory on the battlefront. This conference, held over Veterans Day weekend in 2007, was a magical moment for me. As I sat on stage, I was flanked by two veterans of World War II—Lt. Col. Jerry Coleman, USMC, a Yankee, and Ensign Johnny Pesky, USN, a Red Sox player. It was magic. Not only were these men rivals on the field, but it doesn't get more personal than a Marine and ensign going at each other. It was a priceless, priceless moment for me. You could see how much Jerry and Johnny loved each other.

As part of the celebration that first evening, the Museum presented the attending baseball veterans their "Silver Service Medallions" as a token of esteem from America's only congressionally designated World War II museum. It was an honor and emotional experience for me to be one of the presenters of these medals to these men. However, I had a partner joining me for this presentation— my daughter, Gaby. As she held the tray full of medals, I couldn't help but be struck by the legacy of this great gift of freedom from one generation to another. I guess that is history's way, to leave coexisting generations to define for themselves what freedom means to them. For me, the image of my daughter helping honor these tested men of war made me realize more deeply how much we can learn from those who have gone through fire for us. We can never be reminded too often that freedom is not free. It has come at a terrible price.

As I write this, I am sitting in a Tokyo hotel during the visit of the Red Sox for the 2008 season's opening series. Amazing, isn't it? Some 60-plus years ago, B-29s were raining down a firestorm of death and destruction, and here I am playing baseball with a nation that now values baseball and democracy as passionately as we Americans do. Amazing what those GIs accomplished, isn't it?

It gives me hope for the future.

Curt Schilling
Boston Red Sox
Tokyo, Japan
March 23, 2008

Acknowledgments

◆

This book could not have happened without the enthusiasm and support of the National World War II Museum, its staff, and Board of Trustees—and, in particular the Museum President and CEO Dr. Nick Mueller and Vice President and Chief Operating Officer Stephen Watson.

Thank you as well to Ted Spencer from the National Baseball Hall of Fame and Museum in Cooperstown, New York, for your genuine kindness, support, and belief in this project. Special thanks to Pat Kelly, who oversees all the photographic archives at the Hall of Fame. A huge thanks to Tom Bast and Triumph Books for catching the spirit of this conference, too. And huge thanks to our fellow contributors who, likewise, share a passion and zeal for the greatest game on the face of the earth. Like us, they still get excited every Opening Day! Gary Bedingfield helped oversee all the photo selections and contributed in many, many ways to the success of the project. We're glad we were able to help him make his first visit to both the National World War II Museum and the Hall of Fame.

Thanks to an excellent soundman, Jeremy Haggard, for such a great job assisting on the audio editing. Thanks to a great sports announcer and person—Steve Physioc of the Los Angeles Angels. Steve, your integrity is amazing. We wish to thank our fellow authors—Terry Allvord of the U.S. Military All-Stars, Gary Bedingfield, Frank Ceresi, Merrie Fidler, Linda McCarthy, William B. Mead, Kerry Yo Nakagawa, and Bill Swank.

Thanks for assistance to Steve Netsky at Rounder Books and to a number of people in the Society for American Baseball Research (SABR) who helped in one way or another over the years in assembling information we could draw upon. Thanks as well to Jeremy Collins, Bill Detweiler, and Clem Goldberger of the museum, and Tim Wiles of the Hall of Fame, to Mary Brace/Brace Photo, Warren Corbett, Ralph deButler, Steven Dickson, David Kaplan, William Palmer, Jim Roberts, Ed Washuta, and Lenny Yochim. And to Katie Leighton and to Curt Schilling for the foreword.

We would also like to express our appreciation to Humana for sponsoring the conference and to the Board of Trustees of the National World War II Museum:

When you write a book it can't happen without the support of a loving family. Thanks to my wife, Susan, and my kids, Jamie and Jason, for saying "yes" to another book. There are more to come! Also, lastly, a mention of heartfelt gratitude to my friend, coeditor, and publishing mentor, Bill Nowlin. Your support over the many years has allowed me to believe that dreams are possible, not because of our own doing, but by the power of kindness and generosity to others. Thanks for an important lesson. I hope to pass it on.

—*Todd Anton*

I'd like to thank those all around me—family and friends—who help me keep going. And I'd like to add a few words of what is apparently mutual admiration as well. Todd Anton is an inspiration with his passion and enthusiasm for baseball and for honoring the men and women who served during World War II, which included both of our fathers. Maybe there's a little "conflict of interest" here, but I would strongly urge readers to check out Todd's book *No Greater Love* for its further treatment of several of baseball's World War II vets.

—*Bill Nowlin*

Joe DiMaggio (back row, center) on his way to Hawaii in 1944.

Baseball and War

Our National Pastime

by Dr. Gordon H. "Nick" Mueller
President/CEO, The National World War II Museum

It was December 1944. American forces were facing a German assault in Belgium and Luxembourg commonly known as "The Battle of the Bulge." Many German SS troopers donned American uniforms to cause havoc behind American lines. Their English was perfect: accent-free. How could a GI make sure he was talking to another "Joe" rather than a "Kraut"? The answer was simple: Ask baseball questions. "How did the Dodgers do this year?" "Who is Joltin' Joe?" "What's a Texas Leaguer?" "Where is Ebbets Field?"

You'd better know baseball to stay alive. Americans did. Stories such as this remind us of how baseball's myth and legend are part of popular American culture today. For well over a century, baseball has been the lifeblood of our nation. Even many who aren't fans of the game are familiar with Abner Doubleday's "invention" of the game in Cooperstown, New York, the legend of *Casey at the Bat*, Babe Ruth's "called shot" in the World Series, and the various curses that have hexed the Chicago Cubs for nearly

100 years. Hey, as most Cubs fans say, anyone can have a bad century. That may be true for the Cubs, but for America and its national pastime, that is hardly the case.

Baseball is America's game.

During World War II, heroes from the ballfield reported for duty. Stars such as Hank Greenberg of the Detroit Tigers joined the Army as kids pleaded with him, "Don't let Hitler kill baseball." Radio broadcasts and newspaper boxscores helped create a sense of normalcy on the home front for millions working for national defense. Boys wearing olive drab uniforms—be they from Pennsylvania to South Carolina, from Iowa to California—could pick up a ball, bat, or glove in foreign theaters of war and, if only for the briefest of moments, feel like they were back at their neighborhood sandlot or field with their families and friends. They wanted to be throwing fastballs, not hand grenades. They wanted to hit home runs and "Texas Leaguers," not assault beaches named Omaha or islands named Iwo Jima.

Baseball helped win the war, but not by

inflicting casualties on the enemy or through territorial gains on a map. The game helped remind Americans of the way of life for which they were fighting. It reminded them that they were all on the same team. It reminded them that once victory in this epic struggle was achieved, they could all return to the lives they were used to before the war. Baseball gave veterans their humanity. Baseball reminded them of the boys they once were and were never to be again.

Over Veterans Day weekend in November 2007, The National World War II Museum hosted a baseball conference in New Orleans, "When Baseball Went to War." In no professional sport have more men sacrificed for their country than baseball. This conference was sponsored by Humana and brought to the Museum many of baseball's military veterans, including Jerry Coleman, Johnny Pesky, Bob Feller, Morrie Martin, Lou Brissie, local Negro Leaguer Herb "Briefcase" Simpson who played with the Homestead Grays, and Dolly Brumfield White of the All-American Girls Professional Baseball League.

These presenters were able to provide insight into their lesser-known but just as fascinating stories of their lives in World War II. By sharing their experiences, these veterans of the battlefield and ballfield told a sold-out audience how they felt about their service and how their war experiences changed them both as ballplayers and as men and women. The memories and wisdom of the players who saved baseball reawakened an important image—the greatness of baseball and the character of those who helped save it. It was amazing to see men in their seventies and eighties asking Bob Feller for an autograph as if they were still boys. It was truly a gift to hear the keynote address of legendary Dodgers manager Tommy Lasorda remind us all of the greatness of America and baseball. The conference was as diverse as our nation, but one common theme was as obvious in baseball as it was throughout America—"we're all in this together" and the goal was victory.

In recognition of their service, this conference provided an opportunity to thank these veterans/players. The Museum was honored to do so by bestowing its American Spirit Silver Service Medallion, presented by two members of our Board of Trustees—conference originator and baseball/WWII historian Todd Anton and current baseball pitching ace Curt Schilling of the World Champion Boston Red Sox—to the players in attendance.

The weekend was a grand slam, and as always, the veterans were the stars. Whether the players were in the Hall of Fame or not, the audience was enthralled to hear what these people had done for this nation, baseball, and the world more than 60 years ago. Never once were the baseball veterans bitter over lost records or lost moments on the field. One baseball veteran, when asked about his missing baseball years—those "gaps" in his statistics—responded with typical humility, "Imagine the gaps in my character as a man had I not served." Like all of the other men and women who put aside their normal lives for the duration of the war, they all wanted to—in Bob Feller's words—"Throw a few strikes for Uncle Sam!"

America is glad and grateful that they did!

When Baseball Went to War

by Gary Bedingfield

On September 16, 1940, faced with Japanese territorial gains in the Pacific and Nazi Germany's continued conquest of its neighbors in Europe, President Roosevelt signed the Selective Training and Service Act, better known as the draft. The draft affected every profession, and baseball was no exception. Every American male between the ages of 21 and 36 was required to register for 12 months of military service. These civilian soldiers began arriving at training camps all across the United States in October of 1940. By the end of 1941, nearly 2 million Americans were in uniform. Three hundred of them were professional baseball players.

Major League Baseball was at its zenith in 1941, enjoying a momentous year. Ted Williams batted .406, Joe DiMaggio captivated the nation by hitting safely in 56 consecutive games, and 41-year-old Lefty Grove got his 300th career win. The Brooklyn Dodgers finally made it to the World Series, although catcher Mickey Owen was to be forever immortalized for mishandling a Hugh Casey pitch that cost them the Series against the Yankees. Meanwhile, baseball bid a resounding farewell to the first two major league players to enter military service. Hugh "Losing Pitcher" Mulcahy—a veteran with the Philadelphia Phillies—holds the distinction of being the first major league regular to be drafted in World War II, being inducted on March 8, 1941. The 27-year-old right-hander earned his nickname by losing an astounding 76 games between 1937 and 1940 as a starter with the senior circuit's perennial basement team. "My losing streak is over for the duration," he proudly announced as he reported for induction at Camp Devens in Massachusetts. "I'm on a winning team now."

Detroit slugger Hank Greenberg, one of the first Jewish superstars in American professional sports and a future Hall of Famer, received his draft call on May 7, 1941. "Hammerin' Hank" had played in three World Series and two All-Star Games—he hit 58 home runs in 1938, just two short of Babe Ruth's 1927 record—and was the American League's Most Valuable Player in 1935 and 1940. Greenberg gave up his

Joe DiMaggio reported for duty at Santa Ana Army Air Base in California on February 24, 1943. During the summer, the Santa Ana baseball team compiled an impressive record including a winning streak of 20 straight games. DiMaggio (above) put together a 27-game hitting streak.

$55,000 yearly salary for $21 a month Army pay and reported to Fort Custer, Michigan. "If there's any last message to be given to the public, let it be that I'm going to be a good soldier," he declared.

Despite the deteriorating international situation, these one-year draftees hoped peace would prevail and allow them to return to civilian life having missed just one season. In fact, for Greenberg and former White Sox slugger, Zeke Bonura—who had been inducted by the Army in June 1941—a return to civilian life came sooner than expected. On December 5, they were both discharged after Congress released men aged 28 years and older from service.

Two days later, during the early hours of Sunday, December 7, peace abruptly came to an end as the Japanese launched a surprise attack on Pearl Harbor that sank or damaged 18 warships of the United States Pacific Fleet and claimed more than 2,000 lives. Pearl Harbor sent the nation into a wave of overwhelming patriotism as isolationists and interventionists united in an immediate rush to enlist. Within days, Greenberg and Bonura were back in service. "We are in trouble," said Sgt. Greenberg, "and there is only one thing for me to do—return to the service."

Cleveland's 23-year-old pitching sensation, Bob Feller, was among those who felt an overwhelming need to serve their country. Despite deferment as the only support of his parents, he went to the Navy recruiting office in Chicago on December 9 and, along with thousands of other young men, joined the armed forces of the United States of America. Feller later served in the Atlantic and Pacific as a gun crew chief on the battleship USS *Alabama*.

Hitler's declaration of war against the United States on December 11 merely fueled the enthusiasm. Industrial giants across the nation—including factories, workshops, mills, and mines—swung into action to produce the necessities of war. The vast automobile industry unhesitatingly switched to the production of military vehicles, turning out a steady stream of trucks, jeeps, tanks, and airplanes, while manufacturers that were more accustomed to handling refrigerators and vacuum cleaners turned their straight-line production techniques to the manufacturing of ammunition, guns, and other essential war commodities. Even manufacturers of sporting goods equipment were contributing to the war effort. Hillerich & Bradsby—makers of the famous Louisville Slugger baseball bats—turned their wood-turning skills to the production of stocks for the M1 carbine. Within months of Pearl Harbor, America was impressively living up to the pledge it had given to become the "Arsenal of Democracy."

Although professional athletes were enlisting or being drafted into the armed forces from the beginning, there existed an undertone of disapproval toward seemingly fit men participating in sports and apparently evading military duties. Some thought baseball squandered manpower and should be shut down for the duration. In hindsight, this attitude is understandable, but there is little doubt that for the overwhelming majority, baseball was a major morale booster throughout the war years.

In April 1942, in response to the negative undertones, *The Sporting News* took it upon itself to ask servicemen for their views on the situation: Should baseball continue while they fight and perhaps die for democracy and freedom? An abundance of replies besieged the publication's offices in St. Louis, strongly backing President Roosevelt's January 1942 directive to keep baseball going. Included was a letter from Pvt. John E. Stevenson, based at Fort Dix, New Jersey, who wrote: "Baseball is part of the American way of life. Remove it and you remove something from the lives of American citizens, soldiers, and sailors."

More than 500 major league players swapped their flannels for military uniforms during the war. Some never left the United States, enjoying an almost normal existence playing baseball for service teams as entertainment for military personnel. Others did

The Third Marine Division baseball team was the Little World Series champions of 1944.
James Trimble is in the front row, second from right.

the same in Hawaii and the Pacific Islands. A much smaller group came face-to-face with the horrors of combat and the death of comrades in unimaginable conditions in Europe, North Africa, and the Pacific.

On the home front, major league ballclubs were faced with a huge manpower shortage during the war and overcame this by packing their rosters with youngsters, old-timers, part-timers, and 4-Fs— "physically, mentally or morally unfit for

service." And then there was Pete Gray, a one-armed outfielder with the St. Louis Browns in 1945. There is no doubt Gray could play, and his courage was an inspiration to the veteran soldiers returning home from the war, many of whom were missing limbs. He was featured in newsreels and often visited hospitals and rehabilitation centers, speaking with amputees and reassuring them that they could still have productive lives. Yet, organized baseball continued to overlook the many able-bodied African-American ballplayers who could have helped fill the ranks of wartime rosters. They were allowed to fight and die on the battlefields of Europe and the Pacific but couldn't play baseball on the major league ballfields of America. Fortunately, that injustice was addressed almost immediately after the war when Branch Rickey—possibly fueled by racial tolerance servicemen had witnessed overseas and the existence of integrated service baseball teams in Europe and the Pacific—signed Jackie Robinson for the Brooklyn Dodgers in October 1945.

Late 1945 and early 1946 saw the steady return of servicemen ballplayers, some of whom had been in the military for four years—a vast length of time in any athlete's life. Many—such as Cecil Travis, who suffered severe frostbite at the Battle of the Bulge—were never the same when they returned. The spring in their step had gone, the zip in their fastball or whip in their bat left behind on some far-off battlefield. What once came so easily now rarely appeared at all, and it wasn't only natural ability some were coming home without.

Bert Shepard, a minor league pitcher before the war, had his right leg amputated after his P-38 fighter plane crashed in Germany. Through sheer self-belief and determination, he taught himself to walk and then pitch on an artificial leg—all within the confines of a prisoner-of-war camp. By

February 1945, Shepard was back in the United States and determined to pitch in organized ball. Washington Senators owner Clark Griffith took a look at the amputee's pitching form in spring training and offered Shepard a job as a pitching coach. On August 4, 1945, Shepard became an inspiration to all wartime amputees when he pitched five innings for the Senators against the Boston Red Sox in a major league ballgame, fulfilling a dream that few could have imagined possible.

Adversity also faced Johnny Grodzicki, Lou Brissie, and Bill Fennhahn, all promising young pitchers who suffered serious injuries that should have shattered their hopes of playing baseball for a living. Grodzicki was a promising St. Louis Cardinals prospect before the war. He served in Europe as a paratrooper and was with the 17th Airborne Division when they made their first combat jump east of the Rhine River in Germany on March 24, 1945. Five days later an artillery shell exploded nearby and shrapnel tore into his right hip and leg. Grodzicki was removed to a field hospital, where it was discovered that his sciatic nerve had been badly damaged. There was a good chance he would never walk again. He was hospitalized in England, and then the United States, where he learned to walk again with a cane and steel brace on his right leg. When spring training came around in 1946, Grodzicki was in a Cardinals uniform doing all he

Despite severe injuries, Bill Fennhahn went on to have a
successful minor league career.

could to earn a place on the team's roster.
He pitched briefly for the Cardinals in 1946
and 1947, and then played in the minors
until 1952.

In Italy, Lou Brissie was hit by artillery fire that shattered his left shinbone
into more than 30 pieces and broke his left
ankle and right foot. His leg should have
been amputated, but somehow he was able
to persuade field hospital doctors to send
him to an evacuation hospital where the
limb might be saved. Three years later, in a

specially designed brace, Brissie was on the
mound for the Philadelphia Athletics. He
won a career-high 16 games in 1949.

Bill Fennhahn was with the 5th Ranger
Battalion and hit by machine gun fire in
Germany that broke both his legs, severed
vital nerve fibers, and required 16 months of
hospitalization. Yet Fennhahn still went on
to enjoy a brief career in the minors. Tony
Ravish, Fennhahn's manager when he played
in the Canadian-American League in 1948,
always pitched Fennhahn in seven-inning

Harry O'Neill with the Athletics. *Courtesy of George Brace*

games because he would get tired naturally. "But for seven innings," recalled Ravish, "boy, he could fire that ball!"

Inevitably, some baseball players made the ultimate sacrifice in World War II. Two players with major league experience were killed in action. Harry O'Neill, a young catcher with the Philadelphia Athletics, lost his life in the Pacific, and Elmer Gedeon, a fleet-footed outfielder for the Washington Senators, died in Europe.

HARRY O'NEILL

Harry O'Neill was born in Philadelphia and was a standout athlete at Darby High School before entering Gettysburg Col-

11

lege—a private four-year liberal arts institution—where he studied history. He was a three-sport star at Gettysburg, playing center on the basketball and football teams and helping the baseball team capture the 1938 Eastern Pennsylvania Intercollegiate baseball title as a catcher. O'Neill signed with the Philadelphia Athletics immediately after his graduation on June 5, 1939, and spent the rest of the season with the major league club as their bullpen catcher. He made his only major league appearance on July 23, 1939, as a late-inning defensive replacement for Frankie Hayes against the Tigers.

In 1940, O'Neill was assigned to the Harrisburg Senators of the Interstate League for more seasoning. He entered military service before the year was out. Serving with the Fourth Marine Division, he was promoted to first lieutenant shortly before being shipped out to the Pacific Theater in January 1944, where he made amphibious assaults at Kwajalein, Saipan, and Tinian. In February 1945, he was part of the assault on Iwo Jima and was killed in action against the Japanese on March 6. "We are trying to keep our courage up, as Harry would want us to do," wrote his sister, Suzanna, in a heartfelt letter to Gettysburg College shortly after his death. "But our hearts are very sad and as the days go on it seems to be getting worse. Harry was always so full of life, that it seems hard to think he is gone."

ELMER GEDEON

Elmer Gedeon was a naturally gifted athlete. Born in Cleveland, Ohio, he attended the University of Michigan, where he played baseball, football, and ran 70-yard and 120-yard hurdles. Track was definitely his best sport—twice he was Big Ten champion—but Elmer loved baseball. He was the nephew of former American League infielder Joe Gedeon and signed with the Washington Senators upon graduation in June 1939. The Senators sent him to their farm team at Orlando, but he was recalled in September and made his major league debut on September 18. Gedeon appeared in five games for Washington before the season was over, getting three hits in 15 at-bats.

He was with the Charlotte Hornets of the Piedmont League in 1940 and entered military service with the Army in March of 1941. By May of the following year, he had transferred to the Army Air Force and earned his pilot's wings. Then, in August 1942, his life almost ended in a terrible plane crash. Gedeon was the navigator aboard a B-25 bomber that crashed on take-off in North Carolina. The plane burst into flames and, although he got free from the wreckage, he went back inside to rescue a crewmate and suffered broken ribs and serious burns that needed 12 weeks of hospital treatment. He was awarded the Soldiers' Medal for his exceptional bravery.

Elmer Gedeon (back row, right) with his B-26 crew at Ardmore Army Air Field in Oklahoma in 1943.

In 1944, Gedeon was in England with the 394th Bomb Group as a squadron operations officer. On April 20, 1944, five days after celebrating his 27th birthday, Capt. Gedeon piloted a B-26 Marauder on a mission to bomb German construction works in Bois d'Esquerdes, France. As they approached the target, the plane was hit by anti-aircraft fire and badly damaged. "We got caught in searchlights and took a direct hit under the cockpit," recalled James Taaffe, Gedeon's co-pilot that fateful day. "I watched Gedeon lean forward against the controls as the plane went into a nose dive and the cockpit filled with flames."

Taaffe was the only crewmember to escape the stricken bomber plane. As he hung from his parachute above the French countryside, he watched the burning bomber spiral to the earth along with the Senators outfielder and five other crewmembers.

Death touched the lives of other major

leaguers during the war, including Cardinals manager Billy Southworth, whose son Billy Jr.—himself a minor league player before the war—was killed when the B-29 Superfortress he was piloting suffered engine failure and plunged into Flushing Bay, New York, in February 1945. Frank "Creepy" Crespi lost his brother, Angelo, who was killed in action while serving with the 85th Infantry Division in Italy in September 1944. Former Tigers great Mickey Cochrane lost his son, Gordon, at Normandy on June 6, 1944. Cincinnati coach Jimmie Wilson also lost a son, Lt. Robert Wilson, an Army Air Force bombardier, who was killed when his B-29 Superfortress exploded in mid-air over India in 1944. Hank Bauer, a minor league player at the time who later played for the Yankees and managed in the major leagues, lost his older brother, Herman, who was killed in action while serving with the Third Armored Division in France in July 1944. Lou Brissie lost his uncle, Robert Brissie, who was his catcher when they were growing up. Robert Brissie was with the 354th Coast Artillery Battalion and died in August 1943 in North Africa.

MINOR LEAGUES

The minor leagues, formerly a veritable oasis of baseball talent, were seriously affected by the manpower shortage, with 4,076 players seeing military service. On a daily basis, talent was drained from the game as promising young athletes who had spent summers developing their athletic skills were plucked from baseball diamonds all across the country and taught to fly planes, shoot guns, and maneuver tanks.

Baseball's greatest sacrifice has to be the deaths of more than 100 minor league players during World War II. The stories that follow represent the all-too-brief lives of four of them. Each is unique yet reflective of the common experiences of these up-and-coming young baseball players who gave everything for their nation.

ERNIE RAIMONDI

Ernie Raimondi was a minor league third baseman from Oakland, California, whose brief life was touched by misfortune and tragedy. His brothers Billy, Al, and Walt all played for the Pacific Coast League's Oakland Oaks at some point.

The Raimondis were known as West Oakland's first baseball family. At the age of 16, Ernie caused quite a stir when he signed with the San Francisco Seals. It was 1936, the year after Joe DiMaggio had left to join the Yankees, and after spring training with the Seals, Ernie played his first season with Tucson in the Texas League. By the summer of 1938, he was with Tacoma of the Western International League and leading the circuit in batting when he broke his leg sliding into second base in July. After making a full recovery, Raimondi was called up by the

Not wishing to have the single honor of being the 1938 "pride and joy" of the San Francisco Seals, Dom DiMaggio (standing) passes the buck to Ernie Raimondi, who in turn passes the buck to Bob Lillard.

Seals in the spring of 1939 and was hailed as a major league prospect. Club president Charley Graham said: "This boy Raimondi certainly will be a star. He is fast, has a good arm and is a good hitter." But halfway through the year he went down with appendicitis, prompting the club to release him before the next season. Raimondi signed with his hometown Oakland Oaks for 1940 and batted .274 in 67 games,

Two months after James Trimble's death, Baza Garden Baseball Field, Third Marine Division's home ground on Guam, was renamed Trimble Field.

playing alongside his brother Billy. In November 1940, he married his high school sweetheart, and just two months later their home was broken into. To make matters worse, he got off to a slow start with the Oaks and was released 10 games into the season. At this point, Raimondi seriously thought about giving up baseball. The odds certainly appeared stacked against him, but instead he signed with Oklahoma City of the Texas League.

On April 19, 1944, Raimondi's daughter, Penny, was born, and on the very same day he got his induction notice from the Army. Long before his daughter's first birthday, Pvt. Raimondi was in France with the 44th Infantry Division. On January 9, 1945, as the 44th Infantry Division advanced against German forces near the Maginot Line, Raimondi was fatally wounded. He died two weeks later.

GORDON HOUSTON

Gordon Houston, an outfielder, grew up in Dallas, Texas. He was a highly sought-after semipro ballplayer when he moved to San Antonio in the mid-1930s. Houston signed a minor league contract in 1937 with the Monroe Twins of the Cotton States League, where he batted .320. The following season he was with Texarkana of the East Texas League and led the circuit with an outstanding .384 batting average.

In November 1939, Houston enlisted in the peacetime Army Air Corps and reported to Ontario Army Air Field in California for primary flight training. Somehow, Houston still found time to play professional baseball while learning to fly. During the summer of 1940, he batted .304 in his third season with Texarkana. After Pearl Harbor, Lt. Houston left baseball behind and took up his position as flight leader with the 55th Pursuit Group stationed at McChord Field, near Tacoma, Washington. Piloting his Republic P-43 Lancer—a pre-war fighter plane that never saw combat—it was Houston's job to lead his flight up and down the coast, on the lookout for Japanese submarines. On February 10, 1942, Houston's flight was landing at McChord Field after an uneventful sortie. Attempting to land was another pilot whose radio was not working. He was coming in below Houston's plane. So Houston used the overrun—a grassy area at the end of the runway that was used in case a

plane overshoots a little. What Houston did not realize was that a ditch had been dug during the day to lay some sewer tile. The plane hit the ditch and flipped over. It was like hitting a brick wall at 60 miles per hour.

Gordon Houston died instantly. He was just 25 years old. Services were held at the Fort Sam Houston Post Chapel near San Antonio, and he was buried in the National Cemetery at the fort with full military honors.

JAMES TRIMBLE

James Trimble was from Bethesda, Maryland. He attended St. Albans, a prep school in Washington, D.C., where he was a star athlete. He played football, captained the basketball team, and stunned baseball onlookers with his blistering fastball and hard breaking curve. In his time at St. Albans, Trimble hurled three no-hitters and was never defeated. His coach, Bill Shaw, who was a member of the 1932 U.S. Olympic baseball team, considered Trimble one of the finest prospects he had ever seen.

Senators owner Clark Griffith was keen to get ahold of the youngster and agreed to a $5,000 signing bonus in addition to paying for a four-year scholarship at Duke University. Trimble played baseball at Duke in 1943 and then enlisted with the Marines in early 1944. Within months he was headed to the South Pacific to join the Third Marine Division. He had his first taste of combat on Guam, where he was involved in mopping up the remaining Japanese resistance. Once hostilities ceased on the island, he pitched for the Third Marine Division All-Star baseball team and helped them to a place in the Little World Series.

In February 1945, the Third Marine Divisions left Guam bound for Iwo Jima. After going ashore, they quickly suffered heavy casualties from Japanese artillery fire launched from a hill known as Number 362. Trimble's platoon commander asked for eight volunteers to locate the enemy artillery position. Pvt. Trimble was among the first to volunteer.

The following night, four two-man reconnaissance teams were in foxholes ahead of the rest of the platoon. At midnight, a flare signaled an attack, and immediately Japanese soldiers were among the American Marines in their foxholes. There was shouting and screaming, rifle shots, and grenade explosions. In the chaos, and while still in his foxhole, Trimble suffered a bayonet wound to his right shoulder. Then two grenades exploded nearby. Seconds later a Japanese soldier with a mine strapped to his body jumped in the foxhole, wrapped himself around Trimble, and detonated the mine, killing himself and the young ballplayer.

Two months after his death, the Third Marines ballfield on Guam was renamed Trimble Field. "Pvt. Trimble was an out-standing member of the Third Marine Division All-Star baseball team," announced Major General Graves Erskine, division commander. "His name will not be forgotten and his brave spirit will continue to inspire us in the tough battles that lie ahead."

Lefty Brewer

Forrest "Lefty" Brewer was a pitcher—and a good one. He grew up in Jacksonville, Florida, where life was tough during the Depression years. The family had little money, and they were always moving from slum to slum. But the Brewer boys kept themselves busy hunting, fishing, and, of course, playing baseball.

In 1938, Brewer traveled to St. Augustine for a tryout with the Saints of the Florida State League and promptly won 25 games in his rookie season, including a no-hitter against Orlando on June 6. Brewer was declared "the greatest young prospect to come out of the Florida State League," by league secretary Peter Schaal at the close of the season. Brewer was signed by the Washington Senators in September.

The first major league game he ever saw was from the Senators dugout at Griffith Stadium in September 1938. Brewer was with Shelby and Orlando in 1939, joining the Charlotte Hornets along with Elmer Gedeon in 1940. He was inducted in the Army in March of 1941, and when he volunteered for the paratroopers, he was

Forrest "Lefty" Brewer, 508th Parachute Infantry Regiment,
82nd Airborne Division

assigned to the 508th Parachute Infantry Regiment of the 82nd Airborne Division. He left for Europe in January 1944. The 508th was stationed at Nottingham, England, prior to D-Day. It was there that Brewer played his last ball game. At the request of the people of Nottingham, who were desperate for entertainment after four and a half years of wartime hardship, the 508th staged a baseball game against the 505th Parachute Infantry Regiment at a local soccer stadium. With 7,000 in attendance, Brewer was in fine form. He picked off the first two runners to reach base and the 508th won 18–0.

Eight days later the paratroopers were over the early morning skies of Normandy. Landing in the French countryside, Brewer was with a group of about 80 men who were led by Lt. Homer Jones. They faced a German force at the La Fiere manor house on the Merderet River, not far from St. Mere Eglise. In the words of Bill Dean, who had served with Brewer for more than two years, "One helluva fire fight erupted," and by early afternoon the paratroopers controlled the manor house. Shortly afterward, German tanks and infantry appeared, and the paratroopers had no option but to run for the possible safety of the river. "As I ran for the river," recalled Dean, "I was aware someone was running hard just behind me, and in my panic I took a quick look and saw Lefty, at port arms, running like he was going to stretch a triple into a home run. A split second later I heard a burst of machine-gun fire and Lefty pitched forward, face down into the river."

It was D-Day—June 6, 1944—and Brewer had been killed on the sixth anniversary of his Florida State League no-hitter against Orlando. "I will never forget Lefty," says Dean, "nor how fickle fate is . . . he taught me how to soldier and I made it back . . . he didn't."

THE AMATEURS
Of course, not all ballplayers who went to war played the game at the professional level.

I know only too well how much the game can mean even when it is not played for financial gain. Billy Parish of Celina, Texas, was one such person. Parish was a corpsman with the Third Marine Division in the Pacific, but most of all he was proud of having played for the Third Marine Division All-Star baseball team. Toward the end of his life, Parish was living in a nursing center, where he passed away in October of 2007. Right up until the day he died he would talk of those times, reliving his baseball memories from the hot dusty ballfields of Guam and Iwo Jima.

You won't find the name Billy Parish in any baseball encyclopedia, but the contribution he made to his country, the war, and baseball is just as significant as that of any Hall of Famer.

At first glance, my enthusiasm for baseball might appear somewhat unusual. I was born and raised in Great Britain—not exactly a hotbed for the sport—but I feel I have been blessed having baseball as an integral part of my life since I was 10 years old.

My father introduced me to baseball. He developed a passion for the game as a musician travelling around United States Air Force bases in England in the late 1950s. I was born in 1963, and by the time baseball fans in the States were reveling in the exploits of the Amazin' Mets, my father and

I were more than 3,000 miles away playing catch while everyone else around us seemed to be playing soccer, cricket, or rugby.

When I was 12, my father decided to put together a baseball team of kids from our neighborhood, which was a pretty unusual thing to do since there were only about a dozen teams in the entire country at the time. Something we desperately lacked was equipment—you certainly couldn't buy bats, balls, and gloves from local sporting goods stores—but my father knew exactly how that hurdle could be overcome. A couple of telephone calls to the athletic officers at air bases he'd visited some years before and we soon had all the equipment we needed. He even arranged our first game the same way. I vividly remember how badly we got beat by a team of little leaguers whose parents were Air Force personnel.

For the next 20 years I enjoyed a successful amateur career playing baseball all over Great Britain and Europe. As my playing days came to an end, I developed an appetite for the history of the game, searching for links between baseball and my home country. In 1993, I discovered a World War II-era game program from an all-professional game between U.S. military teams at London's Wembley Stadium. Scanning through the team rosters and dotted between the names of minor league players I noticed Monte Weaver and Lou Thuman of the Senators, Paul Campbell of the Red

Sox, and Ross Grimsley, who would go on to pitch for the White Sox after the war. I was intrigued and excited; I'd had professional ballplayers on my doorstep, albeit half a century earlier!

Finding that program led to me making contact with countless World War II veterans who played baseball in the armed forces. Fifteen years later I remain in awe of these men and of the sacrifices they made. They truly are the Greatest Generation, and I am indebted to them for the help, support, and encouragement they have shown me in telling the story of baseball in wartime.

Thank God Dad Didn't Go to the Polo Grounds

by Todd Anton

This book is a result of a vision started almost six years ago. My World War II/Korean War combat veteran father, Lt. Wallace P. Anton U.S. Army, instilled in me a deep sense of passion for America and baseball—almost in the same breath. Over the years and countless Dodger games I came to know the man who was my dad. He was a man who faced his fears and nightmares and overcame them in the course of his lifetime. And just when I was getting to know my dad, he died on—of all days—D-Day, June 6, 2002.

Shortly before his death, knowing my interest in the subject, he urged me to write about the baseball veterans of WWII. I had told him I thought this would be a great idea for my mentor, Dr. Stephen E. Ambrose, but Ambrose suggested it as a worthy project for a kid full of energy, passion, and enthusiasm. It took five years. Finally, in 2007, my book *No Greater Love* was published.

To me, something more was needed. I wanted every baseball fan to experience what I had and to hear what I heard, not only in my research but also as part of this project. My journey has been an amazing one. I have put on a number of programs over the years, including a discussion of Ted Williams at the San Diego Hall of Champions in 2003, where I met author and Red Sox historian Bill Nowlin. He helped me get my book published. Knowing Red Sox legend Curt Schilling's mutual interest in WWII, Bill and I contacted him to see if he would like to join us in proposing a WWII documentary to various media outlets. To our great excitement, Curt accepted! We then heard from Ollie North's *War Stories* program on the Fox News Channel. Col. North was very interested in the story of baseball at war. As a result, Curt, Bill, and myself were historical advisors and commentators for the show. Not long thereafter, Curt and I were invited to become members of the Board of Trustees for the National World War II Museum, which we both know is a great honor.

As a result of such interest from the media, and Curt's ongoing support, Bill and I approached the National World War II Museum with the idea of a conference on baseball and war. The "When Baseball Went to War" conference in New Orleans and this book are the results.

The museum worked with the National Baseball Hall of Fame, and we brought in the ballplayers you will find in these pages, and more. The subject matter had appeal; the conference sold out.

The pages following, and many audio recordings from my interviews, reflect only a small facet of the service rendered by ballplayers in World War II. The real heroes didn't come home, and the white crosses and Stars of David mark the costly pathway of freedom.

This book reflects the work of a unique collection of historians, authors, and like-minded citizens writing about the greatest game on the face of the earth, all of whom are passionately united in gratitude to this great game. My thanks to all who contributed their time and talents. I'm so thankful to Tom Bast and Triumph Books for catching the spirit, too. This book is a small token of thanks to a generation of men and women who went to bat for Uncle Sam.

Baseball was a game savored by these

Wally Anton returned to New York from combat in Europe and had a chance to attend his first professional baseball game on a 72-hour pass. He had two choices: the New York Giants at the Polo Grounds or the Brooklyn Dodgers at Ebbets Field. Wally chose the Dodgers and generations of Antons are glad that he did!

ballplayers and regular GIs who really wanted little more than to fight off the forces that threatened our society and to come home and pick up where they left off—men like my dad, who sought their humanity in baseball. Upon his return from combat in Europe he was sent to Camp Kilmer, New Jersey. He was given a 72-hour pass. He picked up a copy of the *New York Times* and saw that the Dodgers and the Giants were the two home teams in New York the next day, so Dad went to his first major league game at Ebbets Field. We have all been Dodgers fans ever since. Since then, everyone in my family always says on Opening Day, "Thank God Dad didn't go to the Polo Grounds!"

Stan Musial (left) in the chow line. The location is unknown, but it may have been part of a USO tour in the winter of 1943 to Alaska and the Aleutian Islands.

The 116th Infantry Regiment Yankees were winners of the 16-team ETO World Series in 1943, defeating Eighth Air Force Fighter Command 6–3 in the final game. Lou Alberigo (back row, third from left), Elmer Wright (middle row, second from right), and Frank Draper (middle row, far right) were all killed on D-Day, June 6, 1944.

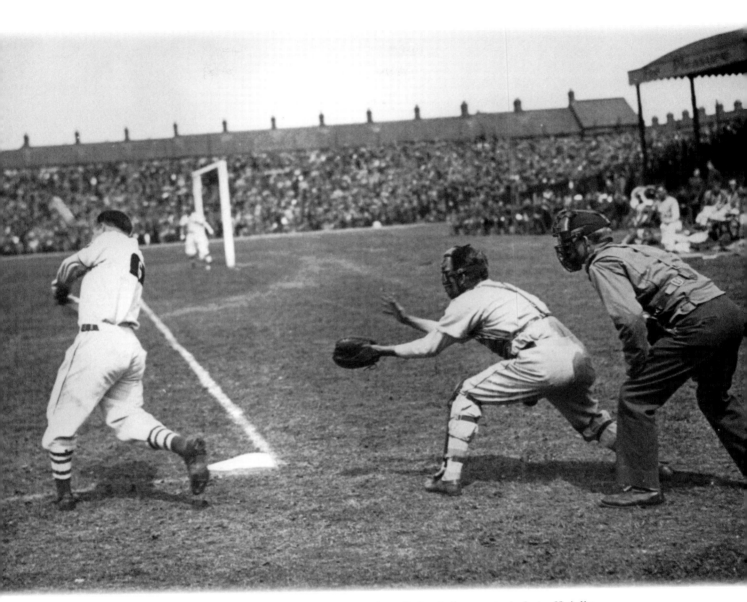

Six months after the first American troops arrived in Northern Ireland, the country's first officially recognized baseball game in 25 years was staged as part of the Anglo-American Independence Day celebrations on July 4, 1942. The Midwest Giants, representing the 34th Infantry Division, defeated the Kentucky Wildcats of the 1st Armored Division 3–2. Here, Sheldon Bowen of the Wildcats is at bat with Orlando Langenfeld of the Giants behind the plate. Captain James Gaynor is the umpire.

The 34th Infantry Division Midwest Giants baseball team in Northern Ireland in July 1942. In December 1942, the division left for North Africa, where they saw combat against Rommel's Afrika Korps. Robert Burns (back row, second from left), Vic Saltzgaver (back row, fifth from left), George Zwilling (back row, seventh from left), and Don Shelton (front row, seventh from left) all lost their lives before the war's end.

Tigers star Hank Greenberg with the team's batboy, Joe Roggin, at Greenberg's May 7, 1941, induction into the Army.

The game goes on. The war always prowled just beyond the foul line. GIs in Luxembourg stacked rifles and helmets on barbed wire for a quick game while comrades demolished munitions charges behind first base.

Upper left: Marine PFC James Bivin (left), formerly of the Pirates and Phillies; 7th AAF 2nd Lt. Tom Winsett (center) of the Red Sox, Dodgers, and Giants; and Corporal Calvin Dorsett (right), formerly of the Cleveland Indians hold a big-league reunion at a camp in the South Pacific in 1945.

Lower left: Jean Jacques de Butler, a captain in the French Army with the 18 Bataillon de Chasseurs a Pied, was present at Rosoy when the 47th Infantry defeated the 39th Infantry by a score of 4–0 in the afternoon of July 4, 1918. *Courtesy of Ralph de Butler*

Babe Ruth, still with the Boston Red Sox at the time, registered for service with the U.S. Army on June 5, 1917, but was exempt from service because he was married. In 1924, however, he was in military uniform with the 104th Field Artillery of the National Guard.

Essays

Chemical Warfare Service: World War I's House of Horrors

The Little-Known Service of Branch Rickey, Ty Cobb, and the Great Matty

by Frank Ceresi

Imagine that you are scared, cold, and hungry, on foreign turf, fighting in the trenches against an enemy that wants nothing better than to annihilate you and your comrades. Imagine that as you inch forward in battle, the enemy begins to lob cylinders of gas in your direction and then follows up immediately by shooting rifle pellets directly at you that are filled with something you vaguely remember as being called "phosgene gas." A sickly smell now fills the air. You are so glad that you had your gas mask on even though it is unwieldy and adds more weight to your tiring body. Now imagine that you look toward your side where your buddy is and see that he could not reach to his belt quickly enough to put his mask on over his face. You see that he took in a small breath of "exposed" air. Then imagine within an instant his terror-stricken eyes opening wide, his face turning purple as he looks through you—and within seconds he is dead. Such scenes of horror dominated trench fighting in France during World War I.

Three of the most influential and celebrated baseball icons of all time—Ty Cobb, Christy Mathewson, and Branch Rickey—served in a special elite unit called the Chemical Warfare Service to combat this terror. They served at the very same time in the same division during the most crucial time of the war. How was it that these three extraordinary men, none of them youngsters pining to show off their youthful mettle, would end up leaving the safety of the baseball diamond and their families and voluntarily join the service to defend their country overseas and battle the enemy in a most brutal fashion?

Precious little has been written about this trio and their link in war, but it is a

The Cleveland Indians train in formation on the ballfield during World War I.

story that reveals much about qualities of character that resonate on the ballfield and in the field of battle. Rickey was 36 years of age and the sole support of four young children. Mathewson, already retired from baseball after notching 373 victories, was 38 years old with a family. And Ty Cobb, fresh from leading the American League in batting, a feat he would do more often than any man in the history of the game, was the "youthful" age of 32. He was also the sole support of his family. Without question, all three could have easily stayed home and aided their country by using their celebrity

to head war bond drives or some similar activity to raise needed capital. But the answer to the question of why they chose the Chemical Warfare Service not only reflects their obvious intense patriotism but also speaks volumes to the strength of their personal character and leadership capabilities. To fully grasp the sacrifices these men made during a time of war, one must first learn of the importance and unique role of the Chemical Warfare Service.

The Chemical Warfare Service, or "The Gas and Flame Division" as it would commonly be called, was created at the height of the war to quell a growing public alarm as news of gas attacks such as the one described previously began to filter home. Soldiers on the front lines wrote their families about "gas attacks," a deadly and virulent horror of war introduced on the battlefields by the Germans two and a half years earlier. At first, soldiers were given simple gas masks to carry as potential protection. But the masks were cumbersome, ineffective, and required the men to breathe through large, unwieldy tubes. By 1918, the military was increasingly concerned and re-doubled efforts to meet the gas threat. After all, more than eight million men had died during the bloody war in just four years! During the summer of 1918, the brass hatched a plan, secret at first, to repel the attacks with a new elite fighting unit officially named the Chemical Warfare Service. Choosing Washington, D.C., as a backdrop to heighten the importance of the plan, they gathered the most influential members of the press to break the news. They wanted news of the unit to receive the maximum amount of coverage possible, not only as a way to scope out men of extraordinary leadership capabilities, but also to inform the public that they would stem the frightening consequence of the German gas attacks in a most effective way.

Major General William L. Sibert told the waiting press corps that the military would combat this "inhuman" form of warfare by recruiting baseball players and athletes with exceptional skill. Significantly, he also said that the Armed Forces would not simply rely on the youngest members of the public to resist these attacks. He emphasized: "We do not just want good young athletes . . . we are searching for good strong men, endowed with extraordinary capabilities to lead others during gas attacks." The die was cast. The "Gas and Flame Division" would only be open to men, strong of body and mind, who had proven themselves to be leaders as athletes and capable of exercising superior judgment in an emergency. Long before Tom Wolfe popularized the phrase, they were looking for men with the "right stuff." What better pool of men to draw from than baseball players who proved their leadership capabilities at the highest level of play? Men such as Rickey, who volunteered to serve in this new and important squad, would be commissioned in as a major. Similarly, his friends Mathewson, nicknamed the "Christian Gentleman" because of his gentle ways, and the fierce Cobb, already American icons, would be recruited as captains. By August all three had been accepted into the Gas and Flame Division.

The pace of the war accelerated quickly. Within a few weeks of their acceptance, the three men's lives intersected in a way much different than when their days were filled with baseball. In September, Cobb and Rickey were told to report for duty

Soldiers trained for the worst with the Chemical Warfare Service during World War I.

immediately and secretly sail with their division to France to join others, including "Matty," who had already been stationed near the front lines for weeks. The war was at a critical stage. The three were to join one another, with Rickey taking command of the unit. They were tasked to prepare for battle with special orders to anticipate German gas attacks where the heaviest trench fighting would be, then turn the tables on the enemy by quickly spraying their flanks with jets of flame from tanks strapped onto their backs. Then, once their tanks emptied they were to lob special "gas grenades" at the fallen Germans and clear the area. The men

were primed! The trio's unit had already participated in several operations supporting Allied tanks and infantry. Now their ranks would swell by a fresh batch of men, including three of baseball's best.

By September the Germans threw caution to the wind and mustered as much of an attack in France as they could. The battles in the northeast of France would be the most decisive in the war. If the Germans could win, the war would continue indefinitely. Then, as the Gas and Flame Division with their famous recruits readying for combat would learn, even preparing and training for dangerous duty could have disastrous consequences. It was during their final training run that tragedy struck one of the three. Cobb, in his autobiography written in 1961, *My Life In Baseball*, graphically described what happened: "I will never forget the day when some of the men, myself included, missed the signal (to snap their masks into position). Men screamed . . . when they got a whiff of the sweet death in the air, they went crazy with fear and I remember Mathewson telling me 'Ty, I got a good dose of the stuff. I feel terrible.' . . . I saw Christy Mathewson doomed to die." Cobb felt that his life was spared only through "the touch of Divine Providence." Cobb was lucky. We shall see that Matty was not.

But fate would have things in store for the trio other than trench warfare. As October turned to November, the rumors of surrender proved true. On Armistice Day, November 11, 1918, the Germans surrendered. The bloodiest world war was finally over. Within weeks, the three, their lives changed forever and inexorably linked by their valor as military men, returned to the United States where they and countless others were met by a war-weary nation wanting desperately to move on. By early 1919, Rickey rejoined the Cardinals and honed one of the shrewdest baseball minds ever. A sick and tired Cobb announced his retirement but after several weeks regained his strength and decided to return to the

game he loved. Cobb would play 10 more years before retiring for good with a .367 lifetime batting average, the highest of all time. The consequences of the gas, however, would linger within Matty's once-strapping system. Upon his return, Mathewson never really regained his health. Sadly, in 1925, after a long series of illnesses, at the youthful age of 45, he succumbed to tuberculosis, his body having been compromised from the exposure to gas from his service to the country and complications inherent from his weakened system.

Today all three men are enshrined in the Baseball Hall of Fame. Their leadership qualities, the very traits that enticed them to join the military elite in the Gas and Flame Division, resonate to this day. Ty Cobb is still widely recognized as being one of the top two or three baseball players of all time. Christy Mathewson, whose life ended prematurely because of his service, is a beloved figure, recognized as being among the top pitchers ever. And the patriotic Branch Rickey's place in our culture grows with each and every year. When he helped set the stage for the civil rights movement by shattering the color barrier, nearly 30 years after his service to his country, the "Mahatma"—as members of the press affectionately called him—opened the door for the equal rights for everyone.

Even the Browns

by William B. Mead

It took a world war to win the St. Louis Browns a pennant, and to me it seemed a small enough price to pay. Like any normal boy growing up in St. Louis during the early 1940s, I had an abiding love affair with the glamorous Cardinals, who, as best I can recall, never lost a game. It seemed that the Browns never won a game until that wonderful war brought the 1944 pennant and in so doing bestowed upon me another love, one that could be indulged while the Cardinals were out of town.

Baseball has long been recognized as a reflection of American values. There is somehow more to it than the playing of a game for the entertainment of spectators. Many fans, myself included, were brought up with a feeling for baseball bordering on the religious. Sportswriters and baseball officials quite naturally do all they can to nourish this attitude, because it enhances their business and magnifies the importance of their work.

This unique role in American life was hard to maintain during World War II, but baseball managed it. Patriotic jingoism was the language of the day. No institution voiced it more loudly, nor identified itself with the war effort more closely, than did organized baseball. Trotting out capital letters in plenty, The Game gloried in its role as the National Pastime, one of the Institutions American Boys were Fighting to Preserve.

This stance contained an element of self-interest bordering on desperation. Baseball officials feared for their business. On January 15, 1942, President Roosevelt laid baseball's fears to rest. In a letter to Commissioner Judge Kenesaw Mountain Landis, Roosevelt wrote: "I honestly feel that it would be best for the country to keep baseball going." It was baseball's green light to continue operating in wartime.

Frivolous activities were frowned upon during the war, and athletes not in military service were sometimes criticized as draft dodgers, though they were not. So baseball adopted a stern wartime visage, did its best to improve morale and inspire the populace, raised vast amounts of money in war bond sales and war charity contributions, and made sure that the game got at least as much credit as it deserved. "Duty and Service and Baseball always have been synonymous," baseball's weekly newspaper, *The Sporting News*, proclaimed in a typically gushy wartime editorial.

Public service and posturing aside, baseball's greatest contribution to the war effort was its manpower. The United States raised armed forces of more than 16 million men and women during World War II, and those drafted first were hale, hearty men in their 20s and 30s. That naturally drained away most of the best professional baseball players, hurting better teams the most and drying up their usual source of replacements, the minor league farm systems.

Many of the best players enlisted, including three of baseball's preeminent stars, Joe DiMaggio, Bob Feller, and Ted Williams. Most of the men left behind to play baseball were physical culls and athletes of extraordinary youth or old age.

With the United States mobilizing for war on two fronts, the 1942 baseball season was expected to be one of steady decline in the quality of play. In fact, draft calls were surprisingly light, and that first wartime season is remembered instead for producing one of the finest teams in baseball history, the 1942 St. Louis Cardinals. The Yankees, managed by Joe McCarthy, won the American League pennant by nine games and were heavily favored to win the World Series. The Yankees won the first game, but the Cardi-

nals won the next four, with rookie Johnny Beazley beating Red Ruffing in the finale on a ninth-inning home run by Whitey Kurowski.

After the fourth game, Enos Slaughter was asked to address the soldiers by radio. "Hi fellows," he said. "We played a great game today and we won again. And we are going to finish this thing tomorrow. Then I'm going to report for duty in the Army Air Corps and join you."

In January of 1943, Judge Landis pulled the prickliest hair shirt of all onto every player lucky enough to escape the draft. He ordered the 16 major league teams to conduct their spring training north of the Mason-Dixon Line. The Florida "Grapefruit League" was replaced by the Indiana "Limestone League." "The wind is cold tonight along the Wabash," commented *The Sporting News*.

The 1943 World Series matched the only two really good teams left in baseball, the Cardinals and the Yankees. Not counting pitchers, the only men in the Yankees starting lineups of both the 1942 and 1943 World Series were Joe Gordon, Charlie Keller, and Bill Dickey. The only Cardinals starters both years were Stan Musial, Marty Marion, Whitey Kurowski, and Walker Cooper. In the fifth and last game, Bill Dickey's homer, only the second Yankee home run of the Series, provided the only runs as Spud Chandler beat Mort Cooper,

Stan Musial of the Cardinals practicing his fielding at the
Bainbridge Naval Base, Maryland.

2-0. Superb Yankee pitching had reversed the outcome of the 1942 Series.

Gradually, this state of affairs made a contender of the St. Louis Browns. Nothing short of a world war could have done so. Among the 16 major league teams, only the Browns had never won a pennant. Most major league teams were listing toward older players, and the Browns were particularly long in the tooth. By the start of the 1944 season, about 340 major league players were in military service, not to mention more than 3,000 from the minor leagues. But not a single player of even the faintest reputation was inducted from the Browns between the 1943 and 1944 seasons. From the Yankees,

Charlie Keller joined the Merchant Marine, while Bill Dickey, although he was 37, and Joe Gordon were drafted.

The Cardinals, unlike the Yankees, were lucky in war. Five of the eight regulars and two of the best pitchers were still on hand in 1944. Whitey Kurowski and Mort Cooper were classified 4-F. Catcher Walker Cooper and shortstop Marty Marion had infirmities that moved them down the draft list because they could only serve in limited capacities.

Stan Musial's deferment illustrated the uneven character of the draft calls from one community to the next. There was no hint that Musial sought or received special consideration; he was just lucky.

The Browns led the major leagues in 4-F players—men physically unfit for military service. The team started the 1944 season with 18 4-Fs, and 13 of them made the squad. Their strength, the experts concluded, was in superior weakness.

The Browns won the pennant that year with 89 wins and 65 losses. Their winning percentage of .578 set a new low in American League history and was indicative of the war's leveling effect. By September 1, a month before the season ended, the Cardinals already had 91 wins and could barely stay awake. Pittsburgh tried, winning 18 of 21 games during an August streak without gaining a single game on St. Louis. The Cardinals were not only better than the Browns, but more experienced.

The first clash between managers Luke Sewell of the Browns and Billy Southworth of the Cardinals was over a place to sleep. With housing short in wartime, the Sewells and Southworths had shared an apartment all season. The Browns and Cardinals were never in St. Louis at the same time. However admirable this display of interleague cooperation might have appeared during the season, it would never do for the opposing managers to sit in the same living room after a World Series game, sipping bourbon and chatting politely with their wives. To the relief of both couples, another resident of the building was out of town in October and graciously let the Southworths use his apartment.

The Cardinals won the Series, four games to two. Browns owner Bill DeWitt complained, "When we won the pennant that year, Landis ruled that half of the proceeds that were to come to the clubs were to be given to Army-Navy relief. I said, 'Jesus, here we are losing money, and for once we get a chance to make some money in the World Series, and we have to give half of it away.'"

National League MVP Marty Marion was unsympathetic. "If the Browns had beat us, that would have really been a disgrace."

With U.S. troops fighting in both Europe and the Pacific, military manpower demands accelerated during the winter of 1944 and 1945. James F. Byrnes, director of War

Mobilization and Reconstruction, instituted draconian measures. "It is difficult for the public to understand, and certainly difficult for me to understand, how these men can be physically unfit for military service and yet be able to compete with the greatest athletes of the nation in games demanding physical fitness," Byrnes said.

If unfit for combat, he said, 4-F athletes could perform less demanding military chores or be put to work in war factories. The result was a draft policy that quite openly discriminated against professional athletes. There were then about 260 4-F players in the major leagues. Even those with serious infirmities were threatened with induction.

J. Edgar Hoover of the FBI rushed to the defense of 4-F baseball players. "If any ballplayers, or other athletes, were attempting to dodge service, it would be our job to look into such cases," he said. "But our records show there are few, if any, such cases among the thousands of ballplayers, and they are entitled to a clean bill of health."

Points toward discharge were awarded to servicemen on the basis of time spent in service, particularly in combat. Bob Feller had been in the service more than four years and had spent most of it as an antiaircraft gunner on a battleship that was in the thick of many South Pacific engagements. Having been given the biggest sendoff of any baseball player, Feller was also accorded the most lavish welcoming ceremony upon his return to baseball in August 1945. He beat Detroit and 4-F Hal Newhouser in his first game and went on to win five games against three losses. Unfortunately for the Indians, Lou Boudreau broke his left ankle again two weeks before Feller's return; Cleveland did not contend for the pennant.

Both pennant races were tight. Thanks to their manager, the Cubs were a light-hearted team. Charlie Grimm was a cheerful man who played banjo, told jokes, and believed that the best players were happy players. He built his 1945 championship team around two veterans of his 1935 Cubs champions, first baseman Phil Cavarretta and third baseman Stan Hack.

Hank Greenberg was discharged from the Army after serving more than four years. He was 34 and had not played baseball while in the service. Detroit went to St. Louis to close its season. Leading Washington by one game, the Tigers had to win one of their final two games to avoid a playoff. The Browns led, 3–2, in the ninth inning of the opener. Detroit loaded the bases with one out, and Greenberg pounded a pitch into the left-field bleachers for a home run. The first baseball star to enter military service had closed the last season of wartime baseball on a dramatic note, and the Tigers were champions of the American League.

Sportswriters were asked to evaluate the two 1945 champs and predict the winner.

Warren Brown, a witty Chicago writer, said neither team could win a World Series. The Series went seven games and the Tigers were World Champions.

A succession of shadowy figures flitted in and out of baseball during the war. The most memorable wartime players were two men and a boy who overcame obstacles to make the major leagues. Bert Shepard, a pitcher, was missing a leg. Joe Nuxhall, a pitcher, was too young. Pete Gray, an outfielder, was missing an arm.

An Army Air Corps pilot and lieutenant, Shepard was shot down on May 21, 1944, while strafing a German truck convoy. He woke up 10 days later in a German hospital for prisoners of war and found that his leg had been amputated between the knee and ankle.

Another prisoner made him an artificial leg, and Shepard was running within a month. He returned home in an exchange of wounded prisoners and was sent to Walter Reed, the Army hospital in Washington, D.C.

To improve the morale of the other wounded men, the War Department sent Shepard, 25, to the 1945 spring training camps of the Yankees and Senators. Washington manager Ossie Bluege agreed to a trial and was not aware of Shepard's artificial leg until he saw him dressing. Shepard was signed as a coach. His pitching was not considered up to major league caliber, although he made one relief appearance in 1945, yielding only three hits and one run in five innings. On July 10, 1945, he beat the Dodgers in an exhibition game played to benefit war charities.

On June 10, 1944, before 3,510 fans at Crosley Field in Cincinnati, manager Bill McKechnie of the Reds sent left-hander Joe Nuxhall to pitch against the Cardinals. At 15, Nuxhall was, and is, the youngest player ever to appear in a major league game. In 1945, with Nuxhall, now 16, farmed out, the Cincinnati pitching staff ranged in age from Herm Wehmeier, 18, to Hod Lisenbee, 46, who in 1927 had won 18 games for the Washington Senators. Nuxhall returned to the Reds in 1952 and pitched 16 seasons in the major leagues.

Pete Gray was born Peter J. Wyshner in Nanticoke, Pennsylvania, a scruffy coal-mining town near Wilkes-Barre. Ethnic names were not in vogue, so the Wyshners changed their name to Gray. At the age of six, young Peter hopped a farmer's provision wagon, fell off, and caught his right arm in the spokes. The arm was mangled and had to be amputated above the elbow.

Despite his handicap, Gray was determined to play professional baseball. He learned to bat from the left side and mixed line drives with well executed bunts. Gray's handicap hindered him more in the field than at bat. With only one arm, he had to catch the ball with a glove and throw it with the glove off. Gray managed this cleverly and deftly.

In 1940, Max Rosner, the promoter-manager of the Brooklyn Bushwicks, an outstanding semipro team, scoffed at Gray when he requested a tryout. Gray handed Rosner a $10 bill. "Take this and keep it if I don't make good," he said. Rosner was impressed. Besides, he knew that a one-armed player would attract fans.

The Memphis Chicks of the Class A Southern Association signed Gray in 1943. He batted .299 and began to receive nation-wide publicity. In 1944, he blossomed into a star and was voted the most valuable player in the league. During two seasons, he struck out only 15 times. The War Department made movies of his play and showed them to wounded servicemen in hospitals.

The Browns, defending American League champions, purchased Gray in 1945 because of his playing skills, not his ability to draw fans. Gray had his heroic moments. He won a game in Detroit with a line drive past third that drove in two runs. Pitchers tried to blow fastballs past him but were unable to. Bob Feller, who later barnstormed with him, said that even he could not get a fastball past Gray. American League pitchers soon found that Gray was a sucker for a change-up.

Many of his Browns teammates disliked him personally and believed he lost a half-dozen to a dozen games because runners often were able to take an extra base while Gray fielded a ball. He returned to the minors and played through 1949.

Wartime baseball ended much more abruptly than it began. As the quality of play returned to prewar standards in 1946, dozens of wartime players were brusquely discarded. Most service veterans regained their baseball skills quickly, but Cecil Travis of Washington, an outstanding hitter before the war, suffered frozen feet in the Battle of the Bulge and could no longer play well.

Lou Brissie, a minor league pitcher before the war, was badly wounded in Italy. Nevertheless, he developed into a star pitcher for the Athletics after the war and became a symbol for handicapped veterans.

The Browns finished seventh in 1946 and never again raised their heads. The team was sold three times until final owner Bill Veeck sold the Browns to Jerold Hoffberger, a Baltimore brewing executive, who renamed them the Baltimore Orioles. The Browns' last season in St. Louis was in 1953. They finished last.

[EDITOR'S NOTE: Condensed from William B. Mead's book *Baseball Goes To War* (originally published as "Even The Browns") with permission of the author. Condensed from the book by Bill Swank.]

Above: To solve a shortage of baseball caps, members of Major Pappy Boyington's fighter squadron offered to down a Japanese Zero for every cap sent them by players in the World Series. Twenty caps from the St. Louis Cardinals arrived and these 20 original members of the squadron accounted for 48 enemy planes, with a large percentage coming after October. The Marine pilots posed on the wings of a Corsair in this December 1943 photograph.

Left: Around the world, baseball infiltrated daily life. Adjacent to a military outpost, youngsters adapt the game to South Pacific terrain.

Leisure time ball games played by American servicemen could be seen all across England throughout the war. Here, Gene Thompson, former California League outfielder, swings at a pitch while playing for the 306th Bomb Group in 1943.

Upper right: Medics at an aid station in France during World War I play baseball with their masks on.

Lower right: Joe DiMaggio (far left) and Pee Wee Reese (second from right) sign baseballs for their commanding officers, Vice Admiral Robert L. Ghormley (second from left) and Brigadier General William J. Flood (far right). Reese's Navy team beat DiMaggio's Army team for the Central Pacific Area Service Championship in 1944.

Phil Rizzuto (far right) talks baseball in the Pacific, where he served with the Navy.

Ballplayers

Moe Berg:
Baseball Player Turned Spy

◆

by Linda McCarthy

". . . It was the toppest secret in World War II, maybe the greatest in any war ever waged. Could and would the Nazis make the atom bomb? That is what they asked me to find out."
—Moe Berg, in an undated page of handwritten notes collected by his sister Ethel

While establishing the CIA Museum, I became familiar with hundreds of inspirational and captivating individuals who had worked for different facets of American intelligence throughout history. Starting with George Washington, considered this country's first spy chief for his strategic use of espionage and subterfuge during the Revolutionary War, there are innumerable patriots whose contributions to our national security seep from the shadows. Many were ultimately featured in exhibits and publications I produced for the Museum, which com- memorated its 20th anniversary in 2008. Of these countless clandestine warriors, none was more compelling to me personally than the baseball player turned spy, Morris "Moe" Berg.

A number of factors spurred what colleagues initially viewed as my curious obsession with Berg. Surely it was his time as catcher for my hometown team, the late, sometimes great Washington Senators. Surely it was his love of books, which helped fuel disdain for Hitler, who summarily burned them. Most assuredly, it was his unselfish service as a member of the World

Moe Berg (center) on assignment somewhere in Venezuela.

War II-era Office of Strategic Services, now considered America's first intelligence agency.

Researching the various OSS artifacts that had been gifted to the Museum, I became intimately familiar with the OSS as an upstart spy organization and as a blueprint for the CIA, its Cold War successor. Dusting the caltrops (designed to puncture tires), limpet (waterproof case for explosives used to destroy enemy ships), and the 16mm Matchbox camera (so named because its size closely resembled a box of penny matches) stoked an unrelenting fascination with all things OSS, most notably, learning what I could about the men and women who willingly volunteered for it.

A number of these eager enlistees were Hollywood and society A-listers, including Academy Awarding-winning film director

Berg was a backup catcher with the Red Sox from 1935 to 1939.

John Ford, motion picture heartthrob Sterling Hayden, and future *French Chef* Julia (McWilliams) Child. Many were drawn to the overseas derring-do promised by the new covert agency; most would later openly credit their involvement to OSS chief, Major General William Donovan, called "Wild Bill" for his Medal of Honor heroics in the First World War.

Another celebrity recruit to the OSS and its unorthodox brand of warfare and intelligence-gathering was Moe Berg, a veteran of 15 seasons in the majors spent principally as a utility catcher.

Like most, I had a hard time understanding at first how a ballplayer better known as Ted Lyons' batterymate could find professional and personal satisfaction as a spy. But there is much, as I discovered while trolling OSS records (now declassified), that suggests just why the life of an undercover operative appealed to Berg and why he was so undeniably good at it.

First and foremost, Berg was a true patriot, ready to place himself in harm's way when, quite frankly, he didn't have to bother. Like many of the Greatest Generation, Berg had established himself in his chosen occupation, that of major league catcher, living out what remained of his career as a player-coach (less player, a little more coach) with his fifth and final team, the Boston Red Sox.

But it wasn't enough.

Taking stock of world events one summer's day a year and a half before the U.S. officially entered World War II, Berg reflected aloud to sportswriter Arthur Daley: "Europe is in flames, withering in a fire set by Hitler. All over that continent men and women and children are dying. Soon we too will be involved. And what am I doing? I'm sitting in the bullpen, telling jokes to the relief pitchers."

Barely a month following the attack on Pearl Harbor, Berg abandoned his comfortable life in the majors, eventually volunteering for the Office of Strategic Services. By that very act, Berg demonstrated his unwavering affection for America at the risk of great personal peril.

Certainly, if one of baseball's first big-time Jewish players, working as undercover operative for the Allies, were caught and his cover blown, Hitler would have made an extreme example of Berg, both for the chance to have such electrifying developments depicted in newsreels playing in movie theaters throughout America and as a bold, unmistakable message to others with similar inclinations.

Despite his many behind-the-lines missions across the European continent, Berg was never captured. Researching his file, it became evident to me how he had managed to evade German counterintelligence rings: Berg was just as adept at calling signals in the field as he was behind home plate.

Effective undercover operatives must think clearly, quickly, and panoramically. These qualities just happen to be the hallmarks of a credible catcher.

Spies must have a strong mental and physical constitution for the work. Sent into occupied Yugoslavia to assess the prospects of rival resistance groups, Berg hiked and climbed his way over miles of rugged mountains to meet with leaders of both warring factions in their respective hilltop hideouts. It was but one instance where Berg the Agent channeled Berg the Athlete.

Field operatives must be able to reasonably tolerate what can, at times, be a lonely and solitary existence. For all the folklore surrounding his social goings-on back in the States, including routine invitations to embassy functions while playing for the Senators, the former ballplayer relished life alone and on the road.

This predilection for the nomadic served Berg well in places such as Italy. While assigned to Rome, he was tasked with obtaining all available information, mainly from disaffected Italian scientists, regarding the location and doings of Germany's considerable brain trust. Werner Heisenberg, winner of the 1932 Nobel Prize for physics, was considered a target of exceptionally high value. Despite the importance of such missions, they sometimes generated consternation among Berg's handlers, who eschewed their inability to bureaucratically keep track of him.

And Berg was smart. Sportswriter John Kieran dubbed him "Professor Moe," for all the cerebral commentary concerning the derivation of words, the position of the planets, and similarly uncharacteristic dugout conversation that came to define some of Berg's more engaging contributions to America's pastime.

As entertaining as Berg's monologues were to bench-riding teammates, it was the game smarts the catcher customarily brought to each inning that earned him a following among some of the premier pitchers of the period. Reading a diamond, much like a chess master analyzes the board and the possible moves it holds, became a noted specialty.

"Counterespionage," he once labeled such game day tactics, a tip of the cap to his spy savvy.

Permanently hobbled by a knee injury suffered while catching for the White Sox, Berg's playing time became markedly sporadic. Still, this did little to detract from his standing with icons such as future Hall of Famer Ted Lyons, who deemed Berg's signal-calling "flawless."

"[I]n the years he was to catch me, I never waved off a sign. Few pitchers did," Lyons declared.

The importance of native intellect to future field agents is not lost on those recruiting them, whether to fight in World War II or in today's war on terror. No matter the unique set of circumstances, a dumb spy is a dead spy.

Berg's brains served him well, from Fenway to France. Of his impressive intellectual pursuits, foreign languages were a particular passion and pleasure. There are disagreements as to the precise number Berg spoke and at what exact level of proficiency. The OSS didn't parse such distinctions when sending Berg on a mission. It cared only that he could effectively communicate with the locals in the battle theater where he was

Berg relaxing between duties in Switzerland. Among his possible duties was the assassination of German physicist Werner Heisenberg. In the end, it wasn't deemed necessary.

operating at any given moment.

All these attributes aided Berg in his most demanding undercover assignment: determining if Germany had anything comparable to America's super-secret Manhattan Project.

It was a continual worry of the Allies that the Third Reich, with its abundance of famed scientists, was creating its own version of an atomic bomb. In December 1944, the OSS dispatched Berg, devoid of any formal schooling in nuclear physics, into Switzerland to hear a talk by Werner Heisenberg—a principle focus of those field interviews Berg had conducted with his Italian contacts.

Although educated at two Ivy League universities—Princeton and Columbia—

most of the eclectic knowledge Berg absorbed he happily learned on his own, through readings and conversations with experts in particular subjects.

To the German he had learned as a Princeton undergrad, Berg added phrases and mathematical formulas characteristically introduced when discussing theoretical and applied physics. These critical intelligence nuggets he obtained during pre-mission briefings and self-tutorials. Berg took this considerable background prep to Zurich, where Heisenberg, probably the guiding force behind any attempt by Hitler to produce his own weapon of mass destruction, was to make a rare public appearance.

Berg was armed with a pistol (to eradicate Heisenberg if he uttered anything alluding to a Wunderwaffe) and a lethal cyanide or "L" pill (for the secret operative, if he were captured and tortured). Scribbling pages of notes, Berg leaned on Heisenberg's lecture. Observing the crowd's reaction to it, as well as Heisenberg's delivery and demeanor, Berg gleaned nothing from the evening's events that hinted Hitler had embarked on a campaign to build an atomic bomb.

Later, at an informal get-together Berg attended, Heisenberg openly despaired of Germany's ongoing reversal of fortunes. To OSS operative Moe Berg, Heisenberg's revealing comments meant Germany had no weapon on the scale of America's Little Boy and Fat Man in production. The baseball player turned spy had, as they say in the intel biz, proved a negative.

The more I learned about Berg, the more I wanted to depict something of his incredible service in the CIA Museum.

When I first set out to honor Berg, his celebrity was limited primarily to Jewish enclaves in cities where he had played, most notably Chicago. Even at the CIA, few had heard of him. While some of Berg's memorabilia had found a fitting home in Cooperstown, a large portion had not yet made it to the auction block.

As representative artifacts, I settled for a couple of Berg ball cards purchased from a local shop. Within a few weeks, they became two of the most popular items on display in the Museum.

To the cards, I later added the bat Berg used during his last season as a player, a rare find that further elevated the former covert operative's public profile. Members of the press began to steadily dun the Agency's Public Affairs Office for access to the exhibit. I lost count of the number of print and broadcast media stories generated by the Moe Show, as I took to calling the phenomenon.

These particular cards and bat are no longer at the CIA Museum. They are mine, and they followed me home when I left the Agency in 1997.

Other "Moe-mentous" collectibles I've been fortunate to acquire include the actual pass issued to Berg, permitting him attendance at the Nuremberg Trials. His signature is clearly evident on the pass, even after all these years.

With my Berg memorabilia safely stored in an underground vault, I use photos of the artifacts in talks I give around the nation, highlighting the extraordinary life of Moe Berg, an intellectually gifted utility catcher who found his true calling as an undercover operative, serving with distinction behind the lines during World War II.

I guess my friends were right. Berg *is* an obsession.

[EDITOR'S NOTE: Because the CIA Museum is housed inside the secured Agency compound in Northern Virginia, it is not open to the public.]

Yogi Berra and the D-Day Invasion

by Bill Nowlin

"I never saw so many planes in my life. It was like a black cloud."
— Yogi Berra

My dad didn't know the first thing about baseball," says Yogi Berra. "My oldest brother was the best ballplayer in the family. He could have gone with Cleveland; my dad didn't let him go." Yogi benefited by being the younger brother, and he signed with the New York Yankees, leading him to an unparalleled 10 World Championships, three MVP awards, and to 15 consecutive years on American League All-Star teams. Berra was elected to the National Baseball Hall of Fame in 1972.

Signed by the New York Yankees early in 1943 as a 17-year-old prospect, Larry Berra was already known as Yogi on the ballfield when he was assigned to catch for the Norfolk Tars in the Class B Piedmont League. There was a war going on, and when he turned 18, he joined the Navy.

He took boot camp in Bainbridge, Maryland, but then was shipped right back to Norfolk. As Berra tells it, "I got tired of sitting around." When a call went out for volunteers to join the "amphibs," he signed up right away, not necessarily knowing quite what he was getting into. He was assigned to train on Landing Craft, Support (Small) rocket boats—small, maneuverable 36-foot flat-bottom boats that were deployed as the first close-up naval offense. Each boat was equipped with 48 rockets, one twin .50-caliber machine gun midship, two .30-caliber machine guns at the stern, and 12 smoke pots to lay a smoke screen upon return. They also provided machine gun support for the troops making amphibious landings.

One of the first successful deployments of these craft in the Mediterranean Theater was during the invasion of Sicily (Operation

Yogi (right) with his brother and father.

Husky) in July of 1943. The crews and officers from that invasion, known as Huskies, returned to the States to help train others in an expansion of the LCS(S) Rocket Boat Program, which was prepared in anticipation of the Allied invasion of Normandy for Omaha and Utah beaches planned for early June 1944. Some 75 crews, comprised of one officer and six crewmen, trained in secret during January 1944, forbidden to write home about the nature of their work. At first, Berra did not know how dangerous the work could be. "I didn't know a damn thing about them," he told Oliver North. "I just wanted to do something, and move out. . . . I kind of enjoyed it. We had our own boat."

After completing training in February, the sailors headed north to Halifax, Nova Scotia, and then shipped out to England in early March 1944 to join in preparation for the Allied invasion of France on D-Day. Seaman Second Class Lawrence P. Berra was assigned to an LCS(S) rocket boat, under Ensign Stoke P. Holmes aboard the attack transport APA-33 USS *Bayfield*, a very active ship in World War II. Commissioned in November 1943, it was the flagship command vessel for the Utah Beach landing during D-Day under Rear Admiral Don Moon and shortly afterward headed through the Straits of Gibraltar to take part in the invasion of southern France on August 15. The *Bayfield* returned stateside for overhaul in September, and traveled to the Pacific in time to help land Marines on Iwo Jima in February 1945. In late 1945 and early 1946, it helped support the occupation of Japan. Later that year, the *Bayfield* was in Bikini at the time of atomic testing there and saw further duty during the Korean War. During Vietnam, the vessel served as a floating barracks off Danang before being decommissioned in 1969.

Early on the morning of D-Day itself, the *Bayfield* lowered various craft into the waters off Normandy, including LCVPs (Landing Craft, Vehicle, Personnel—the so-called Higgins boats) and the four LCS(S) rocket boats on which Berra saw duty. Berra's rocket boat was lowered off the *Bayfield* around 4:30 in the morning and took up a position several thousand yards off Utah Beach, where the rocket boats rendezvoused, 24 in all—12 for Omaha and 12 for Utah. They followed a lead boat and within 300 yards of the beach started

lobbing rockets at targets to try to take out machine gun nests and land mines and to support the troops being landed on the beach with machine gun fire. Berra said, "The Allied airplanes were still pounding the daylights out of the area when we started in. . . . After unloading our rockets onto Utah Beach at 6:00 AM on D-Day, we were diverted between Omaha and Utah beaches as patrol support with our machine guns. . . . We had some confrontations with enemy aircraft over the next several days unloading our 30 calibers and twin 50s." Berra adds, "We stayed on the water for 10 days. They gave us C-rations to eat while we were on it. Slept on it. And we finally got back on the ship." Despite being right in the midst of intense action, he was more in awe than scared. "I enjoyed it. . . . Being a young guy, I thought it was like the Fourth of July, to tell you the truth. I said, 'Boy, it looks pretty, all the planes coming over.' I was looking out and my officer said, 'You better get your head down in here!'" He told North, "I never saw so many planes in my life. It was like a black cloud." Others perhaps better appreciated the dangers. Berra says most of the men called the LCS(S) "landing craft suicide squad."

William Palmer's pioneering book on the subject, *We Called Ourselves Rocketboatmen*, records Ensign Lemuel C. Laney's memories of Berra's crew under Holmes' command: "We drove in at 6:00 AM across

The boat used by Yogi Berra on D-Day. *Photo by Ensign William H. Palmer, courtesy of Bill Palmer*

from Ensign Stoke P. Holmes. We laid all our rockets into the beach. I observed Holmes' crew disappear in all the smoke from the shelling from the battleships but on the way back to the *Bayfield* I saw the Holmes rocket boat coming out of the smoke with crew on their way back safely." Berra has stated, "The officers made it clear that we were not going to be spectators in combat. When we saw the boats themselves we didn't have any doubts. . . . The boat really wasn't much of anything except a platform to carry a whole lot of firecrackers. My job

was firing the machine gun."

Back home in the United States, as soon as word spread that the long-anticipated invasion of the European mainland had begun, all baseball games for the day were canceled in recognition of the gravity of the occasion.

Berra's rocket boat continued its work, taking onboard some of the men who had drowned in attempting to land. After several days, some of the men got off and went onto the beach, but Yogi said, "No, I'm staying on the boat." The rocket boat men only lost one man, S2c Wilton Smith, who was assigned to Laney's crew, who walked onto Utah Beach and was blown up by a landmine three weeks after D-Day. After the role of the rocket boats during the Utah Beach landing operation was done, Berra was transferred on June 27 to the USS *Barnett* and served during Operation Dragoon, the Allied invasion of southern France on August 15, 1944. Ensign Nick Zuras, who commanded the boat on which Yogi served in this invasion, recalls the crew change at Bizerte, where Berra boarded the ship, climbing aboard with a duffel bag that had a catcher's mitt strapped to it. No one could have known that Berra would go on to play in 14 World Series with the Yankees and to win more rings than he could wear. Zuras also recalled, "We would often find him asking the crew to pitch to him. In one instance, when Churchill's entourage came through the camp at break-neck speed to observe the readiness of the LSTs for the invasion, he nearly ran Larry over while in a catcher's stance."

After the work he'd done in support of both invasions, Berra expected to be sent to the Pacific but was returned to Norfolk, where he was informed he was being sent to the submarine base at New London, Connecticut. Taken aback, he declared, "Wait a minute. I didn't volunteer for any submarines!"—only to be reassured that he was being asked to help make up the baseball team under Jim Gleeson. He was still just a prospect but hit a home run in his first pinch-hitting assignment and became a regular from that point on. After discharge, Yogi played most of 1946 with the Newark Bears in the International League, debuting in the big leagues on September 22 for the first of 19 years as a major league ballplayer.

In 2000, Lawrence Berra was awarded the Medale de Jubile by the people of Normandy, France. The medals had been struck on the 50th anniversary of D-Day for all those who had participated in the liberation. Berra was one of several thousand who did not make it to Normandy for the commemoration but were given the medals at a later date.

Sources:
• Palmer, William. *We Called Ourselves Rocketboatmen* (Dorrance Publishing, 2008).
• Interview of Yogi Berra by Keith Olbermann, June 2004. www.msnbc.com.
• Interview of Yogi Berra by Oliver North for the Fox Television show *War Stories*, 2007.
• Alvarado, Monsy. "Not just a Yankee," Bergen Record, February 15, 2000.
• Ivice, Paul. "Berra, baseball have D-Day legacy" MLB.com, June 6, 2004.

Thanks to Dave Kaplan of the Yogi Berra Museum, Montclair, New Jersey, and to William Palmer.

Zeke Bonura, Spreading Baseball Around the Globe

by Gary Bedingfield

"I will give the Army all I've got, just as I did in baseball."
—Zeke Bonura

For some players, military service in World War II was about keeping your head down, getting the job done, and getting back to baseball as quickly as possible. Others, meanwhile, rose to the challenge. Perhaps none more so than Zeke Bonura, whose commitment to the athletic program for U.S. troops in the Mediterranean Theater earned him the appropriate nickname, "the Czar of North African Baseball."

Henry "Zeke" Bonura was born in New Orleans on September 20, 1908. He was a naturally gifted athlete and four-sport star in high school. At 16, he set an AAU National Championship record in the javelin throw at 213 feet and was the most talked-about shortstop in Louisiana high school baseball.

Upon graduation Bonura was inundated with offers to play professional baseball but enrolled instead at Loyola University in New Orleans. He starred in baseball, track, basketball, and football at Loyola. When he graduated in 1929, Bonura signed with his hometown New Orleans Pelicans of the Southern Association. He played there for three years and prompted Larry Gilbert, team manager, to call him "the greatest natural hitter I ever saw."

Bonura was sold to the Dallas Rebels of the Texas League in 1932, and the Rebels sold him to the Chicago White Sox in August 1933. In his first big league season he set a team record for most home runs by a rookie with 27. Bonura was Chicago's first real power hitter and spent seven years in

Bonura with female service personnel softball players in North Africa in 1943

the majors with the White Sox, Senators, Giants, and Cubs. Nevertheless, Bonura's hitting prowess was always overshadowed by his defensive liabilities. Popular with the fans, his personality was affable, engaging, and sincere, but his nonchalant fielding around first base drove managers to despair. "He's not exactly my favorite first baseman," declared White Sox manager Jimmy Dykes, "but he is my favorite character."

By 1941, a steady drop in power output and no improvement defensively put Bonura

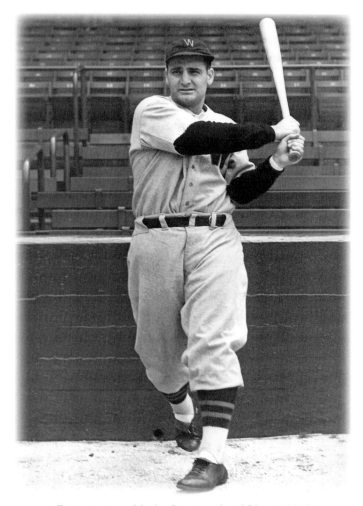

Bonura was with the Senators in 1938 and 1940.

back in the minors. As Joe DiMaggio captured the nation's attention with his hitting streak, Bonura was leading the American Association with a .366 average for the Minneapolis Millers when his Selective Service Board told him to report for Army service on June 19. It had been rumored that he was about to join the Yankees as a replacement for the weak-hitting Johnny Sturm, but he was philosophical about military service. "I will give the Army all I've got, just as I did in baseball," he announced.

Bonura was assigned to Special Services at Camp Shelby in Hattiesburg, Mississippi. He served as assistant to the athletic officer and quickly settled into the Army way of life. "I've never been more at home than I am here," he declared. "I'm in fine condition and I'll be ready for the big leagues again if and when I get out—but I like it so much I'm not sure I want to get out."

That decision, nevertheless, was made for him. On December 5, 1941, six months after he joined the Army, 33-year-old Bonura was honorably discharged after Congress released men aged 28 years and older from service. Then, on January 8, 1942, following the Japanese attack at Pearl Harbor, Bonura was instructed to report back to Camp Shelby. "I might as well kiss baseball goodbye now," he said. "It will be bullets for the Japanese instead of big league baseball for me."

Bonura easily fell back into the Army way of life. During the winter months, he organized wrestling, boxing, and basketball events. When spring came around, he began to think about baseball. Discovering there was no ballfield at Camp Shelby, he promptly helped to build one. "I got down on my hands and knees with these other fellows," he said at the time, "and picked up rock for rock, for over a week, to clear the infield."

Bonura contacted the New Orleans Pelicans and acquired their old uniforms for his players. He petitioned the major league's Ball and Bat Fund for money and equipment and persuaded his former major league teams to contribute their old equipment. By the summer of 1942, he had four servicemen leagues running and earned promotion to corporal.

Meanwhile, seemingly irrelevant events in North Africa were soon to play a significant part in Cpl. Bonura's life. In November 1942, Allied forces invaded Algeria and French Morocco—the first stage in clearing the Axis forces from North Africa, improving naval control of the Mediterranean Sea, and preparing for an invasion of Southern Europe the following year.

In the spring of 1943, Bonura was posted to Algeria, where he organized recreational activities for battle-fatigued troops who were sent to the rear for rest. Bonura had a free hand in developing sports programs, and by the end of the summer, he had set up baseball diamonds and supervised 150 teams in six leagues, involving nearly 1,000 players. "We are playing ball every chance we get," he told *The Sporting News* in August 1943. "I even have some of the Arabs playing the game now. They are not very good players, but they are catching on. The French also have taken to the game, and every time we play, we have a large crowd of French soldiers watching the game."

For his contributions to the morale of troops in North Africa, General Dwight

Bonura was the assistant athletic director at the Camp Shelby, Mississippi, reception center. Pointing out some of baseball's fine points to fellow doughboys in August 1941, he said he was so happy with his work, "I'm not sure I want to get out."

D. Eisenhower presented Bonura with the Legion of Merit on October 26, 1943. The Legion of Merit is one of only two decorations in the United States to be issued as a neck order (the other is the Medal of Honor) and is awarded for exceptionally meritorious conduct in the performance of outstanding services and achievements. His citation read, in part: "By his resourcefulness, enthusiasm and leadership [Bonura] was able to overcome many shortages in needed assistance and construction materials, and he established twenty baseball fields in the area through the use of volunteer assistants and salvaged materials."

The culmination of the baseball season was the North African World Series between the Casablanca Yankees and the Algiers Streetwalkers. Yet again, Bonura's ingenuity and fame came in to effect. He had Gen. Eisenhower sign several baseballs to present to the players of the winning team and arranged for play-by-play coverage to be broadcast by radio to servicemen in the Mediterranean Theater.

"There were no hot dogs and there wasn't any soda pop and it was 4,500 miles to Yankee Stadium," declared *YANK* magazine on November 5, 1943, "but for GIs out here it was almost as important as anything happening back in New York and St. Louis."

Around 3,000 spectators filled St. Eugene Stadium in Algiers to watch the Yankees defeat the Streetwalkers, 9-0, and 7-6, in the best-of-three series.

In the winter months, Bonura organized football and basketball games, and on New Year's Day 1944, he staged the Arab Bowl, a touch football game played in San Philipe Stadium in Oran. The event was preceded by a camel race through the main street of Oran. Halftime entertainment included cowboys, now in the Army, giving rope exhibitions on Arabian horses. The Arab Bowl concluded with the Army defeating the Navy, 10-7.

After 20 months in North Africa, Bonura followed the advancing Allied forces through Sicily, Italy, and southern France. There he staged the first baseball game since World War I, with 10,000 spectators filling Velodrome Stadium in Marseilles on September 24, 1944, to watch an MP unit beat an Infantry outfit, 8-2. Bonura also went out of his way to help French kids learn to play the game. "Everywhere we have a game," he said, "enormous crowds of French flock in. The kids ask a million questions. And in Marseilles they were so interested in our national game that I spent my own time after hours teaching 'em the game."

After two years overseas, Bonura returned to the United States in mid-1945 and received his discharge at Camp Shelby on October 7.

"When the runs, hits and errors of this war are totaled up and they look around for unsung heroes of the ball game, I'm sure they'll pin a medal on the broad chest of Zeke Bonura," wrote Al Schacht—the Clown Prince of Baseball—in *GI Had Fun*. "What he has done for the morale of the American soldier can never be fully revealed except by the GI himself."

In 1946, at the age of 37, Bonura was back in professional baseball. He became player-manager of the Minneapolis Millers but was released on May 5 after the team went into a tailspin. He soon hooked up with another club and continued to play

Corporal Zeke Bonura (right) served as a physical instructor at Camp Shelby in Hattiesburg, Mississippi, during 1942, where he encouraged servicemen to put down their rifles during off-duty hours and play baseball, softball, and basketball.

and manage in the low minors until 1951, including one season (1947) with Stamford of the Colonial League where he batted .385 with 17 home runs and 100 RBIs. Bonura then went back to his home in New Orleans and began breeding and training pedigree beagle hounds, an activity he pursued until his death in March 1987 at the age of 78.

Lou Brissie's Amazing Comeback

by Bill Nowlin

"If someone tells you that you cannot climb the mountain, you set out and find a way to do it." —*Lou Brissie, in* Baseball Digest

Lou Brissie still has the wristwatch he was wearing when a 170-mm German artillery shell exploded near him, breaking the watch and both his feet and also shattering his left tibia and shinbone in 30 places. Shrapnel also pierced his right shoulder, both hands, and both thighs—and, one might assume, crushed Cpl. Brissie's hopes of ever playing professional baseball.

It was December 7, 1944—the third anniversary of Pearl Harbor. Brissie was a squad leader in the 351st Infantry Regiment, 88th Infantry Division, United States Army, fighting against the German 1st Parachute Division in the Appennine Mountains near Florence in the northern part of Italy.

Field surgeons wanted to amputate his leg, but Brissie didn't want to hear that. "I'm a ballplayer! You've got to find another way,"

he exclaimed. "I kept going from hospital to hospital. I don't know if I convinced them but they kept sending me around trying to find a doctor who could do something for me." The idea that he had any shot at playing baseball may have seemed far-fetched to doctors at the time, but the work they did helped make it possible.

Leland V. "Lou" Brissie Jr. was born June 5, 1924, in Anderson, South Carolina but was raised in Greenville and Ware Shoals. His father had a motorcycle shop and then joined Lucky Teeter and His Hell Drivers, an early daredevil thrill show. Lou Sr. ultimately found work running the maintenance department at the Riegel Textile Corporation in Ware Shoals.

Ware Shoals boasted the Riegel company baseball team during Lou's ninth-grade year. Five of his uncles played in textile

Brissie with the Philadelphia A's on July 4, 1949, after he was named to the American League All-Star squad. He finished the season with 16 wins.

league teams in the Carolinas and at one point all five played for the Mauldin, South Carolina, team. "Our heroes were the guys that played in the textile leagues," Brissie recalls. None of them had ever seen—or heard a broadcast of—a major league ballgame.

Lou grew to become a 6'4½" lefthander, and by the time he was 14, he was pitching and played first base for Riegel's "B team" in Ware Shoals. It didn't take him long to graduate to the main team, and by age 16 he was already fielding offers from major league teams. His father greatly admired Philadelphia's Connie Mack, so much so that he even turned down a $25,000 bonus from the Dodgers, a very large sum in those days. The Dodgers pushed the idea that Lou could make the big leagues quickly, but Mack had the reputation he would work with a player who wanted to go to college. Lou traveled to Philadelphia with Presbyterian College student Tom Glade and coach Chick Galloway, a former major league shortstop for the A's and Tigers. They worked out for Mack, and Galloway brought home a contract for Lou's parents to consider. Lou graduated from Ware Shoals High School on May 31, 1941, and signed with the Philadelphia Athletics right afterward. The deal was that Brissie would pitch for the Presbyterian College team for three years, then report to the Athletics. World War II interrupted those plans.

Brissie pitched for the college in 1942 but wanted to enlist in the Army. Twice he tried to enlist but his parents wouldn't sign the necessary paperwork. "They wouldn't talk to me about it. My dad's view was, 'You'll be in there soon enough.'" Presbyterian had a strong military program and all students took ROTC. In late 1942, the students were told they could enlist, stay in school as long as they did the work, and then would be sent right into Officer Candidate School. Staying in college lacked appeal to many, and about 30 percent of the student body failed their coursework almost

immediately. "A lot of us had friends who had gone in the service, family who were in the service, and we just felt like that's where we ought to be. A lot of us just coasted." Brissie enlisted in the Army in December 1942 but got in some time pitching for Presbyterian early in 1943 before he was asked to report in April.

He went through basic training and was stationed at Camp Croft in South Carolina, occasionally pitching for the base team. In the late spring of 1944, he struck out 19 batters in a game against the Greenville Army Air Base Jay Birds. He had topped even that in a game he pitched for the semipro Monaghan textile team while on a day leave, whiffing 22 Easley Mill batters—a game he lost 2–0 on a home run.

It was a few months into training that he learned of his uncle Robert Brissie's death in North Africa after the invasion of Sicily got underway. Robert was a little less than two years older than Lou and was in artillery with the U.S. Army. Robert was a private with the 354th Coast Artillery Battalion. He died on August 4, 1943, and is buried in Tunisia. Lou doesn't know the details of Robert's death but remembers, "He was my first catcher. When we were kids growing up, I always would throw to him and we'd always talk about going to the big leagues together."

In the latter half of 1944, Lou was shipped overseas. Serving with the 88th

Infantry Division (the Blue Devils), his unit saw heavy combat in November 1944. During the 14 months the division was in Italy, they suffered very heavy casualties. When his G Company unit came under exceptionally heavy artillery fire on December 7, eight enlisted men from the company and three of their four officers were killed or wounded that day. His last conscious memory was of himself half in and half out of water and mud in a creek bed, one foot severely damaged and the other seeming to be missing.

Left for dead, Brissie was found unconscious several hours later, and doctors were ready to amputate. In three days of visiting hospitals, he was persuasive enough to convince doctors not to amputate his leg. Dr. Wilbur Brubaker at the Army hospital in Naples worked on saving the limb. "Once he operated on me," Brissie told *Baseball Digest* author Joe O'Loughlin, "I didn't wonder if I could make it back to pitch, but how I could do it."

Brissie had kept in correspondence with Connie Mack. After Mack heard of the injury, he wrote Brissie on December 28, just three weeks after the injury. "He told me that my duty now was to try to get well, and whenever I felt I was ready to play, he would see I got the opportunity. That meant an awful lot to me. It was a tremendous motivator." He would need it.

It took two years and 23 major operations on his leg, with 40 blood transfusions,

but Cpl. Brissie held to the hope of a return to baseball—albeit with a metal plate in his leg. He was perhaps the first soldier in the Mediterranean Theater to be given penicillin in order to fight infection. "They had to reconstruct my leg with wire," he explains.

Strange as it may sound, he was probably fortunate that the German shell hit as close to him as it did. Shrapnel tends to disperse upward and outward. Had it landed even a little farther away, more would likely have cut into him above the knees and could have killed him. Brissie received a Bronze Star and two Purple Hearts.

After months in rehab hospitals, still hobbling around at home on crutches, Brissie told the *Greenville News* that his life's ambition remained "to pitch big league baseball and if I can't make the grade I would at least like to get a job in the big league ball park. And you know the man I want to work for—Mr. Connie Mack. His letters to me were wonderful. He wants me to come to Philadelphia as soon as I am able—just for a visit if nothing more."

It was more than a year before Brissie was able to get to the point he could walk with a cane, but he began throwing a baseball while still on crutches. In July 1945, he traveled to Shibe Park in Philadelphia and worked out for Mack. It was an unusual tryout. "I propped up on one foot with a crutch and threw a few." He stayed for several days, not yet discharged from the Army but on leave between operations. This was a determined man.

On Mack's part, he gave Brissie further encouragement, but there was real doubt in his mind. A year later, Mack confessed, "I'll never forget how he looked last summer, he had just undergone an operation and was about to undergo another one. He was on crutches and I thought, 'Poor boy. He'll never be able to pitch again.'"

Brissie kept working at it, and though he was derailed by a bone marrow infection in 1946, he convinced Mack of both his talent and his spirit. The Athletics owner declared, "If determination can do it, I know he'll make good."

His leg sufficiently stronger, Brissie was signed again by the Athletics in December 1946. Wearing a hard protective brace, he was assigned to pitch for the Savannah Indians in 1947 and started off 13–0. By season's end, he'd put up a 23–5 record. Savannah was in the very competitive Class A South Atlantic League, and Brissie did exceptionally well: he led the league in wins, strikeouts (278) and earned run average (1.91). Brissie struck out 107 batters more than the number two pitcher in the league and far outclassed the second-best at ERA (the only other pitcher under 3.00 came in with a 2.53). The Indians won the league championship.

It hadn't been easy, though. Savannah catcher Joe Astroth said, "Though respect for Brissie was great, opponents gave him no quarter. Foes would probe any weakness, real or perceived. . . . Thinking that his injury limited his mobility getting off the mound to field grounders, hitters began laying down bunts against him to try to get on base." Brissie turned out to be a pretty good fielder, catching several bunts in mid-air and turning them into double plays.

The day after Savannah won the Sally League championship, Brissie was called up to the big league club, and he made his major league debut on September 28, 1947, pitching in the A's final game of the year against the New York Yankees at Yankee Stadium. It was "Babe Ruth Day," and he had the opportunity to meet some great players from the past, such as Ty Cobb, Tris Speaker, Cy Young, and more. It wasn't his best performance. He gave up nine hits, walked five, and threw two wild pitches. He lost that game, 5-3, giving up five runs in seven innings, but enthused, "I thought I had gone to heaven. I lost the game, but it was still a great experience."

Brissie had launched a major league career that saw him win 14 games in 1948 and go 16–11 in 1949, despite struggling with pain every time he took to the mound.

When it came Opening Day 1948, Brissie had made the team and was given the honor of starting the second game against the Boston Red Sox during a Patriots Day doubleheader. The other starter for

Brissie was with the Indians from 1951 to 1953.

Philadelphia was Phil Marchildon, a former Royal Canadian Air Force gunner whose plane was shot down over Germany in August 1944. He was captured and interned as a POW at Stalag Luft III in Poland until Liberation. Both Marchildon and Brissie pitched complete games, and both won their starts. Marchildon had to throw 11 innings, and Brissie had to throw the full nine, holding the Red Sox to just four hits while striking out seven and walking just one. He even drove in the game-winning run with a

From left, Lou Brissie, Lou Boudreau, Fred Bowen (1959 American Legion Player of the Year), and Joe Gordon.

two-run single in the fourth inning.

When Brissie was pitching in the sixth inning against Ted Williams, though, Williams hit a hard shot up the middle, and it hit off the metal plate in Brissie's leg. Williams, Brissie said, could well have had a double but held at first base, called time, and came over to check on him at the mound. "When Ted leaned down, I said, 'Damn it, Ted! Why don't you pull the ball?'" Brissie

won the ballgame, 4–2, but Williams got Brissie later. On May 31, he hit a two-run homer in Shibe Park. "Over the light tower in right field," Brissie remembers. "On his way around the bases, I said, 'I didn't mean pull it that much!'"

After the game in which he got hit in the leg, Brissie was kept overnight in Faulkner Hospital for observation but released in the morning. He did not miss a turn, and he came in fourth in Rookie of the Year voting in 1948. His was such a compelling story that Columbia Pictures expressed interest in making a film of his successful struggle to make the majors and pitch for the Athletics. The chief of staff of the 300th General Hospital in Naples had known Brissie there, and then been reassigned to Walter Reed Hospital. He wrote Columbia and urged the idea on them, but Brissie deflected the inquiry. "They wrote me and I wrote back and told them I just wasn't interested," he explained. "I left a lot of guys in those hospitals and I just didn't feel right about it."

In 1949, Brissie was named to the American League All-Star team and threw three innings, allowing two runs on Ralph Kiner's sixth-inning home run. "I was like a kid in a candy shop, just sitting on the bench with all those guys like Williams, Lou Boudreau and Joe DiMaggio," he told Rich Westcott. "To pitch in the game was an added thrill." Early in 1951, Brissie was traded to the Indians. Even though leaving a last-place team to pitch for the perennial pennant contenders, he wasn't at all pleased to be leaving Philadelphia. For the Indians, Brissie worked primarily as a reliever. After seven seasons in the majors—with Philadelphia and Cleveland—Brissie had a record of 44 wins against 48 losses, almost all of which came while with the Athletics during a span in which the team itself had a losing record. His contract was sold to the Indians'

farm club at Indianapolis, and Brissie wasn't seeing eye to eye with Cleveland general manager Hank Greenberg. Though there was some interest from the new Baltimore club, the Tigers, and the Yankees, Brissie closed his career after the 1953 season with a lifetime 4.07 ERA.

Three weeks after declining to report to Indianapolis, he was named commissioner of the American Legion junior baseball program, where he served for seven or eight years. It was a program in which more than 1 million boys participated. He led a team of boys that played in eight Latin American countries in 1956 and the following year headed to Australia to try to better develop youth baseball there. The Legion released him in 1961 as part of a reorganization. The following spring, he took a position as a scout with the Dodgers and in 1964 began scouting for the Braves.

Brissie then went into private industry, doing some employee relations work and becoming a company rep for United Merchants and Manufacturers, where he represented the firm in discussions and negotiations with regulatory agencies in Washington, D.C. After the company was bought out at the beginning of the 1980s, he served more than a dozen years with the South Carolina State Board of Technical Education, working on job retraining plans as part of the state's development program.

Brissie lost his first wife in 1967 and

married his current wife, Diana, in 1975. He has raised six children. Lou and Diana live in North Augusta, South Carolina, and Lou continues to follow baseball in the area. For a number of years, Brissie joined with Ted Williams and others in trying to get Greenville's Shoeless Joe Jackson off of baseball's restricted list and into the Hall of Fame. Brissie was elected to the South Atlantic League Hall of Fame in 1994.

He continues to require ongoing treatment at Veterans Administration hospitals and maintains regular visits every four to six weeks. The leg, having been broken so badly, is starting to bow a little and there is ongoing concern about osteomyelitis, or an infection of the bone. Only when asked about pain management does Brissie admit that it's been a constant in his life for more than 60 years. He pitched through pain, and it's never been banished; it's with him on a daily basis. It's just a matter of managing the pain. He downplays it, putting it in perspective: "You get up every day and it's like having diabetes—which is something possibly worse, but it is a daily thing that you check and try to deal with, whatever comes up."

Was Lou Brissie a hero? His characteristically modest response: "I don't think I am. I knew some."

Former *New York Times* sportswriter Ira Berkow is completing a book on Brissie's life, with the working title *The Corporal Was a Pitcher*.

Brissie enthusiastically participated in the November 2007 conference at The National World War II Museum and on the final day proclaimed that he had just enjoyed "the most extraordinary three days of my life."

Sources:
• Interviews with Lou Brissie, November 2007 and January 2008 http://www.baseballinwartime.co.uk/player_biographies/brissie_lou.htm, with additional information from Gary Bedingfield.
• Michaux, Scott. "For the love of the game" *Augusta Chronicle*, May 27, 2007.
• O'Loughlin, Joe. "Lou Brissie is an All-American" *Baseball Digest*, June 2005.
• Sapakoff, Gene. "Lou Brissie, the real deal baseball hero" *Charleston* (S.C.) *Post and Courier*, May 29, 2002.
• Westcott, Rich. "Lou Brissie"—for the Philadelphia Athletics Historical Society.

More than a Yankee: Marine Col. Jerry Coleman

as told to Todd Anton

"Seeing friends die and families cry is enough to remind me of the proper place to put baseball." —Jerry Coleman

World War II, baseball, and Korea—all three are an important parts of who and what I am. I'm not special—I tell you that. I just survived, that's all. I was a successful survivor of two wars and a career in baseball, but a hero? Never.

Pearl Harbor changed everyone's life. I was a senior in high school, all set to go to USC [University of Southern California] on a basketball and baseball scholarship, but all I wanted was to become a U.S. Naval aviator. But hell, I was 17—you had to be 18. The only reason I played professional baseball in 1942 was because I had to kill a summer. On my birthday, I went to the San Francisco Trade Building to get into this Naval Aviation V-5 program.

I went to Alamosa, Colorado, for War Training Service, then to Adams State Teachers College, where we got ground school and we flew these little Piper Cubs and first soloed.

Jacksonville, Florida, was home for operational training. I was assigned to the SBD-Dauntless Dive-bomber. Combat flight instruction at Cherry Point, North Carolina. Once I got to Miramar and El Toro, we flew around the clock for 20 days. There was an unbelievable rush of activity. Finally, I was in a replacement ship with the troops crossing the Pacific Ocean. I was still 19 at the time. I was going to war.

They assigned me to a squadron called VMSB 341, on Green Isle, a little north of Bougainville. We flew missions in the Solo-

Coleman at Los Alamitos on May 5, 1952, just after returning to serve in the Korean War.

mon Islands area especially near Rabaul and other Japanese strongholds.

We were the first group of close air support squadrons to be used specifically for helping our brothers on the ground. The Dauntless did the job. I'm only 19, my gunner's 18, but that plane made us men. There's no way to see age in the sky. God, back home, we couldn't get the keys for the family car. Now I was given my own plane.

You grow up fast . . . real fast.

I had visions of sinking a ship. I really wanted to do that. I was carrier-qualified . . . but I was a land-based pilot at Henderson Field, Guadalcanal, in my squadron, the Torrid Turtles.

In all wars you lose people—some good people. It didn't always happen in combat. Every now and then they sent us out on scouting missions to patrol or check a sector over the sea. Since there are no landmarks in the sea, you just went by compass and time readings. You fly an hour and half due north after takeoff, an hour and a half later, turn due west way and an hour and a half back. It was lonely even if I had a gunner at times. We really couldn't talk, as we needed to maintain radio silence. I felt like I was on the moon with nobody there, just water. The sheer vastness of the Pacific really scared the hell out of me. I'd rather dodge traffic than go out there alone. It's terrible. Homer Grasshorn, my best friend, disappeared and never come back on one of those damn patrols. I didn't know where the hell he was. He probably had engine trouble, or ran out of gas, or got lost. It was the first real time I could put a face with death. It was troubling, confusing, and a very real message that I could get killed here.

Combat experiences shaped us and bonded us together. These experiences are very personal and intimate and something you just learn to hide away. Why explain them to anyone who hasn't experienced it? It's kind of like a woman trying to explain having a baby to a man. He just doesn't get it. But when she explains it to another woman, boy, there is an unwritten degree of understanding. So it is with veterans. If you are not a veteran (or a mother), you'll never understand. Never.

Our job in the Philippines was to drop white phosphorous shells from our planes on to Japanese troop concentrations. American ground troops were very close by and they used colored panels as markers of their positions. We had to be careful of the wind. I hated every mission when I used it. I'm sure many of our own guys were burned because of it. Damn!

Finally in July of '45, they took all the qualified carrier pilots, of which I was one, and sent us back to the States.

As I look back at World War II, we were patriots. I was 20. I remember we picked up some nurses and told some lie that I was 22. We walked into a bar, four of us with our dates, and they threw me out. Too young for beer. It was embarrassing. I never lied again. Right here in San Diego, they wouldn't let me into bars. Not that I cared; I didn't drink anyway. It was the principle or the irony. Life is funny that way.

After surviving World War II, my outlook on baseball didn't change. I was still property of the Yankees, and they sent me to Kansas City, Triple A. Being a veteran allows you to see baseball in a different perspective. Baseball allowed me to raise my family and make a living. Baseball was a means to an end. And I happened to be very fortunate: I was a Yankee, and we never came in second. We either won or we lost. Second was losing. The Yankees were not our team, they were our religion. But like Patton said, "Coming in second just means you are a first-place loser."

Coleman keeping in shape with the 1st Marine Air Wing "Deathrattlers" squadron.

World War II and Korea taught me there are more important things than rings. Of course you want to be successful. Sure! But baseball is a game. Living is life. Seeing friends die and families cry is enough to remind me of the proper place to put baseball.

Going to Korea

With the Communist invasion of South Korea in 1950, the Marines needed experienced pilots. Ted Williams and Jerry Coleman were both experienced pilots and Uncle Sam came calling. Coleman remembers…

I never even thought about it, being recalled to duty. I thought, "I'm out of the service."

In October of 1951, I got a call from the Alameda Naval Air Station in California. Major somebody. He said, "We want to talk to you. You wanna have lunch?"

The Marines committed an entire air wing in the defense of Korea. The Marines trained very few pilots from 1945 to 1950. In fact, Truman tried to disband the Marine Corps, in 1947 or 1948. He was going to wipe it out all together. So I was dumbfounded at the moment. I hadn't thought about it. How long? A year and a half, they said. "OK, do me a favor. Take me right now in October 1951 and let me out in March of 1953, and I'll miss a year of baseball."

No. They pulled me at the beginning of '52 and let me out at the end of '53, so I missed two years. In fact, I left for the service in the middle of a doubleheader. I wanted just one more game. I was never that good again. I never played as well.

Some people ask me if have regrets over that. No. Not a whisper. Couldn't care less. My country needed me, and to say baseball was more important or let somebody else do it is wrong. I am an officer of the United States Marines, for Christ's sake. They needed me. I was married. I had two children. In April 1952, about a week before I went back in the service, my son was born. We ended up in Laguna Beach [California]

with our infant. I went over to Korea in the December draft of '52 and came back in August of '53—after personally winning the war, of course.

I joined VMF 323: the Death Rattlers. God, doesn't that sound better than a Torrid Turtle?

My job in Korea was not much different than in WWII, but this time I flew Corsairs. We did dive-bombing missions and close ground support.

One of the highlights of my service in Korea was going into the ready room. The attitude I had to have each time I entered was to act as if I was going into action right then. I say it was a highlight because I knew I was helping my comrades. I was bringing help. I saw it like being on a team.

You could be in that damn ready room from five in the morning till five at night and that damn phone would be going off all day long, and by the time you got done you said, "Jesus Christ, I need a drink or something." But when they had some hot action for us, we responded to any disturbance on the Korean peninsula. One time there was a place called [Haeju]. We were sent half way up to North Korea; it was a bad place to be, because if you're going to get shot down, you're in enemy territory, and it was hell to be a captured airman. They had what they call these long runs, every now and then. Once a month, you'd go out on one of these missions and circle the east coast or the west

Coleman in the cockpit.

coast of Korea with four of our planes. If somebody got shot down, we would go in and help them get out. We would direct the rescuers to them and provide protective fire to keep the enemy away. In fact when Max Harper, my wing man, went down, I think it was an Army group that was on station nearby, and they said, "Can we help? Can we help? We're here; we're ready to go."

And I said, "No, no, there's nothing to be done cause when he got hit, I circled and chased him down and ... shit ... he went straight in and blew up." There was no parachute. But had he gotten out, then you call these guys in, and they can try to get him out. They bring in the choppers and corpsmen to aid the pilot. There is a movie kind of like what we did. Mickey Rooney is in it.

It is called *The Bridges of Toko-Ri*. The choppers were the ones that really took the heat.

I heard Ted Williams go down and his radio calls asking for assistance and his wing man talking to him. That shook me up, too. I knew Ted, of course. Too close to home. We were too far away to help. Ted made it safely back to Earth, thank God.

I'm not really sure how far north we got on our missions in Korea. We were really way up there when Nash, another buddy, got hit. But one area I clearly remember was the Sinanju River. Well . . . there's a place that took a really heavy toll. You know people die in war. It's not pleasant. Sometimes they are your friends. It is a fact of life. Your emotions change, your spirit just . . . well, it kind of dies a little.

I had what I consider a marvelous baseball career even though it was dismantled by the Korean War, and I was with the Yankees for 20-some odd years in one capacity or another, but the defining moment of my life was my time in the service, and, to me, the most important part of my life was my time in the United States Marine Corps. Getting your Navy wings of gold is, I don't know how to express it, except you're walking on air. You are absolutely dumbfounded by the fact that you've become a naval aviator, and that, to me, is the greatest thing that ever happened to me in my life, even the World Series and all the other stuff. Making the Yankees was wonderful, but that was an achievement thing that involved careers and dollars and so forth, whereas the Marine Corps was something that was sacred. It still is.

I flew 63 missions in Korea and then came home in 1953. Hell, I flew 57 missions in World War II, and everyone asks about the medals. Yes, I was awarded two Distinguished Flying Crosses and a few air medals. You know they don't mean that much to me. Merit badges. I was doing my duty. That's what you're supposed to do. I don't listen to the hero B.S.; it isn't about me. But I tell you, the most scary moment of the war is when a guy comes home. It's then that those emotions start hitting you in the head, in your dreams, and even on the field.

What can you do in a situation like that? I followed him down to see if he survived, but he just exploded. He just disappeared. So I returned to base and sat down on my bunk. I had experienced this before, as a combat pilot back in World War II. You know you just learn to stuff it. What the hell can you do? I can't change what happened, but I can change how I choose to deal with it.

"Captain Coleman! Phone!" I went and took the call. It was the owner of the Yankees calling, saying, "We need you, Jerry. We are in a hell of a pennant race and we need you. Now!" *Jesus! I thought. Now?* "Well, uh, I am kind of busy here, sir." After all, I was fighting in a damn war. "Get in touch with your commanding officer." So I did, not knowing what he was going to say. Yankees ownership was persistent; it's the Yankees way. The Yanks knew my tour was just over a few weeks from ending, so ownership thought they would speed up the process.

It's the day before my birthday, September 14, and I'm in the clubhouse dying, like I'm going to save the Yankees. The first day after I worked out, I couldn't get out of bed; I couldn't raise my arms. I had to crawl out of bed.

The Yanks were going to welcome me back in grand style with a "Jerry Coleman Day." Christ, I thought. It's just enough to be home, and I had to make a speech and play on top of that. So I went to my hotel room and sweated it out for the next day nervous and just wanting to get it over with. Jerry Coleman Day arrived. The phone rang . . . with a request from a woman to come down to the lobby. So I did. Her name seemed familiar, but with all the changes and emotions in my mind I didn't put it together. Life at that time was a fog.

Once in the lobby, Jerry recognized a woman he had seen so many times in pic-tures, pictures in which she was surrounded by her five children. Jerry had just come face to face with the wife of his wing man, Max Harper, who asked . . .

"Tell me, Jerry. Is he dead?"

"Yes," was all I could say. That was about all I could say, and then she asked if I could sign some military death benefits papers, which would start the process of care for these kids. She was much stronger than I. She hugged me and thanked me. Thanked me! Can you believe that? That was the worst experience of my life. Now I had to go to Yankee Stadium and play in a game . . . a game!

Heck, in World War II, I was just one of 11 million men who did their duty . . . as a Marine pilot, however. I am very proud of that.

[EDITOR'S NOTE: Jerry Coleman's comments are adapted from an interview he did with Todd Anton and are presented at greater length in the book No Greater Love.]

Murry Dickson, from One Life-Threatening Experience to Another

by Bill Nowlin

When he was just 16 years old, Murry Dickson was on the American Legion baseball team at Leavenworth, Kansas. His team played against Topeka in a 1933 Decoration Day (now Memorial Day) ballgame on the grounds of Kansas State Prison at Lansing. While the game was in progress in front of the prison's 1,861 convicts, one of them made his way under the stands unobserved and seized Warden Kirk Prather from behind, placing a revolver that had been smuggled into the prison to the back of the warden's head. He placed a copper wire with a slip noose around the warden's neck and was joined by several other convicts who seized weapons—including at least one machine gun—from guards who were afraid to open fire for fear of killing the warden. Other guards "with tommy guns surrounded the field, stopped the game, and saved Dick-son from being shot down in defeat."[1] The game was in the fifth inning, the score tied 2–2 at the time. According to a later eyewitness report, a Topeka player was at bat and hit a ball high and over the prison wall for a home run. It was just at that moment that the escapee made his move.[2] The escaped convicts linked up with "Pretty Boy" Floyd and "Machine Gun" Kelly and launched a reign of terror that lasted for months and spread into Oklahoma and other states.

As for Murry Dickson, he went on to pitch briefly in the 1943 World Series, serve overseas in combat during the Battle of the Bulge, help with the liberation of Dachau, and pitch again in the World Series in 1946. Signed by the St. Louis Cardinals in 1936, he appeared in one game each in 1939 and 1940 but first truly contributed in 1942 and 1943, racking up a 14-5 record in the two years before being drafted into the Army

Dickson getting loose at Wrigley Field.

shortly before the 1943 World Series against the Yankees. Dickson, on a 10-day furlough, pitched to the final three New York batters in the Yankees' series-clinching victory in Game 5. He is one of only two members of the armed forces to appear in a World Series while on active duty.

Originally stationed in his hometown at Fort Leavenworth, he was transferred to Fort Riley, Kansas, where he played on the base's strong baseball team. Dickson was part of the 35th Infantry Division and shipped out for Europe a little more than three weeks before D-Day, arriving in Liverpool, England on May 26. He landed on the mainland as part of the ongoing invading force on July 8, 1944, and saw action in France, Belgium, Luxembourg, and Germany. Sgt. Dickson served as driver of a point jeep for a recon group, often advancing ahead of the front line troops to try and spot weaknesses in Nazi defenses. His son Steven reports that at one time Dickson's unit found some German bombers hidden in the woods; the Nazis would bring a plane out to a road to take off and after landing would hide it back under tree cover.

Gary Bedingfield writes that Dickson "was in combat at the breakout at St. Lo, the Battle of the Bulge, the crossing of the Rhine, and the final thrust through Germany."[3] Dickson declined an offer to become General George S. Patton's driver, having met the general when Patton had dropped in on him—literally jumping onto Dickson in a foxhole when a German artillery shell exploded nearby. He was among the first Americans to see firsthand the recently liberated concentration camp at Dachau, and he captured many gruesome photographs. One depicts a group of Polish laborers who were found in a barn, shot to death by the retreating Nazis. Another shows some American MPs overseeing German civil-

ians as they dug graves to bury some bodies wrapped in white sheets.

Dickson stayed in Europe for several months after the war and even had the opportunity to play a bit of baseball in Hermann Goering Stadium in Koblenz. He returned home with a number of souvenirs of war, in good shape and ready to help the Cardinals reach the World Series once again in 1946.

As Warren Corbett points out, not all the Cardinals pitchers who served were able to return effectively. Prospect Hank Nowak seemed to have a great future in baseball and was, like Dickson, a sergeant in the Army; Nowak was killed in the Ardennes during the Battle of the Bulge on New Year's Day 1945. Another, Johnny Grodzicki, had appeared in five games in 1941 (2–1, 1.35 ERA) but suffered wounds in combat and was ineffective in 27 innings in 1946 and 1947.

Murry Dickson, though, posted a 15–6 record (2.88 ERA) and appeared in two World Series games as the 1946 Cardinals beat the Red Sox for the world championship. He was well-launched on a career that saw him pitch 13 more seasons through 1959, become a 20-game winner in 1951 with the Pirates, and appear in his third World Series as part of two games with the New York Yankees in 1958. Dickson won 172 major league games (against 181 losses), with a career 3.66 ERA.

A selection of the photographs he took during wartime were on display at the National Baseball Hall of Fame in 1995–96.

Notes:
(1) Corbett, Warren. Murry Dickson biography, at http://bioproj.sabr.org/. Accounts of the prison breakout come from Associated Press dispatches and a special report to the *New York Times*.

(2) The score was reported in a special by Jack Martin in the October 1 *Atlanta Constitution*. The various exploits of the desperadoes were carried by a number of newspapers of the day, and the story here is assembled from accounts in the *Chicago Tribune*, *Los Angeles Times*, and other newspapers, in addition to the *Atlanta Constitution* and *New York Times*.
(3) Bedingfield, Gary. Murry Dickson biography, at http://www.baseballinwartime.com.

Photo Essay

Murry Dickson's World War II Photographs

"Ernie Pyle Bridge" was a pontoon bridge at Dusseldorf, Germany, and served as a main supply line for U.S. troops.

Above: Dickson with three children, probably in Belgium (note the wooden shoes on two of the children)

Right: Dickson warming up

Dickson
cradling a
.45-caliber
Thompson
machine
gun, with a
.45-caliber
pistol sidearm

Another town freed—Dickson is in front row, first from left

Photograph of Dickson wearing his Santa Fe Division uniform, possibly at Hermann Goering Stadium

Dickson at the wheel, with a .30-caliber machine gun in front and a .50-caliber gun mounted in the back. Dickson's crew would often go into a town after Allied bombings to patrol for any remaining Germans. One of Dickson's brothers said that Murry went through three jeeps during World War II.

Below: On the road to Berlin, 60 km west of Braunschweig

Above: Dickson and friend waiting to play

Above: Baseball along the was—without uniforms, Dickson (center, facing batter) and others stop to play a game on a makeshift field.

Dom DiMaggio Changes Uniforms

as told to Todd Anton

"I just didn't want to be at home playing baseball while all my fellow countrymen were out fighting and serving the country."
—Dominic DiMaggio

Dominic DiMaggio wore eyeglasses, a rarity in professional baseball—and more so in those days. This fellow outfielder was dubbed "The Little Professor" by none other than Ted Williams.

The great Red Sox center fielder is a man of tremendous accomplishments and character and also a man who achieved much on his own despite growing up in the shadow of his brother Joe's celebrity.

I loved my brothers. But we were brothers! It isn't always smooth or perfect. People are always looking for controversy. All I will say about Joe is that I loved him very much, and he was a great player. No doubt about that. I wanted all the best for him. His pressure was nothing like mine. I wouldn't have changed places with him for anything. I was happy to be just where I was, playing center field in Boston with men I loved very much, raising my family, whom I loved even more.

I didn't have any regrets about changing uniforms. None whatsoever. I had to fight my way to get into the Navy to begin with. It was my eyesight. They didn't want to take me. I pleaded with them, and I talked with the optometrist who checked me, and he said, "I'm sorry, they won't take you."

I said, "What are my chances in the Army?" My chances were 40 percent, they said, "Well, if there's any chance, I want to be in the Navy."

Finally, after the longest time, he said, "I may be able to do one thing. Mr. DiMaggio, I could have you draft a letter and have all of the people here at the Federal building on the staff, countersign your signature, and

DiMaggio takes off his Red Sox uniform to prepare to join the Navy.
Courtesy of No Greater Love.

we'll send it to the War Department and recommend that you be accepted. We will tell them that your 'athletic ability will offset your deficiency in eyesight.' So, you want me to do that?"

"Absolutely," I said—and so that's how

I got into the Navy. I wanted to be on the water. I love the water, I live near the water here in Massachusetts, I live near the water, or close to the water in Florida; everywhere I've ever lived, I've always been close to the water and the sea. I love it. I guess that

A rumor that he'd lost the sight in his right eye prompted Coxswain Dominic DiMaggio to point to the eye in question and deny any loss of eyesight. In eight postwar seasons, he hit over .300 for the Boston Red Sox.

comes from being raised in San Francisco. I went in and did my duty. I served in Hawaii, played service ball for the Navy, too.

I just didn't want to be at home playing baseball while all my fellow countrymen were out fighting and serving the country. I wouldn't have felt right about it.

Pearl Harbor changed everything. In World War II, Americans were on the same team. We were so angry—it was not all that different than 9/11—but we knew what we were fighting for and who we were fighting against! Nobody wanted to be left out. The Depression taught us a lot. We as a nation had a sense that we had survived some sort of test, and now we were getting another one. At least that's how I see it today.

I didn't think anything different about guys who stayed home and played ball. That is their business. I wanted to be able to look at myself in the mirror and know I did the right thing. I feel that way even today. Self-respect is an important attribute that can easily be lost.

I never ever had any suggestion in any way, shape, or form from management as to whether or not I should try to get in or enter the services, or that I would be protected. Like I said, I had to fight to get in. It mattered to me as a man, that I serve and do my part. I wasn't going to be left out. I would not allow that. I would not have wanted to be the one player who did not serve. That's why I tried so very, very hard to make sure I got in and to get in to where I wanted to be. My great objective was not to be left out, let me put it that way.

One might think the war changed everything for me. In some ways it did, but it did not change my outlook on baseball in the least. I entered, I did what I wanted to do at the time and completed my service to the Navy and waited for my regular discharge, and fortunately it was in time for me to come back and play in the 1946 season. I had absolutely no regrets. None whatsoever,

I'm very pleased and proud I made the effort to join the service.

I wouldn't have it any other way. I learned a great deal, being in the service. I think I was a better man coming out of the service than I was when I went in it. You're confronted with a lot of different things that you would not have confronted if not in the services.

We were part of a team. You just joined another team—that was all that happened in World War II. I do believe that anyone who goes into the service, for even a short period of time, picks up a lot more for their future as far as living and understanding things a [great] deal better, a maturity, so to speak. It teaches you, yes. It's another avenue of learning.

As a wartime president, I think [FDR] did a fabulous job. I can't recall any presidents off the top of my head that could have done better. He was the right man at the right time. He had a tough job. The man was crippled but taught America to stand again. He started the WPA, and CCC, did many other things. He put people to work, not on welfare.

I guess, all in all, World War II taught me that we're all on the same team working for a common goal and hoping somehow that we could all get back to where we were. I understood that, being a player. I understood it even better in 1946 when, in my first year back with the Red Sox, we made it to the World Series. That was to be my only trip there, but the war gave me a heightened sense of discipline, maturity, and even freedom.

What does freedom mean to me? Oh my! Thank God I was born here. Thank God my folks migrated here.... Look at what America has done for the DiMaggios! How do you expand on that?

[EDITOR'S NOTE: Dom DiMaggio's comments are adapted from an interview he did for Todd Anton and are presented at greater length in the book *No Greater Love*.]

Navy Chief Bob Feller: Throwing Strikes for Uncle Sam

as told to Todd Anton

"Whether it's on the ballfield or the battlefield. We're Americans. We always play to win." —Bob Feller

There is no better example of baseball doing the right thing than Chief Petty Officer and Naval Gunner Bob Feller. Those lessons of doing the right thing began in the farming fields of Van Meter, Iowa, as a lesson between a father and a son.

Bob Feller broke into the majors in 1936. "Rapid Robert" had a fastball that most batters couldn't handle. The right-hander led the American League three years in a row from 1939–41 with win totals almost unheard of today: 24, 27, and 25 wins, respectively. He'd compiled a record of 107–54 and led the league in strikeouts four years in succession, when the Japanese attacked the U.S. Naval base at Pearl Harbor on December 7, 1941. When it came to choose pitching on service to the nation, the answer was clear. It was time to throw a few strikes for Uncle Sam.

I was in Chicago that day to meet the general manager of the Cleveland Indians. He was meeting me that night for dinner to sign my contract for 1942. I found out about the attack just before my meeting. When I met him that night I said, "I already called, and I am going to join the Navy."

All my former boss could say was "Congratulations."

I had called my friend Gene Tunney, who was not only world heavyweight boxing champion, but also head of the U.S. Navy's physical fitness program. Tunney put me in contact with Frank Knox, Secretary of the Navy. Yes, they would be more than delight-

Feller warming up for the Great Lakes team.

ed to have me on their team. So, I volunteered. My mother wasn't all that excited,
but my dad was very proud of me. Even
though he had brain cancer, he said, "Go."

Some people wonder why I didn't sit the
war out, since I had legitimate excuses, but I
still can't understand why anyone would not
want to serve their country. After the Pearl

Harbor attack, I thought: "If you have any
guts, then you are going to do what you can
do, no matter what and how little it may be."

The transition from baseball to the life
of a raw recruit was sharp. I went straight to
boot camp in Norfolk, Virginia.

I came out of the U.S. Navy's War College at Newport, Rhode Island, as a chief

gunner's mate, even though I was always technically a chief specialist, a specialist in athletics.

By summer, I was on the deck of the USS *Alabama*, a brand new state-class battleship and one of the most powerful war machines the world had ever seen. At just 680 feet long and 35,000 tons displacement, it was armed to the teeth. Its main armament consisted of nine 16-inch guns capable of firing a shell weighing as much as a small car 20 miles away. Complementing this awesome salvo was a set of 20 five-inch guns, 48 40-mm cannons, and 52 20-mm cannons. Its firepower was roughly equivalent to an entire army division.

The *Alabama*'s first assignment was to provide escort on the Murmansk convoys. A vital link from Britain to Russia, the convoys kept the Red Army supplied with American weapons to keep the Germans from overrunning the East. But the only way to get to Russia was to sail up the coast of Nazi-occupied Norway—braving the wolfpacks of U-boats and the deadly reach of the Luftwaffe—past the Arctic Circle and on to the northern coast of the Soviet Union.

I was an antiaircraft gunner, spent all of my active duty outside. We had to stay with the slowest Liberty Ship, and, of course, we zigzagged all the way. We had aircraft cover. We had a couple of big carriers with us. We also had land-based aircraft dropping depth charges around the area to protect the cargo-carrying Liberty Ships from German submarines and aircraft. I only ever saw one Liberty Ship go down in a whole year.

Combat? Usually nothing is going on, but you are waiting for something to happen. It was stressful. Naturally, you are scared, you're worried, and you're concerned. We practiced a lot with loading the guns blindfolded so we could do it at night.

War is not glory, but you do see men at their best and a nation at its finest.

Besides leading my gunners, I helped with fitness and morale. My duties aboard ship included giving exercises twice a day, if conditions permitted, to the crew—about 2,900 in all. I had helpers all over the ship do the exercises with their men.

We needed to always remain sharp. With the U.S. and Royal navies effectively countering the U-boat menace, the last real threat to the *Alabama* was the *Tirpitz*, an even more fearsome German battleship. The British had been trying to sink it for years and finally succeeded when a squadron of Lancaster heavy bombers got it hiding in a fjord in Norway and put it to the bottom. They didn't need the *Alabama* any longer; we went to the Pacific.

Task Force 58

As soon as the *Alabama* joined Task Force 58, it was pounding Japanese garrisons with its 16-inch cannon while Marines stormed the beaches on islands throughout the

Feller at the Norfolk Naval Training Station in 1942

Carolines and Marianas. The Americans were steadily and unstoppably island hopping toward Japan. We earned eight battle citations aboard the big ship.

But it wasn't all fighting. We played ball-games on the islands over there in the Pacific when we were in port. These weren't just local sandlots. As often as not, the makeshift ballfields were just cleared of Japanese soldiers. We'd come in for three or four days to rearm, reload, and lick the wounds if there were any, then go back and take another island.

Because of my baseball career I was in charge of the whole Third Fleet's sports program on the beaches when we came into port. I was the one running the show. Mostly all baseball, of course.

I made sure the men had a good time. Baseball in the Navy always was much more fun than it had been in the major leagues. I wasn't all that serious about winning. Not that I took it easy on them. Sometimes we played the battleship *Missouri* or maybe a carrier, or the *South Dakota*, or some of the other big ships.

I got a chance to leave combat and go back to Pearl Harbor to participate in an Army-Navy exhibition series. Capt. Wilson asked me if I wanted to go back. We were way out there between the Philippines and the Marianas at the time. "I don't want to go back," I said. "I am going to stay with you."

He sighed and said, "When I asked you that question, after I received the radiogram from Honolulu, I knew you weren't going back. I knew you were going to stay with me before I even asked you the question."

The flagship of Task Force 58, our ship, protected the carriers—especially the *Yorktown*—from the Japanese by putting our firepower between the Japanese and the flat-tops. The carriers were launching all-important air strikes against Japanese positions on Palau, Yap, Ulithi, and Woleai.

Japanese air attacks weren't uncommon—my men and I had to fight off two attacks in one night more than once—but one night during the Great Marianas Turkey Shoot was a very long night.

For 13 hours, the Imperial Japanese Navy threw every plane it could at our task force. And the 2,900 of us on the *Alabama* fought them off. I was the gun captain on a 40-mm quad, with about 25 sailors throwing in the ammunition. We fired eight

rounds a second and opened up at 4,000 yards. For all 13 hours, we stayed at our guns. We had our C-rations to eat, and we just stayed there and waited for whatever was going to happen.

On the sky just above the sea horizon I spotted dots, four of them. They could be anything—perhaps American SBD dive bombers, Hellcat fighters, maybe. Probably it's just another protective air patrol. I blinked hard, rubbed my eyes. Nope. These were twin engine, high tail. These were Betties—Mitsubishi G4Ms, the enemy's most lethal attack aircraft. When the Betties got close enough, we opened fire.

The sky turned alternately black from smoke and bright white from tracer fire. The smell of cordite overpowered the sea air. The Japanese sent bombers, and we sent up a wall of white-hot metal to meet them.

I kept my four guns blazing. I never hesitated, never thought. I didn't feel fear or have a moment's indecision. Two of the Betties disintegrated, and the others turned around and fled. We were relieved for the moment. Then news came.

A blot as big as a hurricane showed up on radar, and it was approaching the task force. The ships that the *Alabama* were protecting were about to come under a massive and intense attack. The horizon began to blacken with the approaching aircraft. It looked like a swarm of killer bees.

THE DIVINE WIND: THE KAMIKAZES

A combined squadron of torpedo bombers and dive-bombers swung in to attack our group. But they had to get by the fighter cover provided by the *Yorktown*'s Hellcats.

Those enemy planes that got through had to brave the horrifying blast of our guns. Even our own American planes broke off the aerial combat to avoid being chewed up by their own ships' guns.

Two enemy dive-bombers made it through. A 250-pound bomb landed on the *Alabama*'s sister ship, the *South Dakota*, and caused minimal damage.

An hour later, another wave came through. Again the *Alabama* put up a devastating barrage of fire. The two bombs dropped by the one Japanese plane that survived to press its attack fell harmlessly in the water beside the *Alabama*, causing nothing more damaging than waves.

The *Alabama* had just taken part in what later became known as the "Great Marianas Turkey Shoot"—a prolonged and lopsided battle that for all intents and purposes ended the aerial threat of the Imperial Japanese Navy. It was something! Of the 430 Japanese aircraft that attacked the Task Force 58 on July 19, 1944, just 35 came back in one piece. The gunners of the screening ships, including the *Alabama*, claimed 27 enemy planes. The Japanese Naval Air Force didn't exist anymore when the sun went down. We sunk four carriers and shot down almost all of their airplanes. The back of the Japanese offensive threat was broken.

The worst damage the great ship suffered was when one of its own five-inch guns accidentally misfired. Five men died, and 11 more were wounded. That's all I have to say about that. Let's leave that story alone.

Providing cover for the U.S. carrier-based attacks at Cebu, Leyte, Bohol, and Negros, the *Alabama* kept what remained of Japan's air power—including kamikazes—off the carriers.

There would be no period of calm. After a short break for refitting we joined the battle for Okinawa. Although the South Pacific couldn't match the North Atlantic's icebergs, our ship saw its share of weather trouble there, too. One typhoon was a big one that sunk three destroyers because they ran out of fuel. They would have come alongside the battleship to refuel, but they were dead in the water and the swells rolled them over. The typhoon broke off the bow of the USS *Pittsburgh*, about 50 feet of it, took all the airplanes off the baby carriers and smashed in some of the flight decks on some of the big aircraft carriers.

We took over the *Pittsburgh*'s mission. The *Alabama* was the first Allied ship to attack one of the Japanese home islands when we bombarded Minami Daito Shima on June 10, 1945. It was becoming increasingly obvious that the invasion of Japan was imminent. The *Alabama* was going to be at the pointed end of that inevitably bloody battle.

But President Truman made a choice. He dropped two atomic bombs on the Japanese homeland, demonstrating the unprecedented power they were up against.

Truman made the right choice. It saved 5 million lives. It was the right thing to do! Truman was a great president. He had guts. When you go into a war, you have to go in to win. He made a great decision.

A week after the second bomb, we received word that the Japanese had surrendered. The celebration was muted; we still had work to do. As the nearest battleship to the Japanese mainland, the *Alabama* had the curious honor of delivering the first Marines and Bluejackets for the initial occupation of the Yokosuka-Tokyo area.

Nine days after the Japanese had surrendered and a week before the documents were actually signed, I was on the mound in Cleveland.

It was Friday, August 24, 1945. I struck out 12 and give up just four hits in a 4–2 win over Detroit's Hal Newhouser.

[EDITOR'S NOTE: Feller threw a one-hitter before the year was out. In 1946 and 1947 he led the league in wins once more, with 26 and 20 respectively, and broke Rube Waddell's strikeout record with 348 in 1946—and threw his second no-hitter, this time against the Yankees. In 1948, he started Game One of the World Series. Did he feel fear on baseball's biggest stage? "I was facing the Boston Braves lineup, not a squadron

of suicidal torpedo-bomber pilots hell-bent on my destruction."]

ANY REGRETS?

I didn't miss baseball at all. I wanted to do what little I could to help this country. I did what most any good, red-blooded American should have done. This is not to say that I didn't do a lot of praying during my tour of duty. There are times when it sure comes in handy. Like when you see the kamikazes coming at you. Like they say, no one's an atheist in war.

As far as today's athletes are concerned, I don't think September 11 is a situation that is anything close to what the danger was for America during my time. We had a greater emergency then. We had Pearl Harbor and were losing big in Europe. We were getting pushed around, all over the world, and had a "now or never" mentality.

Today is nothing like the days of Pearl Harbor or Hitler. There is no national crisis. But I am sure that if we were threatened with a loss of sovereignty, an awful lot of good, young Americans would probably do what I did, or at least serve their country and go to war.

As for myself, I believe I gained much more than I lost from my military service. There are probably some records I could have had, like no-hitters, wins, or strikeouts. Ted Williams would have been way ahead of almost everyone in batting average, home runs, runs scored, and runs batted in if he

Feller aboard the *USS Alabama* in 1943.

hadn't spent two years in Korea in addition to his tour of duty in World War II. But he served his time, just like I served my time. No regrets. We served our flag and our country without question and with honor.

It is, after all, about winning. Whether it's on the ballfield or the battlefield. We're Americans. We always play to win.

[EDITOR'S NOTE: Bob Feller's comments are adapted from an interview he did for Todd Anton and are presented at greater length in the book *No Greater Love*.]

Hank Gowdy, Hero on Two Fronts

by Frank Ceresi

He saw things no man should see. What an amazing life Hank Gowdy had. He played major league baseball during the rough-and-tumble early years of the 20th century, was the star and most valuable player of the 1914 World Series as a member of the championship "miracle" Boston Braves team, and was a bona fide war hero who served his country in two world wars. Henry Morgan Gowdy was a man who epitomized, through his play on the baseball field and his exploits in the armed forces, the inexorable link between our national pastime and service in the military.

Henry "Hank" Gowdy was born on August 24, 1889, in Columbus, Ohio. His father was Horace C. Gowdy, an independent man of modest means, and his mother, Carrie Burhart. Hank was taught early on to work hard and do his chores. But like so many of his friends, he gravitated toward the playing fields once those chores were done. He played football, basketball, and baseball at Hubbard Elementary and North High School in Columbus. Though he enjoyed all team sports, he loved baseball and convinced an official from the Columbus Senators semipro team to give him a tryout. His talents on the ballfield began to blossom, and he first signed professionally with Lancaster in the Ohio State League. In 1909, New York Giants scout Billy Doyle purchased his contract for $40 back pay due from Lancaster. He was assigned to Dallas (Texas League) for a few months' more seasoning. By this time, Gowdy was a strapping 6-foot-2, 180-pounder who was considered a team leader.

Gowdy's major league career started in 1910, during the height of the "dead ball era," when he briefly played with John McGraw's Giants. He only batted .214 that season, and, after a few games during the 1911 season, he was traded to the Boston Braves. He saw some action in both 1912 and 1913, but still had not quite found his stride, accumulating 101 at-bats for the Braves but spending most of the two years honing his craft as a catcher for the Buffalo Bisons. It was a "make-it-or-break-it" time period for the youngster, but it was at Buffalo that he

Hank Gowdy

hooked up with a man who would become a major influence in his life.

During the latter part of the 1912 season, the young catcher began to make his mark under the watchful eye of veteran manager George Stallings. The son of a Confederate general, Stallings was a larger-than-life character known for his crafty, hardnosed baseball ways. A superstitious and tough man who was never intimidated on or off the baseball diamond, Stallings had been managing in the baseball vineyards for years and had developed a reputation for being a fine judge of baseball talent. He was especially looking for men who not only had the necessary skills to play the game, but who could lead the team on the field as well. Stallings spotted what he wanted in the young Ohioan and became one of Hank Gowdy's most ardent supporters. The two seemed the perfect match. Both were no-nonsense, natural leaders of men. That trait proved to serve both men well.

Even though Stallings left the Bisons in 1913, his "field general" Hank Gowdy ended up batting well over .300 for the year and became the mainstay of the team. By the year's end Gowdy had developed leadership capabilities while playing perhaps the most vital position on the team, that of catcher.

Their separation would be brief. By August of that year, Stallings took the helm for the Braves and quickly recruited young Mr. Gowdy to help him anchor his new squad.

In the late 19th century, the Boston Braves (originally called the Red Stockings, the Red Caps, and the Beaneaters) were at the top of the majors, winning several championships. But by the time Stallings and Gowdy joined the club, the Braves were known as perennial losers in the National League—the senior circuit's doormats. By the time the 1914 season began, they had been absolutely dominated for several years by McGraw's New York Giants. In fact, the Giants were coming off a season in 1913 in which they won 101 games and captured the National League pennant. Stallings' Braves

ended up a distant fifth place. The Boston boys won 69 games but lost 82. Sure, that was an improvement over their last-place finish in 1912, when they barely squeaked out 52 victories, but most people thought that the 1914 season would simply bring more of the same. That is, more misery for the woeful Boston Braves and more joy to the great New York Giants with their star pitcher Christy "The Christian Gentleman" Mathewson, who was at the top of his game.

But fate had other plans for Hank Gowdy, his manager George Stallings, and their team, for 1914 would become a spectacular season that is still considered among the most thrilling single baseball seasons of them all. Not only did the Braves embark on the greatest team comeback in Major League Baseball history—rebounding from 15 games behind the first-place Giants on Independence Day 1914—but the team overtook its old nemesis with ease in September. The Braves then went on to sweep the heavily favored American League champion Philadelphia Athletics in the World Series, four games to none. Hank Gowdy was in his prime.

Much to Stallings' joy and McGraw's consternation, "field commander" Gowdy made several clutch hits against Mathewson during the pennant drive in late August and early September. Gowdy's star burned most brightly in the cool air and gusty winds when summer turned to fall, when baseball is played at its toughest and best, and during the October classic, baseball's biggest stage, the World Series. Having dispatched McGraw's men, this time the duo faced the cunning Connie Mack, the A's grand man who had carefully assembled what was thought to be, by far, the best team in baseball.

Stallings, Gowdy, and their men had other plans. Hank Gowdy proved to be the original "Mr. October," long before Reggie Jackson claimed that moniker. Gowdy hit safely six times and batted .545 for the World Series with three doubles, a homer, and a triple. He was the peerless clutch hitter who anchored a team loaded with characters such as Rabbit Maranville and grizzled vets such as Johnny Evers. He also made key hits and won the third game by going 3-for-4. Later, Stallings himself would state flatly that Gowdy was the most valuable player during the "miracle" run. He called the games well, too. The A's only scored five earned runs in the four World Series games.

For two and a half years, Gowdy continued to catch for the Braves, but the clouds of war soon interrupted the thrills of baseball. Gowdy, a very patriotic man who pined to serve his country, decided to lay down his bat for something more important. Soon he traded his baseball uniform for military garb and became the very first major leaguer to enlist in the armed forces during World War I. On June 1, 1917, Gowdy signed up to serve in the Ohio National Guard and eventually reported for duty on July 15, 1917. He was soon heading for the front lines in Europe. He later said that he saw things "no man should see." Baseball and the cheering crowds from Boston seemed a long way away. The fighting was tough and brutal against the Germans, a determined enemy.

Hank Gowdy's war record was quite impressive. He served with distinction in the 166th Infantry Regiment and became a part of the famed "Rainbow Division," the Fighting 42nd. Gowdy carried the colors during the war for this spectacular fighting unit. Legend has it that Gen. Pershing himself dubbed them the "Rainbow Division" since they had the uncanny "luck" of being surrounded by actual rainbows on their way to and during the heavy combat they saw in France. The men certainly needed all the luck they could muster because they were one of the first American divisions to reach the western front. They fought side by side with the French, and the fighting was brutal. It was trench warfare in the most violent sense of the word as the men engaged in man-to-man combat against the Germans, employing rifles and guns and, when they ran out of bullets, with bayonets and knifes.

Casualties were high, but unlike so many of his counterparts in the Rainbow Division, Hank Gowdy returned to the United States in one piece. By this time,

Hank Greenberg hears from Cincinnati Reds coach Hank Gowdy,
the first ballplayer to sign up for the service in World War I.
Greenberg had just been discharged from the service,
but re-enlisted immediately after Pearl Harbor.

the returning war vet Gowdy was a bona fide war hero, as popular in Boston as the mayor himself. Gowdy gladly laid down his rifle and once again picked up his glove to return to the game he loved. He resumed catching for the Braves from 1919 through mid-1923, when he was traded to his old rivals, the New York Giants, still led by John McGraw. Certainly McGraw remembered Gowdy's clutch hitting as part of the "miracle" team. Gowdy played 187 games for the New York Giants during a two-and-a-half-

115

year stretch. He also played in the 1923 and 1924 World Series contests for the Giants. His team captured the title in 1923 and lost it in seven games to the Senators in 1924. Gowdy stuck with the game as a player for a few more years. After 17 years in the majors as a player, Hank Gowdy, however, was not one to rest on his laurels. Although he never batted the ball for his team after 1930, he would be a coach for three different major league teams—the Boston Braves, New York Giants, and Cincinnati Reds. Also, as unbelievable as it sounds, when World War II broke out, Gowdy served his country for a second time. At the ripe old age of 53, he was commissioned a major in the United States Army. He again served with distinction and became, for an extended period of time, the chief athletic officer at Fort Benning, Georgia.

To this day, the baseball diamond at Fort Benning, where soldiers enjoy playing the national pastime, is called Hank Gowdy Field. Gowdy passed away at the age of 76 on August 1, 1966, while living in Columbus, Ohio. He left no children, but to this day, in and around Columbus, there are relatives and old timers who remember him well. A fine, moral, and modest man who conducted himself with class on and off the ballfield, now we know that without any fanfare whatsoever, he was also a tough military man, who when he left playing baseball at the highest level to serve his country. He saw the terror of war, up close and personal. For that, he deserves our eternal gratitude.

Monte Irvin:
He Could Have Been the First

by Bill Nowlin

"Most of the black ballplayers thought Monte Irvin should have been the first black in the major leagues." —Cool Papa Bell

Hall of Fame ballplayer Monte Irvin admits to being envious that Jackie Robinson got the chance to be the first black player in the major leagues. Branch Rickey of the Brooklyn Dodgers signed Robinson just seven weeks after Irvin was discharged from the Army. Irvin was always generous with his praise for the job that Robinson did. It was only much later, in 1981, that Newark Eagles owner Effa Manley told Irvin he had been the one who was positioned to be the first black player in the major leagues. "She said that I had been selected by her and the rest of the owners for that role. If it had not been for World War II, I might have been the one to break the color line . . . but timing is everything, and fate intervened."[1]

Hubert Irvin was born on February 25, 1919. He was one of 13 children born to his mother and sharecropper father in Haleburg, Alabama. At a very early age, he began working as a water boy in the cotton fields, but by age eight the family had left to Bloomfield, New Jersey, in the wake of some difficulties his father had with a white neighbor who took advantage at a time when recourse was impossible. It was the same year that young Hubert had his name changed to Monford Merrill Irvin.

In New Jersey, Monte saw a lot of baseball. The black semipro team played against the local white team, as did a number of black touring teams. His brother Bob, six years older, bought Monte his first glove while the family still lived in Alabama, and

Monte Irvin in the service. *Photo courtesy of Monte Irvin, thanks to Jim Riley.*

often played catch with Monte. Bob was offered a spot with the Jacksonville Red Caps but had to decline; his mother wouldn't let him go with a team that played ball on Sundays. At the formative age of 13, Monte saw the Pittsburgh Crawfords come through town at a time the team boasted four future Hall of Famers: Josh Gibson, Satchel Paige, Oscar Charleston, and Judy Johnson. It was that same year that Monte began playing for the local Orange Triangles. He became an accomplished multi-sport athlete in high

118

school—fortunate to survive a near-fatal hemolytic streptococcus infection during his senior year.

Under the assumed name of Jimmy Nelson, he signed with the Newark Eagles in 1938 to protect his amateur status as he awaited admission to Lincoln University that autumn on a four-year scholarship. During his sophomore year, Irvin quit school and signed on under his own name with the Eagles, where he played alongside future Hall of Famers Ray Dandridge, Leon Day, Willie Wells, and Mule Suttles. He developed into a truly exceptional ballplayer, often hitting around .400, and was honored to play in five Negro League All-Star games. He played third base in the 1941 East-West All-Star Game in Chicago, getting two hits and a stolen base.

It was a rough existence scraping by in the Negro Leagues, never knowing if segregation might prevent players from getting a meal at a roadside café. Rhubarbs on the field often saw players grab bats before they left the dugout, and more than one umpire carried a pistol. Irvin played some winter ball in Mexico and recalls first hearing of the attack on Pearl Harbor while standing on second base during a game in Puerto Rico. He made his way back to New York and got another season under his belt in 1942. But he is frank in acknowledging the impact the war had on him. "I felt I was really coming into my own. But then I had to go in the

Army and that wiped out everything that I had accomplished."[2] Though he was married and had a five-month-old daughter, Irvin was called to duty in March 1943.

Irvin was assigned to the 1313th Battalion, General Service Engineers, an all-black engineering outfit. Just before he was due to ship out to England, he ran into Tommy Dukes of the Homestead Grays. Dukes told Irvin the colonel was looking for good ballplayers, and they were never going to let the four-time all-star from the Newark Eagles get sent overseas. The colonel was away until Monday, though, and Irvin shipped out on Sunday. While awaiting forward movement to France, his unit was guarding a supply depot near Plymouth. They moved out on a Saturday morning; that evening, the area was heavily attacked by German bombers. "They had really blasted the place," Irvin says. "Thank God we moved because we could not have survived that bombing."[3] Again, the difference of one day or less had made a major difference in Irvin's fate.

The 1313th crossed the English Channel, landing on Omaha Beach on August 1, 1944, and began to move toward Paris, working on building roads and bridges and guarding hundreds of German POWs. During the Battle of the Bulge, Irvin's unit was assigned to guard a major gasoline depot at Reims but admits the unit often felt underutilized. They wanted to fight, too, but ultimately took comfort after hearing how

Monte Irvin broke in with the New York Giants in 1949.
Photo courtesy of Monte Irvin, thanks to Jim Riley.

bad it had been from some of the 101st Airborne who came back from the front. Sgt. Irvin was sent back stateside in August 1945 and rejoined the Eagles in time for part of the winter ball season. It wasn't the same, though. Unlike so many, he had not played ball at all during the war. "After I came out of the service, I was never the same guy that I was when I went in. I had lost my timing, and I was three years older."[4]

The Eagles did well, though, and so did Irvin, with his .394 average leading

Monte with the Newark Eagles.

the Eagles to the pennant. They beat the Kansas City Monarchs in the 1946 Negro Leagues Championship, with Irvin leading the hitters with a .462 average. But despite his success, by this point, Jackie Robinson had been given the nod to become the first to integrate the majors. Cool Papa Bell was among many who realized how close Irvin had come: "Most of the black ballplayers thought Monte Irvin should have been the first black player in the major leagues. Monte was our best young ballplayer at the time. . . . He could hit that long ball, he had a great arm, he could field, he could run. Yes, he could do everything."[5]

Monte Irvin did get his chance, and he made the most of it, breaking in with the New York Giants in mid-1949. He led the league with 121 RBIs in 1951, playing outfield and first base and helping bring the Giants to the World Series. In the Fall Classic, he kicked things off by stealing home in the top of the first inning of Game One. The Yankees beat the Giants in six games, but Monte Irvin led both teams in batting with a .458 average. He was selected to play in the 1952 All-Star Game and was back in the World Series again in 1954. This time,

the Giants triumphantly swept the Indians. After the 1956 season, he called it quits, retiring after eight seasons with a career .293 average. He was named to the Hall of Fame in 1973.

One of many whose career suffered due to war, he remains resolute in his belief that "Freedom is not free. We have to fight for the freedom that we have. Each and every one of us should remember that."

Notes:
1. Irvin, Monte with James A. Riley, *Nice Guys Finish First* (NY: Carroll & Graf, 1996), p. 116.
2. Ibid., p. 97.
3. Ibid., p. 101.
4. Ibid., pp. 102-3.
5. Negro League Baseball Players Association Web site, Monte Irvin biography.

Morrie Martin Takes His Place on the Stage

by Bill Swank

"I don't belong on that stage. They're stars." —*Morrie Martin*

In 1899, at a Navy banquet in Philadelphia, Congressman Willard Duncan Vandiver wryly noted, "I come from a state that raises corn and cotton and cockleburs and Democrats, and frothy eloquence neither convinces nor satisfies me. I am from Missouri. You have got to show me."

Fast forward to 2007. School is out for Christmas break in Washington, Missouri. Morrie Martin's youngest grandchildren, seven-year-old Daniel and nine-year-old Mara, echo the last sentence. "Our teachers tell us that all the time," they confided during an interview alongside their grandfather.

Morris Webster Martin was born on September 3, 1922, in Dixon, Missouri—the Show-Me State—in the heart of the Ozarks. A friendly man, he loves to talk about hunting and fishing, family and base-ball. Family and baseball are the two most important things in his life. Martin detests braggarts, showoffs, and know-it-alls.

There's one other thing he doesn't like. He does not like to talk about his World War II experiences. Before the war, Martin was a promising minor league left-hander who, after leading the Class C Northern League in his rookie year with a 2.05 ERA, made the jump to the highest minors with St. Paul in the American Association. The *Baseball Register* lists all of his teams:

1941, Grand Forks (Chiefs),
   North Dakota
1942, St. Paul (Saints)
1946, Asheville (Tourists),
   North Carolina; St. Paul
1947, Danville (Dodgers), Illinois;
   St. Paul;

Morrie Martin pitched for the Philadelphia A's from 1951 into 1954.

1948, St. Paul

1949, Brooklyn Dodgers

Martin would go on to pitch 10 seasons in the major leagues with the Dodgers, Philadelphia Athletics, Chicago White Sox, Baltimore Orioles, St. Louis Cardinals, Cleveland Indians, and Chicago Cubs.

His best year was 1951 with the Athletics, when he posted the second-highest winning percentage in the American League with a record of 11–4. He beat every team in the circuit that season and particularly savors every sweet victory over the powerful New York Yankees of that era.

The *Baseball Register* also notes that in "1943-44-45," Morrie was "In Military Service." Consider these "stats" for his three years of military service:

1942–43, U.S. Army, Combat Engineer Training, Colorado, Louisiana;

1943, North Africa;

1944, D-Day—Utah Beach, Sainte-Mère-Église, Saint-Lô, Paris, Belgium, the Siegfried Line, Hürtgen Forest and Aachen, Elsdorf, the Battle of the Bulge—Bastogne;

1945, the Bridge at Remagen, Bonn.

It's always tough to play on the road and that was a particularly bad schedule. Morrie Martin fought in most of the major battles of the European Theater of Operations. As a combat engineer, it's a miracle he even survived the war. To return home, rehabilitate, and pitch 10 years in the major leagues defies all odds. Yet few in baseball knew what Martin had been through because he chose not to talk about it.

The WWII baseball conference in New Orleans was neither the time nor the place for in-depth conversation. I made arrangements to visit Morrie at his home. Along with my best friend, Rich Nelson, we leisurely drank some Budweiser, talked some baseball, and shared some laughs about family, friends, hunting, and fishing. Occasionally, I would mention the war. I have tried to put everything into chronological order. I did not ask for elaboration or details. This is Morrie's story:

"I was drafted in 1942 and went to basic training at Camp Carson near Colorado Springs in Colorado. They assigned me to the engineers, because I was good with my hands and could build things. The whole time I was in the Army, I only touched a baseball once. Before shipping overseas, we were in bivouac down in Louisiana. Two guys were playing catch. I asked if I could join them. I'm left-handed, and they said there were left-handed gloves in the truck.

After I warmed up, I started throwing my curve. The lieutenant quit playing catch when one broke so much it hit him in the stomach.

"We went to North Africa in November 1943. We didn't see any combat. We were repairing bridges and roads. Then we were shipped to England to prepare for the invasion.

"Because we were combat engineers, we were the first to land on Utah Beach at H-Hour just as dawn was breaking on June 6th. Artillery was flying overhead, but we didn't fire a shot because the Germans didn't know we'd come ashore. We went around the bluff to get to Sainte-Mère-Église. The paratroopers had landed before we got there. I remember seeing a paratrooper hanging from a church steeple. We thought he was dead. We were fighting, so we just moved on. Sainte-Mère-Église was the first town to be liberated.

"It was hard to fight through the hedgerows. We were sent to fix a bridge but got surrounded by Germans. We hid for a week. We ran out of K-rations, but they didn't taste very good anyhow. Finally the Americans broke through with infantry and tanks and we could move on.

"I got hit by shrapnel guarding a crossroads going into Saint-Lô. They patched me up, put in a few stitches. My index finger on my left hand was hit, too. It's a little deformed, but I could still grip a baseball and

Martin in his service uniform.

throw the curve. In fact, I think my curve ball was probably a little better as a result of the deformed finger. That was my first Purple Heart.

"We liberated Paris that summer. Our outfit kept moving through Belgium. We broke the Siegfried Line and went into Aachen. We got to Elsdorf and the Ger-

mans wanted it back badly. They were bombing us. We went down in the basement of this building and noticed there were steel beams. We thought it would be a good place to spend the night. There were guys who stayed upstairs that laughed at us. I was asleep when the building got bombed. We couldn't see anything and were trapped. The next day, when the sun came out, we saw a pinhole of light. We dug our way out, and nobody was there. Everybody upstairs must have died. When we caught up with our unit, they said, 'Where the hell did you come from?'

"The Battle of the Bulge was the worst. It was the coldest I'd ever been in my life. I didn't have my shoes off for three weeks and I've had trouble with my feet ever since.

"We built the pontoon bridge for tanks at Remagen. The Americans captured the bridge intact, but it was a railroad bridge. It fell apart about 10 days later. It was tough to build the pontoon bridge, because artillery kept coming in. We had to keep repairing it as we were building it. Then the tanks started rolling across. I don't know if that was where Patton pissed in the Rhine. I think it was later because I got hit around that time.

"My cousin Woodrow Hickey was a mailman in the Army. He delivered mail to the front lines. I remember it would take three months to get mail from my folks. Two years ago, Woodrow told me about crossing the bridge we built. He said he saw guys from the 49th Engineers but couldn't stop to talk. He had to deliver the mail. It took over 60 years for him to even tell me this. We just didn't talk about the war.

"Another cousin, Ralph Hickey, was killed on D-Day. He was coming ashore two or three hours after I landed but never made it to the beach. We were born and raised together. He was like a brother. My older brother William—Bill—got a truck blown up underneath him. He recovered from his injuries but got jaundice. He died when he was about 50 of complications from the jaundice.

"I got my second Purple Heart on March 23, 1945 at a crossroads near Bonn. I was shot in the leg. I don't remember much after that. I woke up once and heard a doctor say, 'That's one sick man.' They wanted to saw off my leg. A nurse from Georgia looked at my records and saw I was a ballplayer. She told me not to let them cut my leg off. They had a new drug—penicillin. She told me I had over 150 shots, one every four hours, and that finally stopped the infection. I wish I knew who she was to thank her.

"I don't remember returning to the United States. I don't remember anything from the end of May until the later part of July. I didn't know about battle fatigue then. I do know I couldn't sleep for the first two weeks. I was eventually sent back to Camp Carson and remember asking myself, 'How did I get here?' I was discharged on October 31, 1945.

"My daughters and especially my grandsons, want me to tell them about the war. I can't do it. My youngest daughters, Debbie and Donnie, told me that they remember me crawling on the floor at night when they were young. I don't remember any of that. I do remember one time when I woke up with scissors in my hand. I could have hurt my family. That really scared me. I just don't like to talk about it."

After the war, Martin moved to Washington, Missouri, where his older sister lived. He had a friend who was the local barber. One day, Martin noticed an attractive young lady "with great legs." It turned out the barber knew the young lady, so a double-date was soon arranged. Her name was Loni. Martin jokes that he fought the Germans and then he married a German girl. Loni and Morrie continue to live in the same home on Pottery Road where they raised their four daughters: Kathleen, Deborah, Marilyn, and Madonna (Donnie).

"We still only have one bathroom," said Martin. "I had to get up pretty early to use it when all the kids were at home."

Today, the phone rings constantly as the kids and grandkids check in with Loni and Morrie. The walls are covered with pictures of family and Martin in his various baseball uniforms. Christmas ornaments bear the names of grandchildren and great-grandchildren. There are no reminders of war. Martin has a shadow box that contains his loose medals and ribbons. It is kept in a drawer.

"My best friend from the service was Al 'Aloysius' Link from Cincinnati, Ohio. We landed together on D-Day. After the war, he and his wife came to see me play in St. Paul.

We got together often. Loni and I went to their 50th wedding anniversary, and they came to ours. Al died about five years ago, and his wife just died. We're glad we've still got our health."

Morrie enjoys attending various baseball-related events. He has been to three Philadelphia Athletics reunions and several autograph sessions in the St. Louis area. The baseball conference at the World War II Museum was highly anticipated by Morrie and his family, but it also brought back troubling memories of war.

Todd Anton and I discussed Morrie's misgivings prior to the "Baseball and the Battlefront" presentation at the conference. The other panelists were Bob Feller, Jerry Coleman, and Lou Brissie, combat veterans all. Brissie and Martin were teammates on the '51 Athletics, but Brissie didn't know about Martin's service record.

Martin confided, "I don't belong on that stage. They're stars."

I slowly recited the following, pausing at each comma: "D-Day, Utah Beach, Sainte-Mère-Église, Saint-Lô, the Battle of the Bulge, the Remagen Bridge. . . . I don't think there's a major league player who wouldn't be proud to share the spotlight with you."

Tears filled his eyes as Morrie Martin, combat engineer, took his place on the stage.

Ensign Johnny Pesky

as told to Todd Anton

I just got back from our Louisville minor league season, and we all registered for the draft. I had a high number or I would have been drafted. It was early December, and I was coming home from church in Oregon, and when I finally got in the house, they had the radio on, and the family was listening to it pretty loud.

The Japs had attacked Pearl Harbor.

What can you do? I was waiting my turn like everybody else to get my notice. I went to spring training in 1942 and made the club. Early in the season, a guy named Lt. Fuller approached some of us about this V5 program, a fast track to learning to fly and becoming an officer. I was interested.

It was pretty tough at times in 1942. If you weren't in a uniform, people would say, "What the hell are you doing out of the service?" Unless you were classified 4-F. Well, hell, there was nothing wrong with me. Dominic [DiMaggio] wore glasses, but a lot of guys wore glasses. He had to fight to get in. Ted Williams talked me into joining this V5 program. We signed up together.

Mine was a Navy family. I couldn't see myself in the Army. My father, when he came over to this country, was in the Austro-Hungarian Navy. Many guys were joining the Navy. Dominic went in the Navy, I went in, Ted. When you're 21 years old, you think nothing's ever going to happen to you. I was very fortunate how my Navy career turned out.

Other players joined up, too. Johnny Sain, Joe Coleman, and Buddy Gremp. After the season, Ted and me and the others went up to WTS at Amherst College for three months, and then from there we went to Chapel Hill. Hell, yes, I was nervous.

Ted went on to get his wings, but I was a little . . . in arrears about my navigation, so I had to stay two extra weeks. Flight school was difficult for me. Ted wrote in his book *My Turn at Bat* about one day when I had to make eight approaches to land my Cub observation plane: "It looked like they were going to have to shoot him down. They finally got Pesky out of there. In an airplane he was a menace to himself and everybody else, but he was certainly officer material so they moved him into Officers Candidate

Ted Williams and Johnny Pesky with the Cloudbusters, Chapel Hill, North Carolina, during World War II.

School [OCS] and he actually got his rank before I did. But he couldn't fly an airplane for shit!"

My navigation officer was a pretty good guy, but then the captain of the base called me and some other guys in for an interview. There was a kid from MIT, Harvard, Colby College, and myself, I was the only high school graduate of the four. I'll never forget the captain, Roy Callahan. He said, "Johnny, we're opening this operations school down in Georgia." He said, "I'd like you to go and you'll get your commission there." When he said commission, I was all for it.

"You'll learn how to operate in the field. We go all over the world." We were getting so many kids and so many flyers, they needed guys to work on air stations, casualty units, carrier aircraft service units. They put these Operations officers into areas where they needed someone with a little rank. I said, "Yeah." I just wanted to get my commission. I went to this school, and I really bore down. I never left the base. I wasn't in the top of my class, but I got my commission. That was one of the proudest things I've ever experienced—I made it to the big leagues as a player, and then I got my commission in spite of just having a high school diploma. I could have made it as a flyer, but I was too dangerous. Others washed out, too, but I still had a chance to become an officer.

◆

The hardest lesson that the service taught me? Discipline. When you get a group of people, you have to have certain rules and regulations, and you have to abide by them. The rules were made, and I abided by them. We had duties to do when we first went in. The thing I remember the most about my duties was I had to clean the latrine for a week or two weeks when I was getting my commission. I had to do that until I got my commission.

Our country's survival was at stake. I wished I didn't have to go, of course. But I was like any other kid; everybody in my neighborhood was joining up, and players were going in left and right. I wasn't angry. Nervous? Yes.

On my way to the Pacific I was able to stop by home. The proudest day of my father's life was when I came home with my Navy commission. They gave me 14 days leave so I went back to Portland. I had this great khaki uniform. I thought I looked like Adm. Nimitz. But Dad always got his way. We were going to Mass on Sunday, and Dad wanted me to wear the whites 'cause it had the epaulettes on the shoulders, and those stood out on the white uniform, and the cap looked pretty good to him, too. We're all waiting to go in to Mass, standing outside the church. Dad was standing there, too, with all of his cronies. I said, "Let's go in, Pa, let's get a seat."

He says, "No, wait, wait, the church is starting to fill up." Finally we go in, he's on one side, my mother's on the other, and I'm on my father's side, and we're going down the aisle. He went almost to the front of the church, and he was looking over. He says, "My son, the officer." He was more proud of that than when I played ball. He told me, he says, "Johnny, you're an officer, right? Do you know how long it would take to get what you got in my country? Eight, ten, or twelve years." I said, "But Pa, I'm not in your country. This is America."

◆

Naval aviation recruits Johnny Pesky and Ted Williams pose in a trainer.

Take a look at those kids that gave their lives for this country. A lot of kids got hurt and stayed in veterans hospitals. I was taught by my immigrant parents that if you were born in this country, it was a privilege. When they came over from the old country, they had to work very hard to make a living. So we learned to appreciate everything. Those were our guidelines in a sense . . . appreciation.

You had to have respect for the uniform no matter what jerk wore it, and you went through indoctrination periods of common courtesy to gold braid officers. Officers and rank! Rank is overrated. Let me tell you, the war was run by the Navy chiefs. Every Navy chief that I ever knew was a class guy. They took their jobs seriously, and when your life is on the line, you go on the straight and narrow, and you try to stay out of trouble. It all came down to discipline. The discipline instilled in me was a result of my parents of course, but also, baseball. I didn't really have adjustment problems. . . . I was just a kid just like anybody else. I took my chances, and God was good. He was looking over my shoulder.

At Pearl Harbor, I was a station officer, and many of the guys like me took care of certain things, learned about aircraft maintenance routines. Studied all those enemy aircraft charts and played on a service ball team. Then we were told to get ready for overseas. My group was headed for the big buildup in Okinawa to invade Japan. As I was in our living quarters packing, there was about 45 of us in there: ensigns, JGs, lieutenants, full lieutenants, and so on . . . and they told us to get ready to go. I was getting nervous. This war business was becoming pretty real. Then . . . they dropped the big bomb and that ended everything.

I think Mr. Truman did a very wise thing in using the A-bomb. He saved a lot of lives. MINE! It saved American lives. It saved a lot of people in Japan, too.

But when I think about that war . . . it cost us so much. I don't know what the count was that we lost in the Pacific, but it was big. BIG! I didn't get to see any live action, but my brother did. He was on Guam, the Japs were still over there, he was hiding, having to duck, but . . . we made it home. Safely. Thank God.

You ask about regrets. There was a lot at stake for America in World War II. Hitler was killing all those people. Tojo was killing everybody out in the Pacific. I especially remember the Marianas, and I finally learned some new names for some of those islands I had never heard of before. Then I met some kids that I knew from baseball who were in the Army. As a matter of fact, [one was] a kid that I played ball with, Donny Kirsch was his name, and he was a better player than I was. He was a second baseman and I was a shortstop; we played together for about three years in semipro. He served in the Battle of the Bulge in 1944. I later found out that he was shot up pretty good. There were a lot of Americans lying on the ground. He told me the Germans left [him] for dead, but a medic come by, and Donny happened to twitch, and they got him back to the hospital. He had shrapnel all through his body; he had maybe 15 operations to get that stuff out of his system. He was a great player, and he was a great kid. He gave it all up for you and for me. Makes you feel a little bit guilty at times.

———◆———

I wanted to get home. I missed baseball. I kept up on baseball overseas. You bet! Every day, the games were all over by the time we got the papers, and I'm watching the papers every day. When we could, we listened to the radio. I made it back home and loved playing ball again. Putting on that Red Sox uniform . . . wow, it felt good to be home. 1946 was a great year.

[EDITOR'S NOTE: Johnny Pesky's comments are adapted from an interview he did for Todd Anton and are presented at greater length in the book *No Greater Love*.]

Lt. Bert Shepard: From Terrorflieger to Major League Pitcher

as told to Todd Anton

"I flew every time I could. Hell, if some guy didn't want to fly I would say, 'I'll take your place today.' Goddamnit, I loved to fly. After all…it's my country." —Bert Shepard

Bert Shepard had baseball talent as a youngster but signed up to be an aviator right after Pearl Harbor. That the Japanese used aircraft for their attack inspired many Americans to want to use the same weapon against them. Accepted into the Army Air Force, it turned out he was the only one in his group who had no prior flight experience—not even as a passenger. "Good!" The instructor smiled. "I'll take you first." He learned how to fly the Lockheed P-38 Lightning and was posted to the 38th Squadron of the 55th Fighter Group. Losses had reduced the number of pilots in the squadron from 30 down to 16. More than 30 missions later, Shepard was shot down over Germany.

Our job in the American Eighth Air Force was bombarding Germany and German-occupied cities in increasing numbers. Unlike the British Royal Air Force, which did its bombing under the cover of darkness, our giant B-17s and B-24s flew over the enemy in broad daylight. Although our big bombers were loaded with .50-caliber machine guns, their bloody experience showed that the only effective way to counter German fighters was with a fighter escort. That's where the Lightning came in. I loved being on this awesome team. Damn, that Eighth Air Force did a lot of work.

Bert Shepard preparing to fly. *Courtesy of* No Greater Love.

A "38" wasn't a good airplane to make a head-on pass at. We had four .50-caliber machine guns and a 20mm right in the center of our nose in the 38. We would shoot the hell out of them, and he can't hit us, because he has guns that converge at 300 yards and two more that converge at 400 yards, so at 1,000 yards those Germans flyers can't touch us. At 30,000 feet, we were too high for flak, but typically, when I saw a chance at action, I couldn't pass it up. Once we were on a mission, and I was at about 25,000 [feet], and I saw a P-38 down below me with a German on his tail. I called it into my leader, and he wasn't real eager to join in. So, hell, I just peel off and dove for the German Me-109. He sees me coming, and he breaks off.

We sent up 3,000 aircraft to go in as far as we could and just go to the ground and strafe every damn thing we could, anything that moved. The Germans didn't send up any aircraft because they would have got clobbered, but they took care of us with ground fire. They knocked down 46 aircraft that day. That is a pretty good bunch of aircraft. The 38th, my group, was hit especially hard. Six of the squadron went down, and I happened to be one of them. We all survived. I was the only one that was injured.

The Germans had made a clearing in a small forest and placed an 88-mm anti-aircraft gun among the trees. The only way to see the gun was from above—directly above. I found out about that damn gun when my right foot was blown off.

◆

I guess I slumped over the controls, and I don't remember anything until I woke up in a German hospital about a week later—without my right leg. When German Luftwaffe surgeon Dr. Ladislaus Loidl had arrived at the wreck, it was surrounded by farmers, many of whom were wielding pitchforks and other makeshift weapons. They were going to run me through. Alone, Loidl chased them all away. He set aside his politics and saw a person. One hospital refused me, but he took me to another. They might refuse him over the phone, but

there's no way they'd say no to his face. I was unconscious the whole time!

◆

I remember flying and crashing, I am thinking, "Am I in heaven, you know . . . is this heaven?" I remember, smiling. They pulled back the sheet. There the leg is, off below the knee. There was silence, tension in the room. Here I was, a captured airman, waking up in an enemy hospital, discovering that my right foot was gone. But I surprised them all. I looked up at them and smiled, and I said, "Thank you for saving my life."

As I recovered, I was sent to prison camps farther and farther into Germany as the Allies advanced. I was surprised at the general goodwill of the German people. One guard—this was at the Meiningen camp, the fourth or fifth prison camp I was in—rides by on a bicycle. We would say, "Oh you little fat so-and-so," and "Let's take him out and cut his nuts off." Hell, this Kraut doesn't understand us, we figured. We kept it up for about a week, until one day this guy stops at the fence and asks in perfect English: "How are the Dodgers doing?" After the shock wore off, we started laughing. Turns out he had lived in Brooklyn for 12 years and worked as a policeman there. He came back to Germany to take care of his mother and, the war started. Damn, I still laugh at that one.

◆

I was also impressed with the medical care I received. They did a hell of a job on the surgery, and I had no pain after I had gotten over the numbness. I was in pretty good shape, but when I was released on a prisoner exchange, I only weighed 125 pounds. They took me down to the train station on a two-wheel alley cart because they were short of transportation. The prisoners made me a crude artificial leg for me to walk on, and then I was ready to go down to the interrogation center in Frankfurt. I arrived in New York about a month later. I was given three days' leave and took a train to Washington, D.C., simply because I had never been there. Then I went to Walter Reed Veterans Hospital to see if any of my pals ended up there.

As I arrived, a limousine pulled up, and this officer inside started talking to me. They wanted two officers and two enlisted men to go down and meet Assistant Secretary of War [Robert] Patterson because he wanted to do a press release on our treatment in prison camp, and they heard I was there. I was selected to be one of the officers involved. It changed my life.

We drove down in a big limousine over to the Pentagon to meet Assistant Secretary of War Patterson. The secretary asked all of us what we wanted to do with our lives.

The first guy said loudly he wanted to go duck hunting.

Then he came to me, and I said, "Well, if I can't fly combat in the South Pacific, then I want to play baseball."

Astonished, Patterson said, "Well, you can't play baseball, can you?"

I noticed that Patterson was looking at the crude leg I had on. "Sure I can. As soon as I get a new leg I am pretty sure I can."

Patterson was impressed. He called up Clark Griffith, the owner of the Washington Senators, and said, "He's got a leg off and as soon as he gets a new leg he could play ball."

I knew that Griffith was not going to say no to the assistant secretary of war. He told Patterson, "Send him over whenever his new leg [is] ready." So I got a new leg, and, about four days later, I was behind the barracks practicing throwing and so forth, shifting and getting a balance. Then I go out to work out with the Senators. Of course, nobody, the players, fans, nobody knows I am coming out. I am a little late, and I am in there dressing by myself, and I go out to start to warm up.

With the war still raging, it's still 1945. There were just two sportswriters at Senators training camp that year. One of them noticed me working out and asked who I was.

One of the Senators' bat boys told him, "Well, that is a guy just back from prison camp, and he's got a leg off, but he thinks he can play ball."

That reporter was none other than Ernie Harwell, reporter for the USMC's

Leatherneck magazine. Two hours later, the camp was teeming with journalists and cameramen. I tried to put on a show. I put a uniform back on, going out and doing some running for them. Hell, I hadn't fielded bunts in four years, but I could do pretty damn good with the leg.

I made the Senators! I knew I was there as a token, but I didn't care. I wanted to use my status to make other injured men like me feel better.

Then, on August 4, 1945, we were getting hammered by the Red Sox. Boston broke out to a quick 7–2 lead. Our manager, Ossie Bluege, didn't want to waste any of his regular relievers, so he threw in rookie Joe Cleary. Seven runs and a strikeout later, we were down 14–2, and the fourth wasn't even over yet.

Bluege had nothing left to lose. So I went in. The crowd went wild. Although the Germans had surrendered back in May, the war in the Pacific was still active. Seeing me trot out to the mound was a welcome diversion. I wasn't tearful or scared. Hell, after what I'd been through, I was ready!

I pitched the rest of the game, and I didn't do bad at all. I faced 20 batters in all, allowing three singles, a walk, and an earned run. But I struck out two and recorded a very respectable 1.69 ERA. Much better than Cleary's 189.00—and he had both his legs!

I went to bat three times. I didn't get a hit, but I smacked the ball hard twice, and, by all accounts, I was considered a tough out. I also covered first flawlessly. I was flying pretty high, and even at that moment on the field, my thoughts drifted back to that kindly German doctor who saved my life.

Unfortunately, though, my good job on the mound wasn't enough to get me more playing time as we fought tough to the end and finished 87–67, a game and a half behind the Tigers. Those Tigers went on to beat the Cubs in the 1945 World Series.

It should have been us.

My lack of playing time didn't faze me. My major league debut more or less a success, I went to spring training with the Senators in 1946 assuming I'd make the team.

I pitched three innings three times, and I allowed one hit and no walks each time. I thought I would probably get a better chance this time, but the regular pitchers were coming back from the war and they had already made their mark, so I never got in any more games.

Although I understood my role, the lack of playing time began to get to me. I wanted to earn a spot, so I asked the Senators to send me down to their Triple-A affiliate in Chattanooga. I won two and lost two. I thought I had it made. But the call back to the big club never came.

I did go barnstorming with the American League All-Stars. I played first base. Hell, I hit two home runs in Calgary. I al-

Bert Shepard of the Washington Senators straps on his prosthetic leg
before warming up.

ways thought I could hit—but there wasn't much of anything I didn't think I couldn't do. We played Feller's All-Stars in Seattle, and I got 1-for-2 off Feller, and 1-for-2 off Johnny Sain. I hit the ball hard every time.

I was sure I could make it back to the majors, this time as a legitimate player. All I needed to get ready for next spring was a re-amputation and a new prosthesis. Back at Walter Reed, it took this real lame-ass doctor three times to cut my stump right. He screwed me up royally, and eventually I had to have four more amputations over a period of two years. He did 26 botched operations on the ward that day, and they all had to be done over.

Things got worse before they got better for me. The fourth doctor got the bone spur out but cut too close to a nerve. I would wear the leg a couple of days, and I would start weeping. It really hurt.

I'm not bitter. I was a victim of some very poor surgery, but what can you do about it? You can't sue anybody. You can't blame anybody. That was just the way it happened. By all rights, I should be dead. So what am I going to do . . . bitch about it? Hell no! Be a man, and get on with life. My leg eventually recovered, but other problems set in. Being on crutches all that time just screwed the arm up.

Of course, I didn't give up. The only job [available] was managing. So I went to Waterbury Connecticut Class B, and I took that job just before the season started.

One of my first decisions as manager was to put myself in the starting rotation. I won five and lost five, but my arm just wasn't any good. I have to admit it. I played first base quite a bit because I was the manager! If a guy got hurt I would play first.

I was just 25. I still had dreams about the bigs. One night, I hit two home runs and drove in eight runs.

I honestly think I could have made it, but with my arm growing tired, I packed it

in. I played a few exhibitions after that but nothing serious. I didn't want to play if I couldn't play as well as the others.

I may never have been a star in the major leagues, but you know, I can always say I was there. And I did it my way.

◆

My favorite leg was the one I had back in the late 1940s; it allowed me to become Ted Williams' favorite story. I had my moment in the majors, and then I became a salesman in New York City. I had friends on the Yankees. Phil Rizzuto asked me to come in and throw batting practice to him and Joe DiMaggio. Joe was having trouble hitting left-handers. So I often threw. That was fun. Hell, it was Yankee Stadium! One day, the Red Sox were in town, and it was good to see Ted Williams. He told me to pitch to him, too. He could use the work. Nobody seemed to mind. The Sox were out of it anyway. So I started pitching. Each time I followed through and brought my wooden leg around there was this big cracking sound and a big crack, both coming from my leg.

I threw again and again . . . crack. It was again getting bigger-louder. Ted didn't notice, but each time I could see my fake foot beginning to turn inwards towards a 90-degree angle, totally abnormal to look at. I felt no pain at all. How could I?

Again I threw and followed through . . .

crack! Now I knew the foot was totally disconnected. I was landing on the shaft, you know, a peg leg. Ted was beginning to laugh.

Now I wound up for what I knew would be my final pitch. I lifted my leg and all my foot did was spin around and around.

Ted Williams fell down laughing so hard, I struck him out!

[EDITOR'S NOTE: Bert Shepard's comments are adapted from an interview he did for Todd Anton and are presented at greater length in the book *No Greater Love*.]

Herb "Briefcase" Simpson

by Bill Swank

"Kid, you did pretty good." — Satchel Paige

Like many young prospects in the early 1940s, 21-year-old Herb Simpson was thrilled to sign a professional baseball contract. In fact, he was so thrilled that he signed two contracts. Before playing a single game for the Birmingham Black Barons in 1941, Simpson inked a second pact with the Homestead Grays that would pay him more money.

"The Grays offered me $25 a month more, and that was a lot of money back then," Simpson recalls with a chuckle. This was an early version of free agency that was popular in the Negro Leagues as players would jump from one team to another for a bigger paycheck.

But Uncle Sam had other plans for Simpson and his generation. Instead of playing baseball, the fleet-footed outfielder found himself in the infantry, training for cold weather survival in Wyoming. He was eventually assigned to the quartermaster corps and shipped to England as part of the massive Allied buildup prior to the Normandy landings.

While awaiting the invasion, Herb Simpson played as the only black member of an all-white Army team in what were known as the "battle leagues." Such activities kept the men in top physical shape, and the games were good for the morale of the troops.

Simpson has a particularly vivid memory of a stormy night in England during June 1944. Rain was pounding down on his tent when a loud explosion woke everybody. Simpson recalled, "The next morning I went into a field, maybe 60-70 feet away, and found a piece of a German V-1 rocket." This mangled piece of metal became his wartime souvenir—his buzz bomb "medal."

On D-Day, Simpson's unit, the 2057th Quartermaster Truck Company, was prepared to cross the English Channel on schedule. But once the American beachhead was successfully established, there was no room for additional personnel or material. The 2057th was stopped at the English coast and did not arrive in France until several days later.

After intense fighting, the Allies finally broke through the hedgerows, and General George Patton's "Thundering Third Army" seized the offensive. It was the predominantly black "Red Ball Express" that ran round-the-clock convoys to deliver gasoline to his thirsty tanks. "Red Ball" was an old railroad term used to identify express shipping. Herb Simpson served as a dispatcher in this operation for three months. "We were proud of our service," said Simpson.

Following the surrender of the Third Reich, the 2057th remained in Germany providing continued logistic support in Munich, Frankfurt, and Nuremberg. The troops even got to play a little baseball in Europe, but homecoming remains an indelible memory for Herb Simpson. "As our ship pulled into New York, we were greeted by Count Basie's Band. They were playing 'Sent For You Yesterday (And Here You Come Today).' We were finally back home."

Upon release from active duty, he returned to Louisiana to live with his parents. Simpson recalls that when he would go out for the evening with friends, his mother would admonish him to be home by midnight. His father, Horace Simpson, a New Orleans baseball legend in his own right, argued that Herb was a grown man and could come and go as he pleased. He appreciated his father's support, but said, "I would never disobey my mother."

In 1946, Simpson signed to play ball again with the Birmingham Black Barons. Harlem Globetrotters owner Abe Saperstein held an interest in the Black Barons and decided that Simpson should instead become the first baseman for his Seattle Steelhead team in the newly formed West Coast Negro Baseball Association. The Steelheads were actually Saperstein's Globetrotters baseball team, and the pay was comparable. Simpson drew a salary of $250 per month plus $2 a day for meal money.

When the league folded after a few months, the Steelheads returned to the barnstorming circuit variously known as the Harlem Globetrotters, the Cincinnati Crescents, and Abe Saperstein's Negro All-Stars. Teammates included Sherwood Brewer, Piper Davis, Luke Easter, Dan Bankhead, Paul Hardy, Artie Wilson, Ulysses Redd, and the incomparable Reese "Goose" Tatum, the Clown Prince of Basketball.

Goose shared first base duties with Simpson and performed several comedy routines during the games. As part of their seventh-inning stretch entertainment, the Globetrotters featured a race between 1936 Olympic champion world record holder Jesse Owens and one of the ballplayers.

"Jesse was my friend," said Simpson, and, according to script, Owens was supposed to win the foot races. "Jesse was getting older and he'd say, 'Herb, slow down a little . . . slow down.' We were in Hawaii, and Jesse's daughter was with him. She was real nice looking . . . beautiful. The players asked where she'd sit on the bus from the hotel to the ballpark. Jesse told them, 'She'll sit next to a gentleman,' and he meant she'd sit next to me."

Luke Easter batted clean-up and frequently received a free pass to first base. Simpson hit next in the lineup and laughs softly at the memory. "The Lord was good to me. I'd get my hits, and I'd be right on Luke's heels. He told the manager that I should hit third. That way he could drive me in with his home runs and we could both walk the bases instead of running them."

The first time Simpson's parents and friends got to see him play professionally was in New Orleans at Pelican Stadium against Satchel Paige. The wily Paige yelled down from the hill, "Hey, Kid, whadda ya wanna hit?"

Simpson politely requested a fastball, down the middle, waist high. Paige delivered as ordered. Simpson swung and missed.

The second pitch was in the same location, but this time the youngster drove it into the left field corner for a triple. Afterward, Paige smiled and said, "Kid, you did pretty good."

In 1948, the Trotters beat Paige's Kansas City Royals in an exhibition game. The *Los Angeles Times* proclaimed that the Globetrotters were "generally conceded to be the greatest Negro aggregation in the land."

By this time, Major League Baseball's color barrier had been broken, and the minor leagues were slowly being integrated. After a brief stint on the mound with the 1951 Chicago American Giants, Herb Simpson moved into organized baseball. In 1952, he batted a solid .282 for the Spokane Indians of the Western International League, but it was in Albuquerque where Simpson found acceptance and became a fan favorite. He was the Jackie Robinson of the West Texas-New Mexico League and averaged over .300 for three years.

Dukes manager Eddie Bockman remembers Herb Simpson as "a helluva guy for the situation he was in." Hotels and restaurants were closed to black players in Texas, so boarding homes had to be found. "They always welcomed Herb back, because he was such a nice man. He was very polite. Everybody liked him," recalled Bockman.

Interestingly, Simpson didn't gain his nickname until an Albuquerque sportswriter asked if he was related to major league outfielder Harry "Suitcase" Simpson. There were no family ties, but because Herb was a compact 5 feet, 8 inches, the scribe began calling him Herb "Briefcase" Simpson.

"Briefcase" believes the highlight of his

Herb Simpson with Albuquerque in 1954.

baseball career occurred in 1954, when he married the love of his life, Sophie, at home plate in Albuquerque. After tying the knot, it was time to find a real job. Simpson and his bride returned to New Orleans, where he worked for 20 years in the school system and then another decade for the state of Louisiana.

"We didn't have any children of our own. I was a custodian for the schools, so I had lots of kids. I've always liked kids," Simpson said.

Simpson is now a widower and contin-

ues to reside in his beloved Crescent City. Over the last 50 years, he has remained involved with many civic, religious, and charitable organizations. Most importantly, Herb Simpson has never tired of teaching kids how to play baseball, nor has he tired of expressing his love for his country. He was deeply humbled to represent all of the Negro Leaguers who served during the Second World War at The National World War II Museum baseball conference in New Orleans.

Warren Spahn Overcomes His Challenges

by Gary Bedingfield

"Before the war I didn't have anything that slightly resembled self-confidence . . . but nowadays I just throw them up without the slightest mental pressure." —Warren Spahn

For many, military service during World War II diminished playing skills that could not be resurrected after facing enemy fire on the battlefields of Europe or the Pacific. For Warren Spahn, however, it proved to be the foundation upon which he built a Hall of Fame career.

"After what I went through overseas, I never thought of anything I was told to do in baseball as hard work," recalled the late Warren Spahn, a combat engineer in Europe during World War II and the most successful left-handed pitcher in major league history. "You get over feeling like that when you spend days on end sleeping in frozen tank tracks in enemy-threatened territory. The Army taught me something about chal-lenges and about what's important and what isn't. Everything I tackle in baseball and in life I take as a challenge rather than work."

Warren Spahn was born in Buffalo, New York, on April 23, 1921, the fifth of six children to Ed and Mabel Spahn. A good semipro player in his day, Ed taught Warren to pitch and play first base, and the younger Spahn soon began making a name for himself at South Park High School. He led the school team to two city championships, went undefeated his last two seasons, and threw a no-hitter his senior year.

Nevertheless, he was virtually ignored by major league scouts because he was so skinny. All but one, that is. Bill Meyers, a part-time scout with the Boston Bees (as the Braves called themselves between 1936 and 1940), signed Spahn in 1940 for $80 a month. He was assigned to the Bradford Bees of the Class D PONY League that summer and got off to an uninspiring start. Suffering from a sore arm much of the year, he finished out 1940 with a 5–4 record, although his 62 strikeouts in 66 innings and 2.73 earned run average showed some promise.

Moving up to the Evansville Bees of the Class B Three-I League in 1941, Spahn began to fulfill that promise. He was 19–6 and led the circuit in wins and ERA (1.83). During one stretch he hurled 42 consecutive scoreless innings and contributed three one-hitters to Evansville's pennant-winning campaign.

Spahn's solid performance earned a trip to spring training with the Boston Braves in 1942, where his smooth, overhand delivery secured a place on the club's roster for the start of the season. Four days before his 21st birthday, Spahn made his big league debut as one of five Braves pitchers used against the New York Giants. Hurling two-thirds of an inning before a Patriots' Day crowd of 13,694, he was unable to stop New York's offensive onslaught in the 5–2 loss. He would make one further appearance for the Braves before being assigned to the Hartford Bees of the Class A Eastern League, where he fashioned a 17–12 record and 1.96 ERA, good enough to earn him another trip to

Boston in September. By the close of the season, the Braves were in seventh place and Spahn had pitched a total of just 15⅔ innings with no decisions.

Spahn's fledgling major league career was then put on hold when he entered military service on December 10, 1942. He served with the Army at Camp Gruber, Oklahoma, then Camp Chaffee, Arkansas, where he undertook training in the engineer corps but found time to pitch for the 1850th Service Command Unit baseball team. On August 5, 1943, Spahn pitched a 15–0 no-hitter for the 1850th against the KFPW Broadcasters, striking out 17.

On a bleak winter's day in December 1944, S.Sgt. Spahn arrived in England with the 276th Engineer Combat Battalion (ECB). "Let me tell you," Spahn said, "that was a tough bunch of guys. We had people that were let out of prison to go into the service. So those were the people I went overseas with, and they were tough and rough, and I had to fit that mold."

His time in England would be brief as the 276th ECB was needed in the combat zones of mainland Europe. Hopping the Channel to France and then to the hilly and heavily forested Ardennes region of eastern Belgium and northern Luxembourg, Spahn soon found himself in what later became known as the Battle of the Bulge—the last major Nazi offensive against Allied forces in World War II. In snow and sub-freezing conditions, the Germans inflicted huge casualties but failed to break through the Allied lines. "We were surrounded in the Hüertgen Forest and had to fight our way out of there," Spahn explained. "Our feet were frozen when we went to sleep, and they were frozen when we woke up. We didn't have a bath or change of clothes for weeks."

Furthermore, troops had to deal with German soldiers, dressed as GIs and speaking perfect English, trying to infiltrate Allied lines. Baseball saved many American lives during this time. Jeeps would be stopped at road blocks and the occupants asked such questions as, "What team does Bob Feller pitch for?" "What's the nickname of the team in Brooklyn?"

"The Germans had our equipment, our uniforms, even our dog tags," recalled Spahn. "Our password used to be something like, 'Who's the second baseman for the Bums?' They wouldn't know who the 'Bums' were. I used to pity any guy in our outfit who wasn't a baseball fan because he would be in deep trouble!"

Surviving that ordeal, the 276th ECB advanced toward Germany with the U.S. Ninth Army. To reach Germany, Allied troops would need to cross the Rhine River, and it was fully expected that all the river crossings had been destroyed by the retreating enemy forces.

On March 7, 1945, the 9th Armored Division discovered that the Ludendorff Bridge at Remagen—which led into the German heartland—was still standing. Demolitions were in place but had failed to detonate. By midnight the same day, the bridge had been cleared of mines and explosives, hasty repairs had been completed, and traffic began to cross. On March 10, the 276th ECB took over bridge maintenance. The unit's job was to ensure traffic moved continuously by undertaking any and all repairs that were needed. Among those crossing the bridge at this time was a young major of the 9th Armored who had been a catcher in the Yankees' organization before the war. His name was Ralph Houk, and he would later be a back-up catcher with the Yankees before leading them to three American League pennants and two World Series as a manager.

During this time the Ludendorff Bridge was under almost constant attack from German artillery and dive bombers who were desperate to stop the flow of Allied forces into their homeland. On March 16, Spahn was wounded in the foot by shrapnel while working on the bridge. He got it patched up and went back to work. The following day he narrowly escaped death when the entire structure gave way and collapsed into the river just after he left it. More than 90 Army engineers were injured, and 30 lost their lives, crushed by falling debris or drowned in the river below. The 276th ECB received the Distinguished Unit citation for its efforts to keep the bridge operational. Spahn received

One year after returning from military service, Warren Spahn
won 21 games with the Boston Braves.

a Bronze Star and Purple Heart. He is also one of the few major league players to receive a battlefield commission, being made a second lieutenant. Red Sox left-hander Earl Johnson and Athletics veteran Jack Knott were others promoted on the battlefield.

Continuing to advance through Germany, Lt. Spahn would be attached to the 1257th ECB, 1265th ECB, and 343rd Engi-

neer General Service Regiment before Germany surrendered on May 7, 1945. At that time he was in Giessen, Germany, where a subcamp of the Buchenwald concentration camp was located.

With peace in Europe, Spahn pitched for the 115th Engineers Group on a hastily built ballfield at the University of Heidelberg. In a four-game stretch, he allowed only one run and nine hits while striking out 73 batters. He stopped the 19th Corps in three straight games, allowing four hits and striking out 20 in the first game. He gave up a single and struck out 18 in the second contest, and allowed two hits while striking out 19 in the third game. He then faced the 32nd Anti-Aircraft Artillery Brigade and struck out 17 while allowing just two hits.

Spahn didn't receive his military discharge until June 2, 1946, but he wasted little time and caught up with the Braves in Pittsburgh on June 11. "This is the first time in years I've reported to anybody without saluting," he told the newly appointed Braves' manager Billy Southworth.

It took the 25-year-old four starts to earn the first of 363 major league wins—a 4–1 decision over Fritz Ostermueller of the Pirates on July 14. By the end of the season he had an 8–5 record and a very healthy 2.94 earned run average.

"Before the war I didn't have anything that slightly resembled self-confidence," Spahn explained when reflecting on his newfound success at the major league level. "I was tight as a drum and worrying about every pitch. But nowadays I just throw them up without the slightest mental pressure."

The following year Spahn had the first of 13 20-win seasons, and his emergence coincided with the Braves' resurgence. They won the National League pennant in 1948, and he was immortalized in baseball lore by

the "Spahn and Sain and pray for rain" jingle crafted by *Boston Post* sports editor Gerald Hern.

Spahn continued his winning ways with 20-plus victories in 1949, 1950, 1951, 1953, 1954, and 1956. In 1957, at age 36, he won 21 games, and the Braves met the New York Yankees in the World Series. He lost the Series opener to Whitey Ford, 3–1, but won Game Four, 7–5, in 10 innings. Four days later, a flu-ridden Spahn watched Lew Burdette in his place shut out the Yankees, 5–0, to clinch the Series.

On September 16, 1960, 39-year-old Spahn—at an age when most pitchers are coming to the end of their careers—pitched the first of two no-hitters, a 4–0 win against the Phillies (his second no-hitter came on April 28, 1961, against the Giants).

As the years passed, Spahn kept on top of his game by learning to adapt. When his fastball began to fade, he developed a screwball and later picked up a slider. It seemed his career and dominance of opposing batters would never end. In 1963, at the age of 42, he turned in one of his finest seasons with a 23–7 record and 2.60 ERA, leading the league with 22 complete games.

Interestingly, that same year, Spahn returned to military uniform, albeit under extremely different circumstances. He appeared in an episode of the hit television series *Combat* dressed as a German soldier carrying an automatic sub-machine gun.

Spahn appeared as a Nazi guard in "Glow Against the Sky" on the 1963–64 TV series *Combat*. He is shown here during the filming. After shooting the segment, he beat the Dodgers that same day with a six-hitter.

Several of Spahn's teammates—including Hank Aaron, Claude Raymond, and Ron Piche—came with him to the shoot. "Hope we haven't worked you so hard that you won't be able to do a good job against the Dodgers tonight," director Sutton Roley told Spahn at the end of the day's shooting. As it turned out they hadn't. Spahn beat the Dodgers, 6–1, on nine hits for his 16th win of the season.

Then just one year later his knees betrayed him. His record dropped to 6–13, and the season was further tarnished by ugly run-ins with manager Bobby Bragan. On November 23, 1964, Spahn was sold to the New York Mets. The following spring they purchased 40-year-old Yogi Berra from the Yankees. "I don't know whether we'll be the oldest battery in baseball," Spahn said, "but I know we'll be the ugliest."

Spahn had a 4–12 record with the Mets when he was released on July 22, 1965. He was signed by the San Francisco Giants the same day, and the 44-year-old ended his major league career there with a 3–4 record. Spahn didn't leave gracefully. "I didn't quit," he declared. "Baseball retired me."

Following success as a minor league manager, Spahn returned to the major leagues in the early 1970s as pitching coach for the Cleveland Indians. He was inducted in the Baseball Hall of Fame in 1973—his first year of eligibility. He instructed the pitching staff of the Japanese Hiroshima Carp from 1973 to 1978 and returned to baseball in the United States in 1979 to coach minor-league pitchers in the California Angels farm system. He gave up baseball for good in 1981. After 40 years in the game, he retired to his 2,000-acre cattle ranch in Hartshorne, Oklahoma.

In August 2003, the Atlanta Braves unveiled a nine-foot bronze statue of Spahn outside Turner Field. An ailing 82-year-old Spahn attended the opening ceremony. Three months later, on November 24, 2003, Warren Spahn passed away peacefully at his home in Hartshorne.

Sources:
• Bloomfield, Gary. *Duty, Honor, Victory: America's Athletes in World War II* (The Lyons Press).
• Buege, Bob. *The Milwaukee Braves: A Baseball Eulogy* (Douglas American Sports Publications, 1988).
• Fowle, Barry W. *Builders and Fighters: U.S. Army Engineers in World War II* (US Army Corps of Engineers Fort Belvoir, VA 1992).
• Goldstein, Richard. "Warren Spahn, 82, Dies; Left-Handed Craftsman of the Baseball Mound for 21 Seasons" (*New York Times*, November 25, 2003).
• Rawson, Andrew. *Remagen Bridge: 9th Armored Division* (Pen & Sword Books).
• Silverman, Al. *Warren Spahn; Immortal Southpaw* (Bartholomew House, Sport Magazine Library No. 9, 1961).
• Spahn, Warren. National League Service Bureau Questionnaire.
• *Sporting News*, July 26, 1945.
• *Sporting News*, August 23, 1945.
• *Sporting News*, August 21, 1946.
• *Sporting News*, December 8, 2003.
• Unknown. "Hall of Famer, 82, won 363 games" (Associated Press, November 25, 2003).
• Unknown. "Milwaukee Eagles Honor Spahn at Dinner, April 30" (publisher unknown, April 23, 1966).
• Unknown. "Eagles Club Cites Ex-Soldier Spahn" (*Wisconsin State Journal*, May 1, 1966).
• Unknown. "Spahn Turns in Shutout Game" (*Ogden Standard-Examiner*, August 6, 1943).
• Walfoort, Cleon. "TV Role for *Combat* Vet Spahn: He's Sergeant in German Army" (publisher unknown, September 7, 1963).

Ted Williams at War

◆

by Bill Nowlin

"Ted only batted .406 for the Red Sox. He batted a thousand for the Marine Corps and the United States." —John Glenn

It's difficult to conceive of today. A star ballplayer like Alex Rodriguez flying close air support in Afghanistan, being shot at by al-Qaeda and Taliban fighters as he flies in at 1,000 feet to strafe and bomb their columns in the Panjshir Valley? It almost doesn't compute.

To be fair, though, no one could know how today's men would respond were they situated in the circumstances faced by ballplayers more than 50 years ago.

Ted Williams flew dive-bombing missions over enemy lines during the Korean War, his Panther jet slashing down from the skies while the enemy threw everything they could against him—anti-aircraft and small arms fire alike. These were harrowing combat missions; his Panther jet took hits on more than one mission.

Williams is the only member of the Na-tional Baseball Hall of Fame to serve in both World War II and the Korean War, though fellow Marine pilot Jerry Coleman also saw combat in both wars and is honored by the Hall of Fame as the recipient of the 2005 Ford Frick Award. Times were very different in World War II, the first of two times when Williams and Coleman gave up baseball to serve in the armed forces. Hundreds of major and minor leaguers served, but there were few who were shot at and barely es-caped with their lives.

Williams lost nearly five seasons to war—three in the Second World War and two in the Korean—and there's been specu-lation ever since on how many more than his 521 homers he would have hit had he added another five years to his playing career.

Less than a month after he turned 23, Williams had gone 6-for-8 in a doublehead-

Captain Ted Williams on the flight line in Korea, 1953.
Photo courtesy of Frank Cushing.

er on the final day of the 1941 season—
September 28—catapulting his batting
average from .399 to .406 and becoming in
the process the last man to hit over .400 in
a season. It's a record that's stood for more
than six decades. "The Kid" didn't have a lot
of time to enjoy his accomplishment. Just

10 weeks later, Japanese aircraft attacked
the U.S. complex at Pearl Harbor, Hawaii,
killing more than 3,000 Americans. Hours
later, the United States entered the World
War II.

Williams had a valid deferment as the
sole support of his mother, May, but the

deferment was overturned in the early days of 1942. It was restored on appeal, and some anonymous self-appointed patriots questioned his courage. Williams braved the criticism and was cheered by crowds of servicemen during spring training that year.

Shortly after the season began—perhaps having made his point of principle—Williams and Johnny Pesky both signed up in the Navy's V5 program. This allowed them to play out the 1942 season, but both went on to spend the 1943, 1944, and 1945 seasons in the United States Navy. In Williams' case, he later transferred to the Marines, spending the war as a flight and gunnery instructor serving stateside. He was headed to the Pacific, but before he saw combat, the Japanese surrendered.

Williams was glad to return to baseball in 1946, and the Sox won the pennant and nearly the World Series. Williams won his first MVP and helped power the Red Sox into contention for most of the following five years.

After war broke out in Korea, the Marines were forced to call up large numbers of Reserve pilots in early 1952. Whether by mistake (as his commanding officer in Korea understood) or by design, Williams was among those recalled. He was 33 years old, with a young daughter, and not at all happy about being summoned back. He kept quiet about it, though, because he understood the reason: Politicians did not provide suf-

ficient funding to keep the Marines fully staffed. He took his physical and passed, going through the process with fellow major leaguer Coleman of the Yankees.

When Williams reported for duty in early May (after hitting a home run in his last at-bat before his departure), he decided he didn't want to take the easy route of exhibition baseball and morale-building P.R. tours of bases for the Marines. At some level, he must have wondered how he might have measured up had he ever been tested in combat. He made it clear that if the Marines wanted him back because they needed men to fight, he sought no favored treatment, and he wanted to fight. His instructor, Bill Churchman, urged Williams to put himself forward to fly jet aircraft. They were the best aircraft the Marines had to offer, and Williams always wanted to work with the best of whatever it was he chose: fishing gear, photographic equipment, or aircraft.

He'd only flown propeller craft in World War II. Now he learned to fly the F-9F Panther jet and earned assignment to the elite squadron in Marine Air, VMF-311. He arrived at K-3, the Marine Corps base in southern Korea near the seaside town of Pohang. He flew his first combat mission on Valentine's Day 1953.

It didn't take long for Capt. Ted Williams to make national headlines. Two days later, on his third mission, Williams' plane was hit—apparently by ground fire during a dive-bombing run over North Korea. He'd come in very low and been hit badly. His plane lost its radio and its hydraulics. He couldn't maneuver the plane as well as he would have liked and couldn't put down landing gear. When smoke began to come out from under the fuselage, it was clear there was no way he'd get back to his base. With red warning lights flashing from several spots in the cockpit, Williams' plane began to drift off in the wrong direction. How could Williams ever forget the moment? "When I pulled up out of my run, all the red lights were on in the plane, and the damn thing started to shake. The stick stiffened up and was shaking. I knew I had a hydraulic leak. Fuel warning light, fire warning light, there are so many lights on a jet that when anything serious goes wrong the lights almost blind you. I was in serious trouble."

Fortunately, Lieutenant Larry Hawkins saw a plane drifting off course, heading out to sea and toward North Korea. Not knowing who the pilot was, Hawkins caught up with Williams and signaled him to follow. Hawkins' radio worked; he located an Air Force base and radioed ahead to clear the tarmac. Williams landed his plane, without wheels, scraping metal for hundreds of yards along the tarmac in a shower of sparks and smoke and dirt. When the plane ground to a halt, he popped the canopy and bolted from the plane seconds before it was consumed

in flame. Williams had to hitch a ride back to base that afternoon in a two-seat trainer aircraft. At 8:08 the next morning, he was up again on Mission No. 4, attacking pre-designated troop concentrations.

In all, Williams flew 39 combat missions in Korea. His plane was hit on other occasions but never as badly as on that third mission. In late April, though, the *Boston Globe* ran a five-column front page headline "Flak Hits Ted Williams' Plane" with the subhead "Sox Slugger Lands Safely After Raid." It was Williams' 22nd mission, on April 27. He'd been part of a mission of 23 aircraft that hit the port city of Chinnampo, defended by anti-aircraft fire. Williams' Panther jet was hit in the tip tank, fortunately depleted of fuel at the time. It was, the Associated Press reported, his "second brush with death in 2½ months."

Williams was indeed in the Corps' elite squadron. Among the pilots on the April 27 mission was Maj. John Glenn. The two men remained friends after their service and Glenn said of Williams, "He did a helluva good job. Ted only batted .406 for the Red Sox. He batted a thousand for the Marine Corps and the United States." Generous in his praise, Glenn has on more than one occasion said, "Ted flew about half his missions as my wingman." The two did fly together on several occasions, and at least one mission was just the two Marine pilots on a predawn raid. All told, though, a thorough review of squadron records shows only seven missions in which the two men flew together. Numbers aside, Williams did serve several missions as John Glenn's wingman.

Most books on Williams offer just the obligatory chapter or two on WWII and Korea. Wanting to explore this side of Williams' life more thoroughly for *Ted Williams at War*, I was able to track down and interview 37 pilots who flew out of K-3 in Korea and another 30 Marines who served on the base. The picture that emerges of Williams from these interviews is complex. Like any high profile figure, he engendered a range of opinion, from admiration to envy. Some lionized him; others were deprecatory. Some saw him as an excellent pilot; others disparaged his flying. But Williams kept a low profile on the base, spending considerable time in the darkroom as the squadron photographic officer. Base commanding officer Col. Ben Robertshaw summed up his own appraisal in just eight words: "He stood out because he didn't stand out."

Williams was always outspoken, and some of what he had to say may have ruffled a few feathers among the "regulars"—the Marine Corps lifers. During the course of the research, I came across two different officers who believed that Williams was close to being court-martialed near the end of his stay in Korea and may have been sent home a little early. He had missed several weeks during two hospital stays due to a condition

attributed to too rapid a descent. The full story is explored in the book, but so as not to leave *When Baseball Went to War* readers hanging in too much suspense, the short answer is that the last of his three commanding officers was not enamored with Williams, though his displeasure stopped well short of recommending court martial. With the end of the war just weeks away, and Williams ill, it seemed the better plan was to muster out the pilot that rubbed him the wrong way.

For the record, Williams' other commanding officers accorded him above-average performance ratings and remembered him favorably. It speaks volumes that Glenn chose Williams as his wingman. The April 22 mission, Williams' 14th, departed K-3 at 5:25 AM. At 6:07, the two attacked a road bridge with two 500-pound bombs and 75 rounds of 20mm ammunition. At 6:31, they attacked another bridge, dropping two more 500-pound bombs and 16 rockets. There was meager automatic weapons anti-aircraft fire, but no damage was received. The aircraft returned safely to base. You don't fly on a mission with just one other pilot watching your wing if you don't trust that man implicitly.

Capt. Williams was honorably discharged and returned stateside just in time to be checked out during his third hospital stay of 1953 and make it to the All-Star Game as an honored guest. Despite playing

Williams returns from Korea and plans to switch back to his Red Sox uniform. He hit over .400 in what remained of the 1953 season. *Photo courtesy of Laban Whitaker.*

no baseball at all for about 14 months, despite being frozen in the bitter Korean winter, and despite being shot at and shot down, Williams decided to see if he could get in shape to get in a little baseball in 1953.

He hit .407. Not only did he get in shape, he still had the eye and the talent and the ability to outguess the pitchers he faced.

Teddy Ballgame accumulated 91 at-bats in 37 games, hit 13 homers, and drove in 34 runs. Who needs spring training? It was the third time he'd hit .400 (he'd gone four-for-10 in the six games before leaving for Korea in early 1952).

Ted Williams went on to win two more batting titles—1957 and 1958—and led the league in on-base percentage four more times. After Korea, he added another 197 home runs to his career total and truly left everyone wondering how well he might have done had he not lost nearly five full years of playing time. Most projections put him within a couple dozen home runs of Babe Ruth's record.

As to the Marine Corps, he did spout off once about the "gutless politicians" who wouldn't give the Corps the resources it needed. He found himself in the midst of a tempest for a month or so, but it died down in time.

There is no question that Ted Williams remained proud of his service, and it's likely that his own appreciation for what he had done grew as the years passed. He could well have taken the easy route, but he put himself in harm's way. He escaped serious injury but only barely. He's one of the few major league ballplayers who saw combat, and he almost paid the ultimate price.

In later years, one could even see the pride he felt in the Marine Corps. At any event he attended, he always stood visibly straighter—even if he had to struggle to his feet or be helped to stand up—with pride in his bearing, when the colors were presented and the national anthem was performed.

Asked what he felt best about, looking back on his life, he told Jeff Idelson of the Hall of Fame, "The two things I'm proudest of in my life [are] that I became a Marine pilot and that I became a member of baseball's hall of fame."

[EDITOR'S NOTE: This original article is informed by the research and writing in the book *Ted Williams at War* (Rounder Books).]

A ballgame in progress at Bainbridge.

Above: Sergeant Joe DiMaggio arrives in Hawaii in 1944
and receives his Seventh Army Air Force sleeve insignia.

Left: Soldier Cecil Travis at Fort McPherson, Georgia, January 1942. The former Senators
shortstop had hit .359 the year before, topped only by Ted Williams' .406 in 1941.

American airmen in China fielded a team that included Major General Claire Chennault, Commanding General of the 14th Air Force.

Bob Feller prepares to blast a strike past an opposing batter during a game in which he struck out 18 at Efate in the New Hebrides.

Bad Nauheim internees take the opportunity to play some ball.

BAD NAUHEIM

It had been obvious for months that Germany and the United States would be at war. By December 1941, the only Americans remaining in Berlin were a few dozen government workers and their dependents, military attaches, and 22 journalists. When Hitler declared war on December 11, the Americans were given three days to pack their belongings and prepare to leave the capitol.

Some 114 U.S. citizens were transferred by train to the spa town of Bad Nauheim, about 30 miles from Frankfurt, where they were housed in Jeschke's Grand Hotel, which was reopened for the internees after being closed for more than two years. They were, in effect, under house arrest—albeit in a nice hotel—and under the leadership of embassy First Secretary George Kennan. They were also under what Charles Burdick termed "the watchful, threatening eyes of the feared Gestapo."

By springtime, with food sparsely provided and clothing becoming a little threadbare, the calisthenics program that had been created in winter blossomed into playing baseball four times a week in a municipal athletic field that was not too far away. Major Jack Lowell had brought a regulation softball, a bat, and two gloves with him. They worked to make additional handmade baseballs and formed a four-team league: the Embassy Reds, Embassy Blues, Journalists, and Army & Navy. They scheduled the Bad Nauheim Wurlitzer Cup Baseball Series. Kennan was catcher for the Reds, the ultimate champions. In his report, written after the internment ended when the party was shipped to Lisbon in May 1942, he credited baseball with providing some relief from the individual, personal concerns of the 50 or so on the four teams. —Bill Nowlin

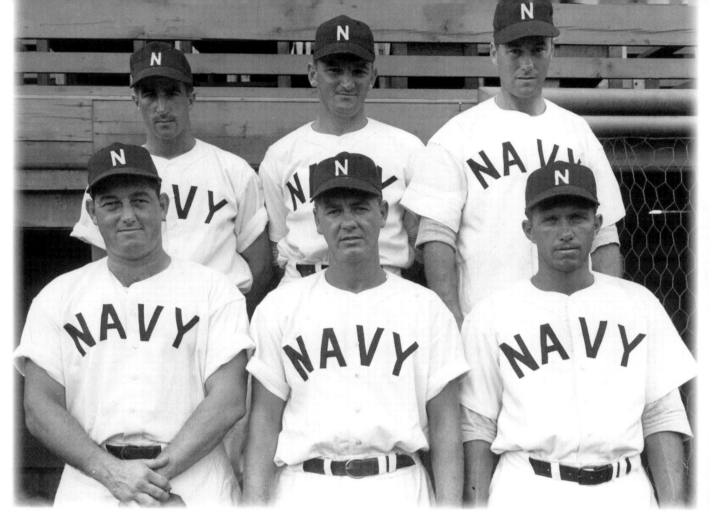

Photo taken during the Army-Navy Service Series in Hawaii in 1944. Back row (left to right): Johnny Pesky, Chet Hajduk, Bob Kennedy. Front row (left to right): Ken Sears, Sherry Robertson, Jack Conway.

Marine pitcher Andy Steinbach congratulates Joe DiMaggio on a Seventh Air Force win.

Photograph taken on September 23, 1944, at Corpus Christi prior to the third game of a four-game series between the Pensacola and Corpus Christi NAS All-Stars. Marine Lts. Bob Kennedy and Ted Williams are first and second from left in the first row. Buddy Gremp is on the far left of the top row. Corpus Christi pitcher Pat McGlothin dealt Williams an 0-for-7 day, pitched all 19 innings of the 5–4 win, drove in the second and third runs, scored the tying run in the 17th inning, and then tripled in the winning run in the bottom of the 19th. In 1949, McGlothin posted a 1–1 record for the Brooklyn Dodgers.

Left to Right: Lefty O'Doul with sportswriter Sotaro Suzuki of the *Yomiuri Shimbun* and Moe Berg, 1932.

Below: Ray Champagne's timely hitting and defensive work at third base helped guide the Third Marine Division to the Little World Series title in the Pacific in 1944. Champagne is typical of wartime players who were offered a professional contract after military service. He signed with the Boston Red Sox in 1946 and went to spring training, but after three and a half years away from home, he chose to stay close to his young family and continued to play semipro ball as he had done before the war.

Mel Ott (fifth from left) and Frankie Frisch (sixth from left) share a laugh with General Patton (third from left) in Europe in December 1944, while on a tour entertaining U.S. troops.

Three prewar National League stars talking things over before an exhibition game on Mog Mog Island in the Pacific. Merrill "Pinky" May (left) was a third baseman with the Phillies, Pee Wee Reese (center) was the Brooklyn shortstop and a future Hall of Famer, while Johnny Vander Meer (right) of the Reds secured a place in the game's history in 1938 by throwing the only major league back-to-back no-hitters.

Perspectives

They Also Served With Valor

by Bill Swank

In 1944, three years before he broke Major League Baseball's color barrier, Lieutenant Jack Roosevelt Robinson was court-martialed for his refusal to sit in the back of a desegregated Army bus at Fort Hood, Texas. Robinson had volunteered for combat with the segregated 761st Tank Battalion. Despite signing a waiver relating to a previous football injury, he was required to undergo extensive medical tests before transfer to the European Theater. It was during this time that Lt. Robinson remained in his seat after being ordered to move by a white bus driver. He was acquitted at his court martial and given an honorable medical discharge. Robinson left the Army to play baseball for the Kansas City Monarchs in the Negro Leagues in 1945.

It is estimated that more than 100 Negro League baseball players served in the armed forces during World War II. The number is undoubtedly higher. Most served in ancillary assignments, because politicians and military leadership did not believe African-Americans would be dependable in combat. By 1944, with a pressing need for increased manpower, Negro units such as the 761st Tank Battalion, 92nd Infantry Division, and 332nd Fighter Group were put into action. When the Germans launched their pre-Christmas counter-offensive (The Battle of the Bulge), Gen. Eisenhower sought volunteers "of all races." About 4,500 black troops answered the call and served with distinction.

After the war, returning veterans, who included Negro League ballplayers, could no longer tolerate their role as second-class citizens. The modern civil rights struggle was born as black Americans fought both the enemy abroad and racial injustice on the home front.

Philadelphia Stars manager Jake Dunn and Memphis Red Sox first baseman Jelly Taylor were among the first Negro Leaguers to answer the nation's call for military service after Pearl Harbor. Although African-American servicemen would be subjected to extreme prejudice, their patriotism was exemplary.

On D-Day in 1944, Newark Eagles pitcher Leon Day and Kansas City Mon-

Sergeant James "Bus" Clarkson on New Caledonia, during the first game of the island championship series with the field artillery unit. Clarkson was a power-hitting infielder who played 14 seasons in the Negro Leagues and boasted a .359 batting average. He appeared briefly for the Boston Braves in 1952, batting .200 in 25 at-bats. He spent three years in military service (1943–45) after being drafted into the U.S. Army.

archs slugging outfielder Willard Brown landed on Normandy beaches with the Army Quartermaster Corps.

Following the war, Day would pitch an Opening Day no-hitter against the Philadelphia Stars in 1946. He was elected to Baseball's Hall of Fame in 1995. Fellow Hall of Famer and WWII veteran Monte Irvin said of Day, "I've never seen a better athlete, never seen a better baseball player all-around."

"Home Run" Brown was a seven-time Negro League home run champion and three-time batting leader. He played for the lowly St. Louis Browns in 1947 and left the team because, "The Browns couldn't beat the

Monarchs, no kind of way—only if we were all asleep." Willard Brown was elected to the Baseball Hall of Fame in 2006, along with 16 others from the Negro Leagues and pre-Negro Leagues.

Fellow Monarch Hank Thompson was also briefly with the Browns in 1947 and would later spend eight years with the New York Giants. Playing in Cuba after the war, his nickname was Ametralladora, which is Spanish for "machine gun." During the Battle of the Bulge, Sgt. Henry Thompson was a machine gunner with the 1695th Combat Engineers.

John Ritchey was another combat engineer at the Battle of the Bulge who earned five battle stars along with staff sergeant stripes. He later served in the Pacific. Playing for the Chicago American Giants in 1947, the left-handed-hitting catcher led the Negro Leagues with a .378 batting average. The following year, he broke the color barrier in the Pacific Coast League.

Newark Eagles pitcher Max "Dr. Cyclops" Manning, Homestead Grays catcher Josh Johnson, and outfielder Herb Simpson hauled gasoline 24 hours a day for the famed Red Ball Express, which fueled Gen. George Patton's tanks as his Thundering Third Army rolled across France and into Belgium. Lt. Johnson would remain in the Army Reserve and attain the rank of major. Manning helped deliver badly needed supplies to the 101st Airborne Division, which

was surrounded at Bastogne during the Battle of the Bulge.

The 92nd Infantry was a highly decorated outfit that fought in Italy. Kansas City Monarchs catcher Joe Greene served with distinction in one of the unit's antitank divisions. During the liberation of Milan, his company removed the body of Benito Mussolini from public display. The former dictator had been executed by Italian resistance fighters who hung him upside down in the piazza.

Late in the 1943 season, 31-year-old Buck O'Neil, one of the game's most beloved ambassadors, left the Monarchs to join the Navy. One morning in the Philippines, as his men were loading ammunition aboard a destroyer, reveille sounded. A white officer shouted at the black stevedores, "Attention, Niggers." First Class Petty Officer O'Neil calmly replied, "I believe you could have addressed us a little better than that, sir." The officer apologized. It was during this time that O'Neil learned his old baseball team had signed a football star named Jackie Robinson.

It is no accident that all five African Americans who broke the major league color barrier in 1947 were World War II veterans. Larry Doby of the Cleveland Indians was in the Navy, and Dan Bankhead of the Brooklyn Dodgers served in the Marine Corps. In an ironic double standard of the times, Negro Leaguers would be more acceptable to white fans if they had served their country.

Military records of Negro Leaguers are difficult to confirm. The following players served in the European Theater of operations: Russell Awkard, Skeeter Banks, James Brown, Elmer Carter, Frank Duncan, Jake Flowers, Bob Griffith, Johnny Hayes, Monte Irvin, Byron Johnson, Red Moore, Charlie Parks, Ulysses Redd, Joe Scott, Herb Simpson, and Lonnie Summers. Those who served in the Pacific included Jeremiah Bennett, Charlie Biot, Sherwood Brewer, Ernest Burke, Marlin Carter, Bus Clarkson, Sammy Hughes, Leonard Pigg, Slick Surratt, Bob Thurman, Andy Watts, and Apples Wilmore. Several other prominent black players were in the military, but it is not known if they were shipped overseas.

Only two white major league players were killed in action during World War II.

Numerous minor leaguers died in combat, but ballplayers from both races spent most of the war years playing baseball to help boost morale among the troops. This was not always met with favor by those on the front lines.

After the war, when new Baseball Commissioner A. B. "Happy" Chandler was told that Branch Rickey had signed Jackie Robinson to a major league contract with the Brooklyn Dodgers, he said, "If they can fight and die on Okinawa, Guadalcanal . . . in the South Pacific, they can play ball in America."

Negro League ballplayers had fought and earned the right to compete in the big leagues. Today, they are still remembered as outstanding baseball players, but we should not forget that many of them also served our country with valor.

Baseball Behind Barbed Wire

by Kerry Yo Nakagawa

"To keep the flow of goodness coming, always be thankful."
—Nakagawa proverb

I am blessed to have uncles who competed and teamed up with Hall of Famers Lou Gehrig, Babe Ruth, Tony Lazzeri, Lefty O'Doul, Biz Mackey, Frank Duncan, Jackie Robinson, and many other world-class, diverse ballplayers in America and Asia. These early pioneers were our courageous American ambassadors for baseball, diplomacy, and race relations. They made prewar tours to Japan, Korea, and Manchukuo, China, in 1924, 1927, and 1937.

Baseball has been in my family for four generations. My grandpa Hisataro Nakagawa played on a sugar cane plantation team in Hilo, Hawaii, and then immigrated to the mainland in 1886. His ability to speak and read English gave him the advantage to combat the alien land laws, anti-immigration, and anti-miscegenation laws of the times. He was wise enough to put the deeds of his farm in his two American-born (Nisei) sons' names and helped to sponsor many more families from Hawaii this way. His 20 acres of grapes never expanded like the many other Issei farmers he helped. It was the size of his heart, not the amount of acres he accumulated, that makes our family so proud of his legacy.

My uncle Johnny was considered the Babe Ruth of the Nisei and was part of the Fresno Athletic Club, one of the best semipro teams in the nation. The FAC toured Japan in 1924 and in 1927 faced the all-stars of the Negro League when both teams were undefeated. Such irony for an African-American team to play a Japanese-American team for the championship in Tokyo at Meiji Stadium. Since these "other" Americans could not cross the color line in Major League Baseball in the U.S., they

From left, Johnny Nakagawa, Lou Gehrig, Kenichi Zenimura, Babe Ruth, Fred Yoshikawa, Harvey Iwata. October 29, 1927, at Fireman's Park, Fresno. Gehrig and his Nisei teammates beat the Babe's team, 13–3. Photo by Frank Kamiyama, courtesy of Kerry Yo Nakagawa.

played in leagues of their own and opened up a positive "bridge across the Pacific," which I feel inspired Japan to start its professional baseball leagues in 1936.

My dad pitched a nine-inning no-hitter in 1928 for his Caruthers Blue Raider high school team. He never got to play with the

Nisei teams or travel to Japan, however, due to work commitments on our farm. When 15 former prewar Nisei ballplayers were honored at the Baseball Hall of Fame in Cooperstown, New York, in 1998, I announced my dad as the starting pitcher for the all-star Nisei team: "You made it to the

Hall of Fame, Dad, and I'm so proud to be here with you."

I was an all-star shortstop, and my son Kale was an all-star catcher. On his mom's side of the family we had great pioneering ballplayers but also a very significant and compelling military dynamic as well. Kale's grandpa George Suzuki used to caddy for Gen. Patton when Patton would visit Honolulu. George's father was Patton's chef, so Patton would take George to caddy for him and even tip Georgie a dime after his 18 holes of golf.

Suzuki was with his friends on the mountainside of Pearl City, Honolulu, on December 7, 1941. They thought at first "war games" were being conducted until they saw the ships in the harbor going down. Suzuki enlisted and was sent to Fort Benning, Georgia, where he became part of the I-88th parachute infantry regiment of the 11th Airborne. He made 13 jumps during the war. One post-war jump in Japan almost impaled him when he clipped a tree on the way down.

All three of Suzuki's brothers joined the military, and brother John T. was Sen. Daniel Inouye's radioman with the famed Japanese-American 442nd Regimental Combat Team. The Go For Broke National Education Center reports, "The 442nd Regimental Combat Team was the most decorated unit for its size and length of service, in the entire history of the U.S. Military. The 4,000 men

Joe Takata

who initially came in April 1943 had to be replaced nearly 3.5 times. In total, about 14,000 men served, ultimately earning 9,486 Purple Hearts, 21 Medals of Honor, and an unprecedented eight Presidential Unit Citations." Many of the "Go For Broke" regiment, 100th and MIS (Military Intelligence Service) volunteered straight out of the 10 internment camps to fight for our country as their families were imprisoned in the desert purgatories across the United States.

In 1942, because of Executive Order 9066, about 120,000 Japanese-Americans on the West Coast lost their freedom, fortunes, education, and dignity. For six months my family was housed in the animal stalls of the Fresno Fairgrounds as permanent camps were being built across the U.S. My mom told me the story of how they were herded and transported to Jerome, Arkansas, on a four-day train ride, blinders on all the windows. She was constantly being reminded by my grandma during their journey, "This is the greatest country in the world, and all immigrants have to pay a price for freedom . . . this is our test, so don't be bitter, and we will prove how loyal we are." She never made it back to her home or restaurant in Fresno, California.

Joe Takata (see photo, opposite) was a legendary ballplayer in his native Hawaiian Islands during the prewar era. A shortstop with power, he enlisted in the Army on November 15, 1941.

The 100th battalion (comprised primarily of Hawaiians) formed a baseball team that played various local teams in Wisconsin ,where they were based. Joe often played outfield for the base team. In February 1943, the battalion was sent for advanced training at Camp Shelby, Mississippi. That June, they journeyed to the Jerome Detention Camp to play an exhibition game against the Nisei internees.

On September 2, the 100th landed in Oran, Algeria. Ted Hirayama was the manager of the 100th/Aloha Squad and he tells a story about Takata:

"From Arkansas we were supposed to head to Europe to begin our battle in Italy, but Milton Eisenhower (head of the War Relocation Authority) had heard that we had this great baseball team, so General Ryder (34th Division) requested that our 100th/Aloha team go to North Africa first to play the 34th Division of the 168th Regiment Team that was also one of their powerhouse baseball clubs.

"So before we got ready to do combat in Italy, we played this last game at the North Africa Army base.

"It was a close game all the way to the ninth inning and they had been pitching away from Joe Takata and his power, either walking him or setting him up with breaking balls. Because we got into the late innings, they had to replace [the starter] with a relief pitcher. Joe settled into the batter's box and set himself. The pitcher rocked and tried to throw a fastball by him. Crack! Joe smacked a ball out of the stadium for a walk-off home run!"

This would be Takata's last home run and his last at-bat. Shortly after arriving in Italy, Sgt. Takata faced combat. On September 29, 1943, at Monte Milleto, while heroically taking out two pillboxes single-handedly, Joe was hit with flying shrapnel from an enemy artillery shell and killed. He became the first of the 100th battalion to be killed in action. He was posthumously awarded the Distinguished Service Cross. His family's reaction back in Hawaii was to raise money for the Red Cross and war relief efforts.

Ted Williams, at his last major league at-bat, hit a home run to end his career. Joe Takata's story ran parallel but with a much more tragic ending.

In June 2003, the baseball field at Hawaii's Fort Shafter was named Joe Takata Field in his honor.

Action during a game at the Tule Lake, California, camp as the
Manzanar catcher takes the throw just a bit too late.

Her body was cremated in Hattiesburg, Mississippi, and her ashes were delivered to their barracks in a coffee can. On top of this progressive and visionary woman's ashes was a piece of paper which said "Jap woman."

Three and a half years later my family arrived at the Sacramento train station. Our farm neighbors, the McClurgs and Ravens, had been egged and spat on for being friends to our family. They drove my family back to our farm and presented my grandpa with a cigar box filled with cash. Not only did Grandpa Raven take care of our 20 acres, he gave back the profits the farm made for the three-plus years they were gone. Most Japanese-Americans lost their civil liberties, homes, businesses, college educations, and professions, but luckily we had neighbors who were an extension of our family despite race, religion, and the xenophobia of the times.

For Japanese-Americans interned during World War II, playing, watching, and supporting baseball inside of America's concentration camps brought a sense of normalcy to very abnormal lives and created a social and positive atmosphere. It fostered the skill level year-round for the athletes and helped maintain their self-esteem despite the harsh conditions of desert life and unconstitutional incarceration.

It was ironic that these so called "enemy aliens" were able to travel from Gila River, Arizona, to Heart Mountain, Wyoming, Tule Lake, California, or even Amache, Colorado, just by putting on a baseball jersey. On the other hand, if a relative passed away, you could not leave the camp to attend the service. Mothers and daughters tore up mattress ticking to make uniforms, and thousands would line up all around the baseball field to cheer on their favorite team and players. The government had taken everything from the internees—but instead of rejecting the all-American pastime, there were 32 teams and three divisions at Gila River, Arizona, on a Pima Indian reservation. Japanese-Americans kept the national pastime alive, even behind barbed wire.

In their world, life was a desert, and they built diamonds in the rough. Former Nisei ballplayer and scout for the Houston Astros

George Omachi said, "Without baseball, camp life would have been miserable. . . . It was humiliating, demeaning, being incarcerated by our own country."

Here are some of my heroes and their special moments during WWII:

Nisei Ard Kozono was a staff sergeant in charge of a 24-man team of interrogators at the Canlubang central Luzon, Philippines, Japanese POW camp. A pickup baseball game between the MIS soldiers and the Japanese prisoners was being played. With the MIS leading in the game, the sergeant in charge of camp No. 1 pulled Ard aside and told Ard he was going to be reprimanded for playing with the "enemy."

"They would cut your throat if they had a chance," he said. Ard explained that it was his duty to gain intelligence, and this was his way to express fellowship and humanity toward the prisoners. Ard was never reprimanded for his actions, and his team was responsible for processing more than 50,000 Japanese soldiers during World War II.

Back home at the Jerome, Arkansas, camp, pitcher Herb "Moon" Kurima shut out Arkansas A&M 6–0. He had pinpoint control and threw 21 strikeouts in a semipro game against Grass Valley in the 1930s. At Fort Snelling, Minnesota, Bill Tsukamoto hit a triple off of Yankees great Spud Chandler to help his Nisei MIS team win, 4–2.

Guadalupe all-star Masao Iriyama won the camp batting championship in 1943 by

The Tule Lake Nippons beat the Manzanar Aces 12-6 on May 4, 1944.
Manzanar traveled to Tule Lake internment camp to play this game.

hitting .421. Handmade wooden trophy in hand, he was given a telegram to take to his parents at their barracks. The telegram revealed that their other son, Masao's brother Minoru, was killed in action as a pilot for Japan during the Doolittle raids over Tokyo.

One of the greatest upsets in Arizona history was when the three-time state champions from Tucson played the Gila River camp high school team. The Badgers had a 53-game winning streak going, and

their starting pitcher, Lowell Bailey, had a 0.00 ERA. It was 10–10 in the 10th inning with the bases loaded when Harvey Zenimura ripped a single past the third baseman to win the game. Seven thousand fans attended this amazing game played on a "Field of Dreams" built by "the Father of Japanese-American Baseball," Kenichi Zenimura.

All-star Joe Takata from the Hawaiian Asahi volunteered and joined the 100th Infantry Battalion. They were shipping out to Europe when Milton Eisenhower diverted the 100th to a North African army base. The 100th faced the 34th Division team, and Takata hit a walk-off home run to win the game for the 100th. Like Ted Williams, Takata's last career at bat was a home run. The 100th landed in Italy, and Joe Takata became the first Japanese American to be killed in action in Italy.

"I'll never forget as we were boarding our train to go to the Assembly Center, I was in my Cub Scout uniform with my prize possessions, my baseball bat and glove," said Norman Mineta, former U.S. secretary of transportation, congressman and ex-mayor of San Jose, California. "A military police soldier stopped me and took my bat away from me, saying it was a lethal weapon. This was my favorite bat, and he took it away."

Years later, Mineta, as a U.S. Congressman, would have another traumatic experience with a baseball bat. He was named an honorary fellow by the American Society of Engineers. Norm Emerson, having heard the story of this young child back in the internment days, presented Mineta with a baseball bat signed by Henry Aaron and Sadaharu Oh, who were the respective home-run leaders in American and Japanese baseball and Mineta's heroes. After expressing his gratitude, Mineta took the bat back to his office. A journalist reminded the congressman that this bat was valued over $250 and would therefore be illegal to accept. For the

second time in Norman Mineta's life, his most prized possession, a bat, would have had to be returned to the government. He declined the gift and returned it to Emerson, who held onto it until Mineta retired from public service and then surprised him by re-presenting him with the gift. The signed bat and ball are proudly hanging in Mineta's office in Washington, D.C.

Henry Honda, an all-star ace for the San Jose Asahi, signed a contract with the Cleveland Indians. Unfortunately it was in December of 1941, and Honda never got to prove himself at the major league level.

Women played a high level of softball in the camps, too. Jane "No-Hit" Ota from Jerome, Arkansas, Rose Kakuuchi from Manzanar, California, and Babe Oshiki were just a few women who could have played at the college level.

During the war, the Quaker religion outreached to 500 Nisei in the 10 detention camps and sponsored their college educations. Kay Kiyokawa was one of the all-star pitchers for the Hood River Nisei who qualified out of Tule Lake's camp and chose the University of Connecticut. At 4-foot-10, Kiyokawa went on to become the starting pitcher and running back for this Division I college football team. His first at-bat against the University of Maine was greeted with a chant of "Tojo, Tojo," and he laced a double down the line. He was greeted for his second at-bat with the chants, "Tojo, Tojo," and quickly hit a triple to right center. On his third at-bat, both stands started chanting, "Slugger, Slugger," and with just three at-bats, Kay Kiyokawa broke down barriers and changed perceptions.

Baseball behind barbed wire demonstrates that an understanding of history can overcome the fear and misunderstanding that wakens intolerance. The arts and sports practiced by the internees were not entertainment but approaches for finding, articulating, and preserving meaning in a senseless situation. Baseball serves as a lens through which to examine camp history. This baseball lens can provide an opportunity to discuss the delicate and troublesome stories of internment because baseball provides a common element with which all diverse cultures can identify. American citizens who were of Issei and Nisei generations were imprisoned by their own government primarily because they looked like the enemy, while German- and Italian-Americans did not. As a result, internment camps are central to the great ideal of Japanese-American culture. Once again, Japanese-American baseball is a story of inclusion within the context of exclusion. Against the backdrop of exclusionary laws, baseball was passionately played within the community by local teams before, during, and after World War II.

Japanese-American soldiers in the 442nd Regimental Combat Team and the 100th Infantry Battalion were the most highly decorated combat unit for its size and length of service. They also suffered the most casualties in the history of the World War II. The Nisei soldiers/translators of Military Intelligence Service saved thousands of lives and helped to shorten the war in the Pacific. Of the 120,000 men, women, and children of Japanese ancestry who were forcibly removed and interned in detention camps, not a single act of espionage or sabotage was ever reported in America.

After September 11, 2001, thoughts such as "If we don't learn by our mistakes, we are bound to repeat them" or "History hasn't changed, only the names" were commonly heard. History is not repeating itself because after September 11, it was Sikhs, Muslim-Americans, and Arab-Americans going through racial profiling of the times, not Japanese-Americans.

The beauty of the immigrant experience is to embrace other cultures, customs, and all that this land of opportunity offers to its people. Tolerance, patriotism, valor, redemption, and especially humanity are the key principles that have surrounded my family for more than four generations. I am guardedly optimistic these themes will prevail many more decades for all cultures and faiths. Loyalty to family, country, baseball, and to the ones who went before us. Bases covered.

World War II and the All-American Girls Base Ball League

by Merrie A. Fidler

Jean Faut, a child of the mid-1920s, was destined to become one of two All-American Girls Base Ball League players to earn MVP honors twice. She noted that during the Great Depression and the beginning of World War II, there wasn't much for kids to do in East Greenville, Pennsylvania, except play ball or go swimming because "You couldn't go anywhere. You couldn't get any gas. So I played a lot of baseball." While Jean grew up playing baseball, most future All-American players including Cincinnati's Dorothy "Kammie" Kamenshek, Detroit's Sophie Kurys, the L.A. area's Dorothy "Snookie" Harrell Doyle, and Canada's Mary "Bonnie" Baker grew up playing a lot of softball.

From its inception in the late 1880s, softball was touted as a sport for girls and women as well as for boys and men. In concert with the Great Depression of the 1930s, softball mushroomed into one of the major participant sports in the country, with more than 2 million male and female players, young and old. During the 1930s, the Works Progress Administration contributed to the construction of more than 8,000 parks that could incorporate the smaller softball field size; the Amateur Softball Association and the National Softball Association emerged to promote men's and women's national championship tournaments; industrial semipro teams proliferated; and the innovation of lighted fields and enforced leisure provided the unemployed and those with shortened working hours the opportunity to emulate participation in the national pastime.

When World War II engulfed the United States in December 1941, the country's first massive military manpower mobilization began. The loss of men in the workforce necessitated the employment of women in traditionally male occupations throughout society. "Women were riveters, spot and torch welders, hydraulic press operators, crane operators, shell loaders, bus drivers, train conductors, bellhops, lifeguards,

185

lumberjacks . . . cowgirls, section hands, coal mine checkers, car washers, filling station operators, taxi drivers, barbers, policemen [and] ferry command pilots."

Women were also employed to fill in for draftees in the sporting world. "They worked as jockeys, umpires, bowling pin setters, caddies, horse trainers, and even football coaches."

In January 1942, President Franklin D. Roosevelt assured baseball commissioner Judge Kenesaw Mountain Landis "that it would be best for the country to keep baseball going," but by the fall of 1942, the message from the Office of War Information's representative Ken Beirn was not so encouraging. The War Office's plan to place 3 to 4 million more men in uniform by the summer of 1943 would force millions more to "transfer from their non-essential occupations to war jobs." Major League Baseball team owners were advised that this manpower push could endanger their non-essential professional sport and quite possibly necessitate its postponement for the 1943 season.

The war turned the country's gender roles in the workforce topsy-turvy. It also resulted in the imminent postponement of Major League Baseball in deference to increased war manpower demands. These factors, combined with a broad talent base of skilled female softball players throughout the U.S. and Canada, coalesced to make

conditions ripe for the creation of a women's professional softball league. It was left to the Chicago Cubs' innovative owner, Philip K. Wrigley, to envision filling major league ballparks with women players in the absence of men, just as women were already filling in for men in every other imaginable occupation throughout the nation.

Wrigley was well aware of the increased employment and status of women in American society during World War I and World War II. In a statement to the press in February 1943, he explained, "World War I showed to the world for the first time on a large scale what women could and did do, and World War II is going to carry this even further. American women have taken a very definite share of the load in the country's progress, and in the fields of science, business and sports they are now also working in ever increasing numbers."

Additionally, Wrigley was aware of the popularity of both men's and women's softball in the 1930s and early 1940s: "In the late 1930s, softball was attracting more spectators than baseball in several cities, including Los Angeles and Chicago, where Wrigley owned baseball parks. A survey conducted by one of Wrigley's employees revealed the existence of 9,000 softball teams within a 100-mile radius of Wrigley Field in L.A. in 1938. One thousand of these were women's teams. As a means of stimulating interest in baseball in Los Angeles, Wrigley

Field in L.A. was offered "free each year for the windup double-header to decide the championship in both men's and women's softball leagues." These games drew up to 30,000 fans and netted as much as $7,000 at the gate. The Chicago Metropolitan Girls Major Softball League had similarly attracted Wrigley's attention by the rise in attendance at its games through the summer of 1942.

When investigating the feasibility of establishing a women's softball league, Wrigley's committee learned that "Without a doubt, softball, particularly among women, [had] the greatest potentialities from both competition and spectator standpoints of any of the growing sports. . . . The game itself should have a tremendous development in popularity due to the huge increase in the number of women war workers and the natural desire of industrial management to find some means of providing esprit de corps in their respective plants." Thus, during the winter of 1942–43, Wrigley's baseball scouts recruited the best female softball players in the U.S. and Canada to compete for 60 positions in a four-team league. When public sentiment for Major League Baseball did not result in its postponement in 1943 despite the turmoil caused by the new manpower push, Wrigley's four-team All-American Girls Soft Ball League was settled in war production communities within a 100-mile radius of Chicago rather than in major league parks. Appropriately, publicity for the league focused on "Recreation for War Workers."

Along with an approximate $250,000 outlay from Wrigley, All-American team guarantors in Rockford, Illinois, South Bend, Indiana, and Kenosha and Racine, Wisconsin, contributed $22,500 each to establish All-American teams in their communities. Some of these guarantors, who also served on team boards of directors, owned factories recently converted to war production. They faithfully attended league games and encouraged their employees to attend also. In fact, they even organized special factory nights, which incorporated incentives for each industry to outdo others for an attendance record. League publicity in local papers further encouraged workers to forget their cares and worries by attending an All-American game to enjoy watching major league-style play, which would boost their morale and provide the best recreation on the home front.

Besides recognizing their role in providing entertainment for war factory workers, players' memories of their contributions to the war effort included lining up in a "V" for victory during the pregame playing of the Star Spangled Banner, playing exhibition games at nearby military bases, and visiting veterans' hospitals. Kurys and Kamenshek recalled two of the most historic All-American war-related promotions, which took place on the nights of July 1, 1943, and July 18, 1944, under temporary lighting in Wrigley Field. The first was an All-American All-Star game featured as part of a large Women's Army Air Corps sports and recruiting rally attended by 7,000 fans free of charge. The second was an All-American double header free to Red Cross blood donors and service personnel, which over 16,000 fans witnessed. Thus the first night games in Wrigley Field were actually played by Wrigley's "girls" rather than his "men."

Wrigley's establishment of the All-American League on the highest professional and social standards of his day is reflected in the trustee nonprofit structure developed for league operations; the creation of the skirt-style uniform; the rigorous player's code of conduct he established; the employment of ex-major leaguers as managers; the institution of team chaperones; the professional wages the players were paid; the major league-style newspaper coverage teams were accorded in league cities; the national publicity garnered by his advertising agent, Arthur Meyerhoff; and even the emphasis on players' femininity in league publicity.

When Wrigley withdrew from the All-American League after the completion of the 1944 season "to be free of the detail involved in the management of the league" and "because of the pressure of other activities," there was no interruption in league affairs because Arthur Meyerhoff assumed the role of league commissioner. Meyerhoff, who was integrally involved in the All-American League's organization and promotion from its beginning, looked at the 49 percent increase in attendance from 176,612 in 1943 to 259,658 in 1944 and was interested enough in the league's expansion potential to purchase its assets for $10,000. He was also successful in persuading team guarantors that he would carry on Wrigley's legacy.

Meyerhoff, like Wrigley, was an innovative, creative, and professional person. Under his tutelage, the All-American Girls Soft Ball League (AAGSBL), renamed the All-American Girls Professional Ball League (AAGPBL) at the end of the 1944 season, became the All-American Girls Base Ball League (AAGBBL) in name and in fact. In three years' time, the base path and pitching distances were lengthened to ¾ those of regulation baseball, the ball size was reduced from 12 inches in circumference to 10 inches—only an inch larger than regulation baseball—the pitching style was converted from underhand to overhand, and Major League Baseball rules were adopted *en toto*.

As AAGBBL commissioner, Meyerhoff did everything within his power to promote and develop the All-American League. After wartime travel restrictions were lifted, he instituted league spring training in southern climes followed by exhibition tours through northern league cities. These spring tours served the dual purpose of affording players intensive preseason game play and allowed the league an opportunity to recruit new players along the way. In 1945 and 1946, Meyerhoff conceived of establishing a "Southern Division" of the league in Alabama and a "Western Division" in Southern California. If these plans had transpired, the established Midwestern teams would have comprised the "Central Division."

In 1947, Meyerhoff expanded the league to eight teams and held spring training for all teams in Cuba. This undertaking eventually led to a Latin American tour of AAGBBL and Cuban players to Central America, Venezuela, and Puerto Rico from late January through March of 1949. As an outgrowth of these Latin American excursions, Meyerhoff proposed but was unable to realize the organization of an "International League of Girls Baseball," which would operate in Florida during December, in Venezuela during January, in Puerto Rico during February, and in Cuba during March. Closer to home, Meyerhoff established an AAGBBL four-team minor league which operated in Chicago during 1948–1950, and two rookie teams that toured through the South and up the East Coast in 1949 and 1950. Like the spring training tours, the rookie tours were designed to train rookies and recruit new players. True to his advertising expertise, Meyerhoff incessantly publicized and promoted the league in team cities and through nationwide publications.

After the 1950 season, team boards of directors were erroneously convinced that Meyerhoff's extensive publicity and promotional activities were draining their pockets. They chose to purchase their teams from Meyerhoff and attempted to go it alone without the benefit of professionally conceived and funded promotional and player training programs. They failed to fathom that funding top notch promotional and player training programs was more crucial for their teams' and their league's survival than ever before. Ideally, their budgets should have expanded rather than cut these programs.

However, in the early 1950s, team owners were faced with recession conditions: community corporations or slowed production, unemployment increased, and the available recreation dollars decreased. Team owners no longer enjoyed lucrative war-industry income; their community members were no longer restricted to available community recreational pursuits by the war's rations of rubber and gas; they competed for spectators with television, renewed migrations to Major League Baseball parks, and other recreational pursuits; and by this time, the league's talent base of softball players needed time and training to be converted into good baseball players. In the end, the AAGBBL suffered the same fate in the 1950s, for the same reasons, as did many men's minor leagues.

Why then did team owners choose to continue operating from 1951 to 1954? The answer may rest in the fact that during the war years and after, players for the Comets, the Peaches, the Daisies, the Belles, the Blue Sox, the Lassies, the Chicks, and others became household names in their communities. Teams became part of the culture of the cities in which they existed, exceptionally skilled players continued to captivate fans, and perhaps team owners kept dreaming of that championship season. Whatever the reasons, team owners continued to support their franchises through the 1954 season until the financial picture became too bleak to surmount.

World War II, Wrigley, Meyerhoff, and individual team owners provided women's professional softball/baseball for 14 different Midwestern cities for 12 years. Initially, the dash and drama of female players in skirted uniforms playing ball with the skill and finesse of male major leaguers provided recreation for war workers, then for captivated community members, for southern and eastern seaboard city populations, and even for some Latin American baseball fans. Most importantly, from 1943 through 1954, World War II, Wrigley, Meyerhoff, and individual team owners afforded more than 600 young female ballplayers the opportunity to realize their dreams of playing a game they loved professionally. The war, Wrigley, Meyerhoff, and individual team owners for-ever proved that women could play a rigorous schedule of professional-caliber baseball. The AAGBBL, therefore, stands as an historical beacon to testify that given proper planning, adequate funding, professional administration and promotion, and social approbation, women's professional baseball has the potential to be a viable enterprise in its own right.

[Editor's note: This material was adapted from the book *The Origins and History of the All-American Girls Professional Baseball League* by Merrie A. Fidler (Jefferson, N.C.: McFarland & Company, Inc., Publishers, 2006). Refer to this volume for information on the sources consulted in preparing this chapter.]

An American Life in the 9/11 Generation

by Terry Allvord, USN (Ret.), President U.S. Military All-Stars

[About the U.S. Military All-Stars: Founded in 1990, the U.S. Military All-Stars are a 501(c)(3) nonprofit organization dedicated to the proud tradition and growth of military baseball worldwide. We are the largest, fastest growing, most successful, and only joint armed forces program in the world. The historic "Red, White, and Blue Tour of America" has been enjoyed by more than 25 million people, making more than 350 appearances annually and providing the absolute finest patriotic atmosphere possible.]

The first time I met Hall of Fame pitcher and former Navy Chief Bob Feller, he was in shorts and a t-shirt autographing baseballs while surrounded by reporters in the locker room at Bright House Networks Stadium. I couldn't help but wonder how many times he had been asked the same question in his lifetime. Approaching the table I wanted my first question to be new and different, and even though he was a generation past his prime I ended up asking one that he had probably heard more than any other: "It's an honor to meet you, sir. Are you starting tonight?" The most surprising response is the one he delivered, saying flatly, "Well, that's what I'm here for, kid. Nice uniform!"

Less than an hour later, I was sitting next to Tommy John in my full "USA" camouflage uniform peering out of the dugout as Feller toed the rubber to start the Major League Alumni Legends Game at the spring home of the Phillies. As great as that was, I was even more pleased to see two of our U.S. Military All-Stars involved—ABE2 Ray Judy leading off against him and fellow

U.S. Military All-Stars player Johnny Hernandez drives a home run during the July 4, 2008, game in Leesburg, Florida.

Navy Chief Jason Mauloni catching him.

Judy did his first deployment in 2001 working the catapults onboard the USS Constellation CV-64. I have done seven deployments during my 23-year career, all of them in the Middle East. The water in the Gulf is always calm and temperatures on the flight deck can reach over 140 degrees. The heat takes its toll after weeks of Alert-5 duty. The long hours force flight deck personnel to sleep wherever and whenever they could. Many found refuge in the catwalk, enjoying the shallow wind that would crawl through the space between the beams. Judy

was exhausted and searching for the breeze on 9/11 when he heard his commanding officer Capt. John Miller over the ship's 5MC. He learned about the attacks on the World Trade Center and the Pentagon. Like all Americans, he will never forget where he was. Judy was on the other side of the world at that moment and played a role in how his crew and America responded to the tragedy that changed the world forever.

Even though we had spent most of the day with these legends during media events and kids clinics, watching Feller's third pitch being ripped by Judy and chased down by former Detroit Tiger Darrell Evans in deep right field made me finally realize just how far our program had come. It was good to have him, Mauloni and many of our other players back. What a thrill it was to be a part of this event, which was hosted by Wade Boggs.

In 1990, as an ensign in flight school, I had the opportunity to talk baseball with President George H. W. Bush. Once he realized that military baseball had waned after World War II and been snuffed out all together following Vietnam, he was clearly disappointed. As a World War II veteran, he knew the value and tradition of baseball in the military and encouraged me to begin it again. He kept his promise to check our progress the following year; by that time we had established Navy and Marine Corps teams in Pensacola. As the founder of military baseball in the modern era, I had a mission to communicate the significant responsibility to our players to represent everyone who ever wore a uniform in defense of our country. With our teams built, we established the Southwestern Baseball League in Pensacola, Florida. That league led to the Navy vs. Marine Corps Baseball Challenge and, eventually, the U.S. Military All-Stars of today.

Nineteen seasons later, our historic program is the fastest growing, largest, most successful, and only joint armed forces baseball program ever created. More than 35 military programs have been established in all services worldwide in an effort to assemble the most talented U.S. Military All-Stars to compete against the finest professional, independent and summer collegiate programs in the world. It began with more than 100 players showing up at the University of West Florida after seeing a 3x5 index card posted in the base gym.

Midway through that first season, an All-Star game was played. As you might imagine, the first meeting between the two teams was extremely competitive and required 14 innings to determine a winner. More than 2,000 people were on hand that day to witness a hard-fought 9–8 Navy victory. Immediately following that contest, conversation centered around a rematch. Less than three months later, they met again. This time it was a standing-room-only affair built on weeks of hype in the community. It lived up to the billing as the teams once again battled into extra innings before Navy finally exploded in the 12th inning to post a 13–7 victory. It would turn out to be the second of six in a row tallied by Navy.

In February 1993, control of the league and Challenge passed to HM2 Chris Jabs. Meanwhile, I was hard at work founding the San Diego Military Baseball League (SDMBL). Soon we were ready to face off again, this time on the west coast. Thanks to the support of Dr. Carroll Land, the next Challenge was played at Point Loma

Nazarene University and seen by more than 3,500 spectators who were treated to yet another competitive contest that exuded the intense rivalry the event has come to represent. Appearing were the Commander, U.S. Navy Air Forces Pacific, U.S. Navy Band, U.S. Navy "Leap Frogs" Parachute Demonstration Team, U.S. Navy Chaplain, Captain W.R. Begg, Ronald McDonald, and the San Diego Padres mascot. In San Diego, I had the unique opportunity to recruit and coach both teams, as Navy stretched its winning streak to six straight victories.

In 1995, after the success of the Challenge, I began work to play the event immediately following a San Diego Padres game at Jack Murphy Stadium. The timing and desire of the new Padres ownership to reach out to a very large military community made the event a perfect fit for the team and the City of San Diego. In the inaugural game at the "Murph" over the Fourth of July weekend, it was time for the Marine Corps to shine.

Behind the dominant pitching of St. Louis Cardinals prospect Kevin Lucero (signed 1991), the Marines went on to claim their first of six consecutive victories. In fact, the Navy didn't wrestle the trophy back until the summer of 2002, when three pitchers combined to throw 8⅔ innings of no-hit baseball, downing the Marines by the score of 5–1. Navy won again in 2003 by the score of 5–3. The Marines battled right back

in 2004. Down to their last strike, a high fastball from Navy's Alex Pino landed in the seats to top off a dramatic 6–5 Marine Corps victory in the bottom of the ninth. The Marines tied the series at 8–8 with another come-from-behind 5–3 victory at the 16th annual game during the inaugural season at PETCO Park in San Diego on July 17, 2005.

On July 7, 2006, the U.S. Military All-Stars dominated the Marines winning 12–1 in their first meeting at Tony Gwynn Stadium. The Marines were only one of 47 teams to fall to a very strong U.S. Military All-Stars team that also won three of five against teams from the Golden Baseball League, an independent professional league. They earned victories over the San Diego Surf Dawgs, Long Beach Armada, and the Yuma Scorpions. The program also achieved a milestone by posting its first win over a team from the prestigious Cape Cod Baseball League, winning 12–11 in extra innings.

During the annual "Red, White and Blue Tour of America," during which the team visits more than 40 states and four countries, the U.S. Military All-Stars shoulder a unique responsibility to promote the awareness of all Americans in support of the honorable sacrifices our brave men and women make each and every day at the "Tip of the Spear."

Operational commitments remain our top priority. Active duty, reserve, and veteran players pay all expenses. Each year, the majority of the players have recently returned from deployment in direct support of Operation Iraqi Freedom and the global war on terrorism. Our players are among the most talented athletes in the military and have been selected among thousands of personnel worldwide to represent the armed forces. Players and staff alike understand our scope of responsibility far exceeds the games won or lost on the field. In 2008, the U.S. Military All-Stars led a Baseball Diplomacy Tour to Central America, visiting the Dominican Republic, Panama, and Nicaragua on behalf of U.S. Southern Command and the State Department. The tour will further build the reputation of an extremely successful program on and off the field.

2008 RESULTS

+ More than 150 armed forces players participated worldwide. Most played for a limited time. In some cases, just one inning.
+ 25 million people learned about our mission at events and through the media.
+ 366 organizations in 40 states and four countries hosted an event or appearance.
+ More than 20 tons of sports equipment collected through our Operation Slugger II partnership with Louisville Slugger will be enjoyed by thousands of troops currently deployed.

+ More than 400,000 care packages were sent by our primary charity partnership with Operation Gratitude.
+ 131 Americans who saw our event made a commitment to serve our country as a member of the armed forces and two of our former players are currently SEALS.
+ Purple Heart recipients: Sgt. Isaac Rodriguez, USMC, led our pitching staff in ERA and Cpl. Cooper Brannon, USMC, was signed by the San Diego Padres
+ Military players drafted or in professional baseball: Nick Hill, USA—Seattle; Milan Dinga, USA—L.A. Angels; Matt Foster, USN—Toronto; Mitch Harris, USN—St. Louis; Cole White, USA and Chris Simmons, USA—Pittsburgh; Drew Clothier, USA—Florida; ENS Jonathan Johnston, USN deployed in 2007 after being drafted by the Oakland A's in the 42nd Round of MLB Draft. He played in Central America for the U.S. Military All-Stars and was later assigned to the Class "A" Kane County Cougars; BMSN Johnny Hernandez hit over .300 playing for the Bridgeport Bluefish in the Atlantic League coached by Tommy John.

For more information please visit: www.usmilitaryallstars.us

These "Yankees" played in Melbourne, Australia, in 1942, the first American team to win a Premiership there.

An American bazooka team gathers on the outskirts of Rizal Stadium in the Philippine capital of Manila in 1945.

Ball team of Japanese-American detainees at the Fresno Assembly Center, September 30, 1942.

Former Cubs first baseman Eddie Waitkus bats in a ballgame at bomb-damaged Rizal Stadium in Manila, a Japanese strongpoint during World War II.

The U.S. Navy All-Star baseball team, 1944, at Exhibition Grounds, Brisbane, Australia.

Championships

The 1943 All-Pro Game in England

by Gary Bedingfield

When a pitcher comes off the ballfield after an outstanding performance, teammates and fans commonly congratulate him. When that pitcher is an Army Air Force sergeant, he doesn't expect to be told by a general that it was the best game he had ever seen. But that is exactly what happened to Bill Brech of Secaucus, New Jersey, after he threw a 1–0 no-hitter against a hand-picked Army team in England during the summer of 1943 and was met by Major General Ira C. Eaker, commander of the Eighth Air Force.

Billed as the first all-professional game to be played in England since the New York Giants and Chicago White Sox were there in the fall of 1924, two hand-picked teams representing the U.S. Army and Eighth Air Force met before 21,500 fans at London's Wembley Stadium on a overcast Sunday afternoon on August 7, 1943. While both lineups were dominated with minor league players, a number of former major leaguers now in military service were involved. Paul Campbell of the Boston Red Sox and Lou Thuman of the Washington Senators were there, along with Monte Weaver—a 22-game winner with the Senators in 1932—and Ross Grimsley, who would pitch for the Chicago White Sox in 1951.

With all the professional talent in the Army lineup, no one expected Brech, a 21-year-old semipro righthander, to retire the Army hitters in order through the first six innings of the seven-inning contest. In all, he allowed only two runners to reach base, faced just 23 batters, and struck out six as he secured his no-hitter and a place in the hypothetical European Theater Baseball Hall of Fame.

Pitching for the Army was St Louis Browns' farmhand Ralph Ifft, who allowed five hits and the deciding run in the first two frames before being replaced by Lou Thuman.

Maj. Gen. Eaker, who had been involved in the organization of the all-professional game, rewarded the victorious Air Force team with a 30-day tour of military bases around Britain and personally wrote to each player telling them how they "contributed materially to the morale and high spirit of

The 1943 Eighth Air Force All-Stars. Pictured, from left to right, are (front row): Al Slakis, Joe Gradisher, Larry Toth, Paul Campbell, Joe Rundus, and Floyd Lancaster. (middle row): Hugh Gustafson, Nick Fracaro, Andrew Dzuris, Gene Thompson, Ross Grimsley, James Beane, Jack Gaston, and Stanley Stuka. (back row): Monte Weaver, Ed Hawkins, Bill Brech, Louis Tabor, Ed Gatlin, James Vance, and Bill Moore.

the Eighth Air Force by [their] personal example and great professional skill."

"There are a lot of combat crews in those stations who haven't seen a ballgame this season," said Bill Moore, the All-Stars' manager, as they prepared for the first of 29 games, "and this is our opportunity to do what we can for them." They won 28, with Joe Rundus, formerly with Tyler of the East Texas League, hurling the team's second no-hitter, a 9–0 win over a Photo Intelligence squad.

Chuck Eisenmann demonstrates his pitching techniques with two school-boys in England in 1943. Eisenmann had been with the San Diego Padres before the war and would probably have been the starting pitcher for the US Army All-Stars had he not had an appendectomy shortly before.

Nevertheless, a war still had to be fought and two of the Army team players—Lou Thuman and Walt Hemperly, a third baseman formerly with Gloversville-Johnstown of the Canadian-American League—saw combat duty in Europe the following year. Both sustained injuries that ended their playing careers.

And what became of Bill Brech? He was discharged from service in 1945 and returned home to Secaucus, where the 24-year-old signed a contract with

Monte Weaver, a tall, laconic right-hander, was a 20-game winner with the Washington Senators a decade before arriving in
England to serve with the Eighth Air Force in 1943.

Harrisburg of the Interstate League but decided he was too old to pursue a career in pro ball. Brech continued to play semipro baseball in New Jersey for many years. During the When Baseball Went to War confer-ence at the National World War II Museum in November 2007, Brech was remembered for his accomplishments in 1943. His son, Brad, was in attendance.

EIGHTH AIR FORCE ALL-STARS

NAME	POS	PRE-WAR AFFILIATION
Bill Brech	P	Otto Mack, Secaucus, NJ (semipro)
Paul Campbell	1B/OF	Boston Red Sox (American League)
Andy Dzuris	SS	Lima, OH (Ohio State League)
Nick Fracaro	OF	Joliet, IL (amateur)
Jack Gaston	OF	Lindale, GA (Northwest Georgia Textile League)
Joe Gradisher	3B	Muskegon, MI (semipro)
Ross Grimsley	P	Independence, KS (Ban Johnson League)
Hugh Gustafson	1B	Milwaukee, WI (American Assocation)
Ed Hawkins	OF	Seneca, SC (amateur)
Floyd Lancaster	2B	Fairfield Manufacturing, IN (semipro)
Joe Rundus	P	Tyler, TX (East Texas League)
Al Slakis	SS	Kinston, NC (Coastal Plain League)
Stanley Stuka	C	Allentown, PA (Interstate League)
Lou Tabor	P	Martinsville, VA (Bi-State League)
Gene Thompson	OF	Santa Barbara, CA (California League)
Larry Toth	2B	Lima, OH (Ohio State League)
Monte Weaver	COACH	Washington Senators (American League)
Bill Moore	MANAGER	Greenville, SC (South Atlantic League)

US Army All-Stars

Name	Pos	Pre-War Affiliation
George Burns	1B	Sylacauga, AL (semipro)
Chuck Eisenmann	COACH	San Diego, CA (Pacific Coast League)
Amey Fontana	OF	Medusa, PA (semipro)
Walt Hemperly	3B	Gloversville-Johnstown, NY (Canadian-American League)
Ralph Ifft	P	Butler, PA (Penn State League)
Maurice Jacobs	2B	Binghamton, NY (Eastern League)
Lou Kelley	OF	Stoughton, MA (semipro)
Bobby Korisher	2B	Scranton, PA (semipro)
Walt Novick	C	Shreveport, LA (Texas League)
Joe O'Donnell	OF	New Iberia, LA (Evangeline League)
Pete Pavich	SS	Clinton, IA (Three-I League)
Red Shapiro	MANAGER	Unknown
Lee Taggert	3B	Unknown
Lou Thuman	P	Washington Senators (American League)

The 1945 GI World Series

by Gary Bedingfield

Following the surrender of Nazi Germany, the summer months of 1945 saw 200,000 American servicemen playing baseball in Europe. The race was on to find the 1945 European Theater champions.

A series of regional tournaments eventually narrowed the competition down to two teams, and on September 2, the best-of-five games GI World Series opened at Soldiers' Field in Nuremberg, Germany, with the 71st Infantry Division facing the OISE All-Stars.

A crowd of 50,000 gathered to see the two best teams in Europe. The 71st Infantry Division had a formidable lineup, including Cardinal outfielder Harry Walker, Cincinnati pitcher Ewell Blackwell (who was unbeaten going into the series), and Pittsburgh outfielders Johnny Wyrostek and Maurice Van Robays. The Overseas Invasion Services Expedition (OISE) All-Stars had to rely on the determination and guile of manager Sam Nahem—a former Phillies pitcher—whose lineup consisted predominantly of minor leaguers and semipro players, together with Negro League stars Leon Day and Willard Brown. What followed was one of the biggest upsets in military baseball history.

GAME 1: SEPTEMBER 2, 1945
Soldiers' Field, Nuremberg, Germany
71st Infantry 9, OISE All-Stars 2
Before a crowd of 50,000, undoubtedly the biggest crowd to see a baseball game in Europe during the war, the 71st Infantry easily defeated the OISE All-Stars, 9–2. Ewell Blackwell allowed five hits and was never in trouble, although Emmet Altenberg homered to right field in the eighth.

GAME 2: SEPTEMBER 3, 1945
Soldiers' Field, Nuremberg, Germany
OISE All-Stars 2, 71st Infantry 1
Negro League star Leon Day was in sensational form and allowed just four hits while striking out 10 to lead the OISE All-Stars to a 2–1 victory and even the series at one game a piece. Tony Jaros led the OISE hitters with three doubles and Sam Nahem contributed two hits.

The OISE All-Stars, 1945 ETO champions.

GAME 3: SEPTEMBER 6, 1945
Headquarters Command Athletic Field, Reims, France

OISE All-Stars 2, 71st Infantry 1

In front of a home crowd, the OISE All-Stars beat the 71st Infantry to take a two games to one lead in the series. Despite Blackwell's outstanding efforts in holding the All-Stars to three hits, he was beaten by Nahem, who allowed just four hits. Nick Macone's fourth-inning two-run double gave the All-Stars the runs they needed.

GAME 4: SEPTEMBER 7, 1945
Headquarters Command Athletic Field, Reims, France

71st Infantry 5, OISE All-Stars 0

The 71st Infantry evened the series at two games each behind the pitching of Bill Ayers. Harry Walker homered with a man on, and Bob Ramazzotti was outstanding defensively, as Ayers scattered five singles.

GAME 5: SEPTEMBER 8, 1945
Soldiers' Field, Nuremberg, Germany
OISE All-Stars 2, 71st Infantry 1
The underdog OISE All-Stars clinched the 1945 GI World Series crown in a tightly fought contest. Lew Richardson broke the 1–1 deadlock in the ninth with a deep drive to center field to score Frank Smayda. Nahem and Bobby Keane combined for the win, while Blackwell took the loss.

71ST INFANTRY DIVISION (3RD ARMY)

NAME	POS	PRE-WAR AFFILIATION
Bill Ayers	P	Atlanta (Southern Association)
Charlie Bamberger	3B	London (PONY League)
Ewell Blackwell	P	Cincinnati Reds
Al Brazle	P	St. Louis Cardinals
Herb Bremer	C	Little Rock (Southern Association)
Jim Gladd	C	Jersey City (International League)
Ken Heintzelman	P	Pittsburgh Pirates
Russ Kerns	SS	Superior (Northern League)
Garland Lawing	OF	Birmingham (Southern Association)
Ansel Moore	OF	Beaumont (Texas League)
Walt Olsen	P	Dayton (Middle-Atlantic League)
Larry Powell	P	San Diego (Pacific Coast League)
Bob Ramazzotti	SS	Durham (Piedmont League)
Walter Smith	P	Petersburg (Virginia League)
Milt Ticco	2B	University of Kentucky
Ken Trinkle	P	New York Giants
Maurice Van Robays	OF	Pittsburgh Pirates
Harry Walker	OF	St. Louis Cardinals
Johnny Wyrostek	OF	Pittsburgh Pirates
Benny Zientara	2B	Cincinnati Reds

OISE All-Stars (Com Z)

Name	Pos	Pre-War Affiliation
Emmet Altenberg	OF	Petersburg (Virginia League)
Russ Bauers	P	Pittsburgh Pirates
Willard Brown	SS	Kansas City Monarchs (Negro American League)
Leon Day	P/OF	Newark Eagles (Negro National League)
Marv Gluckson	P	Brooklyn Bushwicks (semipro)
Joe Herman	OF	Green Bay (Wisconsin State League)
Tony Jaros	1B	University of Minnesota
Bobby Keane	P	Unknown
Nick Macone	OF	Sydney Mines (Cape Breton Colliery)
Roy Marion	OF	Nashville (Southern Association)
Sam Nahem	MGR-P	Philadelphia Phillies
Lew Richardson	C	Hopkinsville (Kitty League)
Frank Smayda	IF	Unknown

The 1945 All-Star Game—
Baseball Navy World Series

◆

by Bill Nowlin

There was no All-Star Game in the summer of 1945. But in late September, the service stars of the American League and those of the National League squared off in what might be called a combination All-Star Game and World Series. It was a best-of-seven game series played at Honolulu's Furlong Field in the 14th Naval District.

World War II had ended with the surrender of Japan on September 2, but few of the ballplayers in the service had yet been demobilized. There was a high caliber of players participating. The games included Ted Williams, Stan Musial, Billy Herman, Bob Lemon, Johnny Pesky, and Bob Kennedy. Gayle Hawes of the *Honolulu Advertiser* wrote that the Navy series would "present more individual stars than even the World Series on the mainland. . . . [A] titanic battle between some of the best known players in baseball."

The series began on September 26. Additional stands were erected, programs were printed, and all military personnel were "invited to the battle." The National Leaguers worked out at Peterson Field's Aiea Barracks, under the leadership of manager Billy Herman. Herman and his team were up against Schoolboy Rowe's squad of American Leaguers. Rowe's men drilled at the submarine base.

The announced starting lineups give some idea of the quality of play that could be expected. Most of the men were in decent form, having played a number of exhibition ballgames during their time in the service.

"I'm still a little rusty, but I hope to be ready for this big series," Ted Williams told the *Honolulu Advertiser*. "I think every man on our squad is anxious to win, and every one of our boys will be ready to go Wednesday afternoon. It should be quite a series." Bill Dickey agreed the teams were well-matched and said he was "looking forward to seeing seven games of the best baseball you'll have a chance to see anywhere this year."

The *Advertiser*'s Hayes picked the American League as favorites. The starting lineups looked like this:

NATIONAL LEAGUE

Charley Gilbert, CF
Jim Carlin, 3B
Billy Herman, 2B
Stan Musial, RF
Whitey Platt, LF
Wimpy Quinn, 1B
Ray Lamanno, C
Ray Hamrick, SS
Clyde Shoun, P

AMERICAN LEAGUE

Jack Conway, 2B
Johnny Pesky, SS
Chet Hajduk, 1B
Ted Williams, RF
Dick Wakefield, LF
Jack Phillips, CF
Bob Kennedy, 3B
Rollie Hemsley, C
Freddie Hutchinson, P

An overflow crowd of around 26,000 fans watched Game 1 of the series. The matchup was a good one. Hutchinson was a key prospect for the Tigers, who had paid the then-enormous sum of $75,000 to purchase him in 1938. Shoun had thrown a no-hitter for Cincinnati against the Boston Braves the year before, on May 15,

1944. Ted Williams, incidentally, wore No. 23—not No. 9—and Musial wore No. 14.

Stan Musial led off the scoring with a line drive over the right-field fence. Later, Ray Lamanno "smashed a towering drive over the right center field stands." Shoun surrendered the 2–0 lead he'd been handed. He walked Williams in the bottom of the second, gave up a single to Dick Wakefield, and then Bob Kennedy hit the first pitch into the left center field seats for a three-run homer. After seven, the AL held a 4–2 lead.

The Nationals tied it in the top of the eighth and built a 6–4 lead in the ninth. With men on first and second and one out, Williams—who'd beaten the National League in the 1941 All-Star Game with a dramatic home run—hit the ball sky-high but straight up. The catcher, Lamanno, camped under it to make the catch. Wakefield whiffed to end the game.

The National League won the next two games, 4–0 and 6–3, then took a big 12–1 loss in game four. The AL again held the Nationals to one run and took Game 5, 4–1, but lost the series in six, staving off a ninth-inning AL rally to win 4–3 behind Lou Tost's pitching. An anticlimactic seventh game was played; the AL won that one, 5–2.

COMPOSITE BATTING STATISTICS,
MINIMUM 10 AT-BATS:

AMERICAN LEAGUE
Hemsley, 6-for-15, .400
Pesky, 9-for-26, .346
Hajduk, 4-for-12, .333
Kennedy, 6-for-21, .286
Sears, 4-for-14, .286
Wakefield, 5-for-18, .278
Williams, 3-for-11, .273
Lyons, 3-for-12, .250
Phillips, 3-for-12, .250
Marks, 4-for-17, .235
Conway, 5-for-25, .200

NATIONAL LEAGUE
Lamanno, 6-for-14, .429
Quinn, 9-for-27, .333
Carlin, 7-for-25, .280
Platt, 6-for-24, .250
Hamrick, 4-for-20, .200
Musial, 4-for-20, .200
Gilbert, 4-for-27, .148
Herman, 2-for-20, .100

HR
(AL): Glenn, Kennedy, Lyons, Lutz, Pesky, Phillips, Rowe, Sears, Williams.
(NL): Brack, Carlin, Gilbert, Lamanno, Musial.

RBI
(AL): Kennedy 5, Sears 4, Lutz 3, Pesky 3, Glenn 2, Hemsley 2, Rowe 2, Wakefield 2, Williams 2, Lyons 1, Phillips 1.
(NL): Gilbert 3, Lamanno 2, Musial 2, Platt 2, Schenz 2, Brack 1, Carlin 1, Casey 1, Hamrick 1, Herman 1, Quinn 1, Scheffing 1, Tost 1, West 1, Wilson 1.

[EDITOR'S NOTE: Thanks to fellow SABR member Duff Zwald for researching both the *Honolulu Star-Bulletin* and *Honolulu Advertiser* at the author's request. A longer version of this article, including game-by-game accounts, was published as "The 1945 All-Star Game" The National Pastime, #26, published by SABR, 2006.]

Major Leaguers Who Served in World War II

A

Clifford A "Cliff" Aberson, OF, Army, USA; George A Abrams, P, Navy, Pacific; Calvin R "Cal" Abrams, OF, Army, ETO; Joseph L "Joe" Abreu, IF, Navy, USA; Marion D "Bill" Adair, Manager, Army, ETO; Robert H "Bobby" Adams, 2B-3B, USAAF, USA; Richard L "Dick" Adams, 1B, USAAF, USA; Robert G "Bob" Addis, OF, Marine Corps, Pacific; William G "Bill" Akers, IF, USAAF, Pacific; Edward J "Ed" Albosta, P, Army, USA; Harold J "Jack" Albright, SS, Navy, Pacific; Dale L Alderson, P, Navy, USA; Robert S "Bob" Alexander, P, Navy, USA; Ethan N Allen, OF, Army, Mediterranean; Baldomero M "Mel" Almada, OF, Army, USA; Thomas E "Tom" Alston, 1B, Navy, USA; Wayne H Ambler, SS, Navy, ETO/Pacific; Andy H Anderson, IF, Army, ETO; Alfred W "Alf" Anderson, SS, Navy, USA; Arnold R "Arne" Anderson, P, Navy, Pacific; Ferrell J "Andy" Anderson, C, Army, ETO; Harold N "Hal" Anderson, OF ; William E "Bill" Anderson, P, Army; Arnold R "Red" Anderson, P, Navy, Pacific; John E Andre, P, USAAF, Pacific; Ernest H "Ernie" Andres, 3B, Navy, Atlantic; Herbert C "Hub" Andrews, P, USAAF; William M "Bill" Andrus, 3B, Army, USA; William J "Bill" Antonello, OF, Navy, Pacific; Peter W "Pete" Appleton (Jablonowski), P, Navy, USA; Lucius B "Luke" Appling, SS, Army, USA; Angel V, Jr "Jack" Aragon, C, Coast Guard, USA; George A Archie, 3B-1B, Army, ETO; Rinaldo J "Rugger" Ardizoia, P, USAAF, Pacific; Henry I "Hank" Arft, 1B, Navy, Pacific; Morris "Morrie" Arnovich, OF, Army, USA; Joseph H "Joe" Astroth, C, Coast Guard, USA; James

C "Jim" Atkins, P, Marine Corps, Pacific; William F "Bill" Atwood, C, USAAF, CBI; Leycester D "Leslie" Aulds, C, USAAF, USA; Martin G "Chick" Autry, C, Marine Corps; William O "Bill" Ayers, P, Army, ETO; Richard J "Dick" Aylward, C, Army, ETO.

B

Frederic J "Fred" Baczewski, P, USAAF; James C J, Jr "Jim" Bagby, P, Merchant Marine; Edson G "Ed" Bahr, P, Navy; William P "Bill" Baker, C, Navy, USA; Eugene W "Gene" Baker, 2B/3B, Navy; Robert R "Bobby" Balcena, OF, Navy; Harold E "Hal" Bamberger, OF ; George I Bamberger, P, Army, MTO/ETO; Daniel R "Dan" Bankhead, P, Marine Corps, USA; John D "Red" Barkley, IF, USAAF, USA; Albert J "Al" Barlick, Umpire, Coast Guard, USA; Rex E Barney, P, Army, ETO; Victor D "Vic" Barnhart, SS, Army; Richard "Dick" Bartell, SS, Navy, USA; Boyd O Bartley, SS, Army; David R "Dave" Bartosch, OF, Coast Guard; Romanus "Monty" Basgall, 2B, Army; Hubert E "Bud" Bates, OF, Navy, USA; Matthew D "Matt" Batts, C, USAAF, USA; Henry A "Hank" Bauer, OF, Marine Corps, Pacific; Russell L "Russ" Bauers, P, Army, ETO; Frank C Baumholtz, OF, Navy, Atlantic; Cramer T "Ted" Beard, OF, Army, Pacific; Henry E "Gene" Bearden, P, Navy, Pacific; John "Johnny" Beazley, P, Army, USA; Joseph E "Joe" Becker, C, Navy; Clarence S Beers, P, USAAF; Joseph S "Joe" Beggs, P, Navy, Atlantic; Henry "Hank" Behrman, P, Army, ETO; Alojzy F "Ollie" Bejma, IF, Navy; Fernando J L "Fern" Bell, OF, Navy, Pacific; Roy C "Beau" Bell, OF, Army; Raymond A "Ray" Benge, P, Navy, Pacific;

Joseph R "Joe" Bennett, 3B, Army; Vernon A "Vern" Benson, OF, Army; John A "Al" Benton, P, Navy; John "Johnny" Berardino, 2B, Naval Reserve, USA; Morris "Moe" Berg, C, OSS, ETO; Louis W "Boze" Berger, IF, USAAF, USA; Walter "Wally" Berger, OF, Navy, USA; John G "Johnny" Bero, IF, USAAF; Lawrence P "Yogi" Berra, C, Navy, ETO; Joseph H "Joe" Jr Berry, Marine Corps, Pacific; Cornelius J "Neil" Berry, IF, USAAF; Herman A Besse, P, Navy; Louis E "Lou" Bevil (Bevilacqua), P, Army; Henry A "Hank" Biasatti, 1B, Canadian Army; Vernon E "Vern" Bickford, P, Army, Pacific; James M "Jim" Bilbrey, P, Navy; Frank S "Porky" Biscan, P, Navy, USA; Charles T "Charlie" Bishop, P, Navy; Hiram G "Hi" Bithorn, P, Navy, Pacific; James N "Jim" Bivin, P, Marine Corps, Pacific; Joseph "Joe" Black, P, Army; Wayne T Blackburn, Coach, Army; James R "Jim" Blackburn, P, Army, ETO; Ewell "The Whip" Blackwell, P, Army, ETO; Louis N "Buddy" Blair, 3B, USAAF, USA; Edward J "Ed" Blake, P, Army, Pacific; Lincoln H "Linc" Blakely, OF, Navy, USA; Prosper A "Al" Blanche, P, Army; John L "Johnny" Blatnik, OF, USAAF, USA; Robert G "Buddy" Blattner, IF, Navy, Pacific; Seymour "Cy" Block, 3B, Coast Guard; James H "Jimmy" Bloodworth, 2B, Army; Michael J "Mike" Blyzka, P, Army; Milton F "Milt" Bocek, OF, Army, Pacific; Joseph E "Eddie" Bockman, 3B, Navy, USA; John E "Jack" Bolling, 1B, Army; Donald R "Don" Bollweg, 1B, Army, USA; Cecil G Bolton, 1B, Army; William C "Cliff" Bolton, C, Army; Julio G Bonetti, P, Army; William J "Bill" Bonness, P, Army; Henry J "Zeke" Bonura, 1B, Army, MTO; Raymond O "Ray" Boone, IF, Navy; Edward J "Red" Borom, IF, Army; Melvin E "Mel" Bosser, P, Army; John C Bottarini, C, USAAF; David T "Tim" Bowden, OF, Army; Grover B Bowers, OF, Army, ETO; Charles J "Charlie" Bowles, P, USAAF, USA; Robert R "Bob" Boyd, 1B/OF, Army; Cloyd V Boyer, P, Navy, USA; Gilbert H "Gibby" Brack, OF, Navy, Pacific; Henry

V "Vic" Bradford, OF, Navy, USA; William D "Bill" Bradford, P, Navy; Fred L Bradley, P, Navy; George T Bradshaw, C, Marine Corps; Robert R "Bobby" Bragan, SS-C, Army, USA; Albert "Al" Brancato, SS, Navy, Pacific; Norman D "Norm" Branch, P, Coast Guard; William G "Bill" Brandt, P, Navy, USA; Alpha E "Al" Brazle, P, Army, ETO; William R "Bill" Breckinridge, P, Army; Herbert F "Herb" Bremer, C, Army, ETO; John H "Jack" Brewer, P, Navy; Thomas J D "Tommy" Bridges, P, Army, USA; Leland V "Lou" Brissie, P, Army, Mediterranean; John A "Jack" Brittin, P, Navy, Pacific; John J "Johnny" Broaca, P, Army; Kenneth L "Ken" Brondell, P, Army; Sigmund T "Sig" Broskie, C, Navy; Giuseppe G "Joe" Brovia, Army; James R "Jimmy" Brown, IF, USAAF; Willard J "Big Bill" Brown, OF, Army, ETO; Mace S Brown, P, Navy/Marine Corps, Pacific; Norman "Norm" Brown, P, Army; Hector H "Hal" Brown, P, USAAF; Robert W "Bobby" Brown, 3B, Navy; Walter G "Jumbo" Brown, P, Navy, USA; John L "Lindsay" Brown, SS, Navy; Walter R "Roy" Bruner, P, Navy, USA; William H "Bill" Bruton, OF, Army; Harold F "Hal" Bubser, PH, Army; John G "Johnny" Bucha, C, Navy; Garland M Buckeye, P, Navy; Michael J "Mike" Budnick, P, Navy, Pacific; Cyril O "Cy" Buker, P, Army, USA; Nelson E Burbrink, C, Navy; Forrest H "Smoky" Burgess, C, Army; William M "Bill" Burich, SS-3B, Army, Mediterranean; Robert J "Bobby" Burke, P, Navy; George H Burpo, P, Navy, USA; Paul R Burris, C, Army; Edward F "Moe" Burtschy, P, Navy; James F "Jim" Busby, OF, Army; Joseph H "Joe" Buskey, SS, Army; Wilburn R "Bill" Butland, P, Army, Pacific; Ralph S Buxton, P, Navy; Samuel D "Sammy" Byrd, OF, Navy; Harry G Byrd, P, Army; Thomas J "Tommy" Byrne, P, Navy, Mediterranean.

C

Thomas "Tom" Cafego, OF, Army; Robert M "Bob" Cain, P, Navy; Bruce Caldwell, OF, Navy; Frederick

J "Fred" Caligiuri, P, Army, ETO/MTO; Henry R "Hank" Camelli, C, Army; Alexander S "Al" Campanis (Campani), 2B, Navy, USA; Paul M Campbell, 1B, USAAF, ETO; Clarence "Soup" Campbell, OF, Army, Pacific; Bruce D Campbell, OF, USAAF, USA; John M Campbell, P, Navy; Mario C "Milo" Candini, P, Army, Pacific; Michael J "Mike" Cantwell, P, Marine Corps; John B Carden, P, Marine Corps, USA; Thomas F A "Tom" Carey, 2B, Navy, Pacific; James A "Jim" Carlin, OF, Navy, Pacific; Edwin E "Ed" Carnett, OF, Navy, USA; Daniel J "Dan" Carnevale, Coach, Army, ETO; Robert L "Bob" Carpenter, P, Army, USA; Walter L "Kit" Carson, OF, Army; Frank W Carswell, OF, Marine Corps, USA; Hugh T Casey, P, Navy, Pacific; Jack D Cassini, 2B, USAAF, USA; James V "Jim" Castiglia, C, Army, USA; Peter P "Pete" Castiglione, 3B, Navy, Pacific; Hardin A Cathey, P, Army; Rex R Cecil, P, Army; Marvin A "Pete" Center, P, USAAF, USA; Bill Chamberlain, P, Army; Spurgeon F "Spud" Chandler, P, Army, USA; Edward O "Ed" Chandler, P, USAAF, Pacific; Samuel B "Sam" Chapman, OF, Navy, USA; William F "Fred" Chapman, SS, Navy, Pacific; William B "Ben" Chapman, OF-P, Navy, USA; Paul Chervinko, C, USAAF; Robert V "Bob" Chesnes, P, Coast Guard; Mitchell "Mitch" Chetkovich, P, Army; Louis P "Lou" Chiozza, IF, Army; Robert H "Bob" Chipman, P, Army; Walter J Chipple (Chilipala), OF, Navy, USA; Emory N "Bubba" Church, P, USAAF, CBI; Nestor L, Jr Chylak, Umpire, Army, ETO; Thaddeus W "Ted" Cieslak, 3B, Army, USA; Albert J "Al" Cihocki, IF, Coast Guard; Louis A "Lou" Ciola, P, Navy, Pacific; Alfred A "Allie" Clark, OF, Army; Melvin E "Mel" Clark, OF, Navy, Pacific; Michael J "Mike" Clark, P, Army; William S "Stu" Clarke, IF, Navy; James B "Buzz" Clarkson, SS, Army; Joseph C "Joe" Cleary, P, Army; Chester S "Chet" Clemens, OF, Navy; William M "Bill" Clemensen, P, Army; Thomas K "Tom" Clyde, P, Army; David L "Dave"

Coble, C, USAAF; Gordon S "Mickey" Cochrane, C, Navy, Pacific; Andrew H "Andy" Cohen, 2B, Army, Mediterranean; Richard R "Dick" Cole, IF, Army; Edward W "Ed" Cole (Kisleauskas), P, Army; Gerald F "Jerry" Coleman, 2B, Navy/Marine Corps, Pacific; Joseph P "Joe" Coleman, P, Navy, Pacific; Raymond L "Ray" Coleman, OF, Navy, MTO/Pacific; Edward T, Jr "Eddie" Collins, OF, Navy, Pacific; Joseph E "Joe" Collins (Kollonige), 1B, Navy; Merrill R "Merl" Combs, IF, Army; Richard "Dick" Conger, P, Marine Corps; William W "Bill" Connelly, P, Marine Corps, Pacific; Mervin T "Bud" Connolly, SS, Navy; Mervin J "Merv" Connors, 3B-1B, Army, ETO; Kevin J A "Chuck" Connors, 1B, Army, USA; William G "Bill" Conroy, C, Navy, USA; Jack C Conway, SS, Navy, Pacific; Herbert L "Herb" Conyers, 1B, USAAF; Rollin E Cook, P, Army; Allen L "Dusty" Cooke, OF, Navy, USA; Raymond F "Bobby" Coombs, P, Navy, Pacific; Robert D "Bob" Cooney, P, Army; William W "Walker" Cooper, C, Navy, USA; Orge P "Pat" Cooper, 1B-P, Army; Calvin A "Cal" Cooper, P, Navy; Henry P Coppola, P, Navy; Claude E Corbitt, IF, USAAF, USA; Edward C "Ed" Cotter, IF, Navy; Clinton D "Clint" Courtney, C, Army, Pacific; William D "Bill" Cox, P, Army, USA; William R "Billy" Cox, SS-3B, Army, ETO; Harry F Craft, OF, Navy, Pacific; Howard O Craghead, P, Navy; Henry C "Shag" Crawford, Umpire, Navy, Pacific; Patrick F "Pat" Creeden, 2B, Navy; Bernard O "Bernie" Creger, SS, Navy; Robert A "Bob" Cremins, P, USAAF; Frank A J "Creepy" Crespi, 2B, Army, USA; Walker J Cress, P ; John M "Jack" Crimian, P, Army; Joffre J "Jeff" Cross, IF, Navy, USA; Frank D "Dingle" Croucher, SS-2B, USAAF, USA; George D Crowe, 1B, Army, CBI; Alfred E "Al" Cuccinello, 2B, Coast Guard; Bernard A "Bud" Culloton, P, Army; Benjamin B "Benny" Culp, C, Navy; Vernon E "Vern" Curtis, P, Navy.

D

Nicholas D "Dom" Dallessandro, OF, Army, USA; Frederick C "Tony" Daniels, 2B, Marine Corps; Harry "The Horse" Danning, C, USAAF, USA; Clifford R "Cliff" Dapper, C, Navy, Pacific; Alvin R "Al" Dark, SS, Marine Corps, Pacific; Frank Dascoli, Umpire, Coast Guard; Robert F "Bob" Daughters, PR, Navy; James B "Jim" Davis, P, Marine Corps; John H "Red" Davis, 3B, USAAF; Lawrence C "Crash" Davis, 2B, Navy, USA; Otis A "Scat" Davis, OF, Navy, USA; Thomas O "Tod" Davis, IF, Army; George A Davis, P, Army; Woodrow W "Woody" Davis, P, Navy; Ellis F "Cot" Deal, P, USAAF, USA; Alfred L "Chubby" Dean, P-1B, USAAF, Pacific; Paul D "Daffy" Dean, P, Army; Michael D "Mike" Dejan, OF, Army; William C "Bill" DeKoning, C, Merchant Marine; Garton L Del Savio, SS, Coast Guard; James H "Jim" Delsing, OF, Army, ETO; William L "Billy" DeMars, SS, Navy, USA; Samuel J "Sam" Dente, IF, Army; Eugene A "Gene" Desautels, C, Marine Corps, USA; Robert S "Ducky" Detweiler, 3B, Army, USA; Melvin E "Mel" Deutsch, P, Army; Charles "Charlie" Devens, P, Navy; George W "Skeets" Dickey, C, Navy, Pacific; William M "Bill" Dickey, C, Naval Reserve, Pacific; George E "Emerson" Dickman, P, Navy; Murry M Dickson, P, Army, ETO; Charles E A "Chuck" Diering, OF, Army, Pacific; William J "Bill" Dietrich, P, Navy; Lloyd A "Dutch" Dietz, P, Army; Robert B "Bob" Dillinger, 3B, USAAF, Pacific; Dominic P "Dom" DiMaggio, OF, Navy, Pacific; Joseph "Joe" DiMaggio, OF, USAAF, Pacific; Robert L P "Bob" DiPietro, OF, Army; Raymond J "Ray" Dobens, P, Navy, CBI; Andrew J "Jess" Dobernic, P, Army; Joseph G "Joe" Dobson, P, Army, USA; Lawrence E "Larry" Doby, OF, Navy, Pacific; Robert P "Bobby" Doerr, 2B, Army, USA; August "Augie" Donatelli, Umpire, USAAF, ETO; Willard E "Bill" Donovan, P, Navy; Harry "Fritz" Dorish, P, Army, Pacific; Calvin L "Cal" Dorsett, P, Marine Corps, Pacific;

John F Douglas, 1B, Navy; Howard J "Danny" Doyle, C, USAAF, USA; Thomas K "Tom" Drake, P, Navy; Clemens J "Clem" Dreisewerd, P, Navy, USA; John J Dudra, IF, Army; Grant L Dunlap, OF, Marine Corps; Elmer C "Red" Durrett, OF, Marine Corps, Pacific; Ervin F "Erv" Dusak, OF-P, Army, Pacific; James R "Jim" Dyck, 3B-OF, Navy.

E

Thomas F A "Tom" Earley, P, Navy, USA; Jacob W "Jake" Early, C, Army, ETO; George L "Moose" Earnshaw, P, Navy, Pacific; Gordon H "Hugh" East, P, Navy, USA; Luscious Luke "Luke" Easter, 1B, Army; Zebulon V "Zeb" Eaton, P, Army; John G "Johnny" Echols, PR, Army; Charles W "Charlie" Eckert, P, USAAF; Henry A "Hank" Edwards, OF, Army, USA; Charles Bruce "Bruce" Edwards, C, Army; Foster H Edwards, P, Army; Elmer A Eggert, 2B, USAAF; Jacob H "Jake" Eisenhart, P, Army; Harry Eisenstat, P, USAAF; Henry K "Heinie" Elder, P, Army; Peter "Pete" Elko, 3B, Army, USA; Charles W "Red" Embree, P, Army; William F "Bill" Endicott, OF, Army; Charles D "Charlie" English, IF; Delmer "Del" Ennis, OF, Navy, Pacific; Russell E "Russ" Ennis, C, Army; Albert P "Al" Epperly, P ; Harold F "Hal" Epps, OF, Marine Corps, Pacific; Aubrey L "Yo-Yo" Epps, C, Marine Corps, Pacific; Edward L S "Eddie" Erautt, P, Army, USA; Joseph M "Joe" Erautt, C, USAAF, Pacific; Harold J "Hal" Erickson, P, USAAF, Pacific; Calvin C "Cal" Ermer, 2B, Marine Corps, USA; Carl D Erskine, P, Navy, USA; William L "Bill" Evans, P, Army, ETO; Alfred H "Al" Evans, C, Navy, USA; Russell E "Red" Evans, P, Navy; Walter A "Hoot" Evers, OF, USAAF, USA; George L Eyrich, P, Navy, Pacific.

F

Everett J Fagan, P, Army; Ferris "Burrhead" Fain, 1B, USAAF, Pacific; Bibb A Falk, OF, USAAF, USA;

George D "Flash" Fallon, SS-2B ; Luvern C "Vern" Fear, P, Navy; Alfred "Al" Federoff, 2B-SS, USAAF; William P "Dutch" Fehring, C, Navy, USA; Edward I "Eddie" Feinberg, SS, Army, ETO; Marvin W "Marv" Felderman, C, Navy, Pacific; Robert W A "Bob" Feller, P, Navy, Atlantic/Pacific; Edward P "Ed" Fernandes, C, Navy, USA; Froilan "Nanny" Fernandez, 3B, USAAF; William J "Bill" Ferrazzi, P, Navy; Thomas J "Tom" Ferrick, P, Navy, Pacific; David M "Dave" Ferriss, P, USAAF, USA; Wilson L "Chick" Fewster, IF, Merchant Marine; Stephen C "Steve" Filipowicz, OF-C, Marine Corps; Thomas M "Tommy" Fine, P, USAAF; Charles W "Carl" Fischer, P, USAAF; Joseph P "Joe" Fitzgerald, Coach, Army, USA; Walter L "Wally" Flager, SS, Army; John F "Red" Flaherty, Umpire, Marine Corps; Albert D "Al" Flair, 1B, Army, Pacific; Raymond A "Ray" Flanigan, P, Army, ETO; Leslie F "Bill" Fleming, P, Army, USA; Elburt P "Elbie" Fletcher, 1B, Navy, Pacific; Charles W "Wes" Flowers, P, Navy; Stuart M "Stu" Flythe, P, Army; Dee V Fondy, 1B, Army, ETO; Richard J "Dick" Fowler, P, Canadian Army, CANADA; Charlie F "Irish" Fox, C, Navy, Atlantic; Frederick M "Fred" Frankhouse, P, Army; James W "Jack" Franklin, P, Army; Murray A "Moe" Franklin, 3B, Navy, USA; Herman L Franks, C, Navy, Pacific; Joseph F "Joe" Frazier, OF, Coast Guard; Edwin C "Ed" Freed, OF, Army; George W Freese, 3B, USAAF; Vern D Freiberger, 1B, Navy; Antonio "Tony" Freitas, P, USAAF, ETO; Lawrence "Larry" French, P, Navy, ETO/Pacific; Walter E French, OF, Army; Linus R "Lonny" Frey, 2B, Army, USA; James R "Jim" Fridley, OF, Army; Fred F Frink, OF, Marine Corps; Charles A "Charlie" Frye, P, Army; Carl A "Skoonj" Furillo, OF, Army, Pacific; Lester L "Les" Fusselman, C, Army.

G

Frank H Gabler, P, Coast Guard; Kenneth H "Ken"

Gables, P, Army; Leonard H "Len" Gabrielson, 1B, Navy; Willard R "Nemo" Gaines, P, Navy; Milton "Milt" Galatzer, OF, Army; Dennis W "Denny" Galehouse, P, Navy, USA; Joseph E "Joe" Gallagher, OF, Army; Stanley J "Stan" Galle (Galazewski), 3B, Coast Guard; Lee J Gamble, OF, Army, USA; Joseph S "Joe" Gantenbein, IF, Army; Joseph H "Joe" Garagiola, C, Army, Pacific; Alexander "Alex" Garbowski, PR, Army; Edward M "Mike" Garcia, P, Army, ETO; David "Dave" Garcia, Manager, Army; Arthur E "Art" Garibaldi, IF, Coast Guard; Virgil C "Cecil" Garriott, OF, Army; Robert F "Ford" Garrison, OF, Navy, USA; Ned F Garver, P, Navy; Sidney A "Sid" Gautreaux, C, Army, Pacific; Eugene F J "Huck" Geary, SS, Navy; Peter "Pete" Gebrian, P, Army; Elmer J Gedeon, OF, USAAF, ETO; Charles L "Charlie" Gehringer, 2B, Navy, USA; Paul A Gehrman, P, Army; Charles M "Charlie" Gelbert, SS-3B, Navy, USA; Joseph E "Joe" Genewich, P, Navy; George M Genovese, SS, Army; Samuel C "Sam" Gentile, OF, Navy; Stephen P "Steve" Gerkin, P, Army, USA; John G "Johnny" Gerlach, IF, USAAF; Floyd G Giebell, P, Coast Guard, USA; Charles M "Charlie" Gilbert, OF, Navy, Pacific; Andrew "Andy" Gilbert, OF, USAAF; George L Gill, P, USAAF; Paul A Gillespie, C, Coast Guard; Myron N "Joe" Ginsberg, C, Army, Pacific; Albert F "Al" Gionfriddo, OF, Army, USA; James W "Jim" Gladd, C, Army, ETO; Roland E Gladu, 3B, Army; Thomas G "Tommy" Glaviano, IF, Coast Guard; James J "Jim" Gleeson, OF, Navy, Pacific; Joseph C "Joe" Glenn (Gurzensky), C, Navy, Pacific; Alban "Al" Glossop, IF, Navy, Pacific; Leslie E "Lonnie" Goldstein, 1B, Army; Isadore "Izzy" Goldstein, P, Army; Stanley "Stan" Goletz USAAF; Mike M Goliat, 2B, Army, Pacific; Joe M "Smokey" Gonzales, P, Navy, Pacific; William D "Billy" Goodman, 2B-3B, Navy, Pacific; James P "Jim" Goodwin, P, Army; Raymond D "Ray" Goolsby, OF, Army; Sidney "Sid" Gordon, 3B-OF, Coast Guard, USA; Joseph L "Joe"

Gordon, SS, USAAF, Pacific; Thomas D "Tom" Gorman, P, Army, Mediterranean; Herbert A "Herb" Gorman, OF, Coast Guard; Henry F "Hank" Gornicki, P, Army; John J P "Johnny" Gorsica (Gorczyca), P, Navy, USA; Nicholas E "Nick" Goulish, OF, Army; Henry M "Hank" Gowdy, Coach, Army, USA; Joseph L "Joe" Grace, OF, Navy, Pacific; Robert E "Earl" Grace, C, Army; John B "Jack" Graham, OF-1B, USAAF; Newton M "Mickey" Grasso, C, Army, N Africa; Ted G Gray, P, Navy, Pacific; Henry B "Hank" Greenberg, OF-1B, Army/USAAF, CBI; Kent Greenfield, P, USAAF; Paul E Gregory, P, Navy; Lewis E "Buddy" Gremp, 1B, Navy, USA; Ross A Grimsley, P, USAAF, ETO; Lee T Grissom, P, Army, USA; Marvin E "Marv" Grissom, P, Navy; John "Johnny" Grodzicki, P, Army, ETO; John T "Johnny" Groth, OF, Navy, USA; Ernest W "Ernie" Groth, P, Marine Corps, Pacific; Sigmund S "Sig" Gryska, SS, Navy; Benjamin J "Ben" Guintini, OF, Army; Witt O "Lefty" Guise, P, Army; Louis J "Lou" Guisto, 1B, Navy; Harry E "Gunboat" Gumbert, P, Army, USA; Randall P "Randy" Gumpert, P, Coast Guard.

H

Berthold J "Bert" Haas, 1B-3B, Army, Mediterranean; Robert J "Bob" Habenicht, P, USAAF; Warren L Hacker, P, Marine Corps, Pacific; Richard F "Dick" Hahn, C, Navy; Samuel "Sammy" Hairston, C ; Chester "Chet" Hajduk, 1B, Navy, Pacific; George S Halas, OF, Navy; Robert L "Bob" Hall, P, Coast Guard; William A "Bill" Hallahan, P, Army; Jack P Hallett, P, Navy, Pacific; Ralph C Hamner, P, Navy, Pacific; Granville W "Granny" Hamner, SS, Army; Raymond B "Ray" Hamrick, 2B-SS, Navy, USA; Morris M "Buddy" Hancken, C, Marine Corps; Andrew V "Andy" Hansen, P, Army; Donald T "Don" Hanski (Hanyzewski), P, Army; William E "Bud" Hardin, IF, Army, Mediterranean; Francis J "Red" Hardy, P, Navy; William B "Bill" Harman, P, Marine Corps; Charles B "Chuck" Harmon, 3B-OF, Navy, USA; Maurice C "Mickey" Harris, P, Army, CANAL ZONE; Robert N "Ned" Harris, OF, Navy, Pacific; Robert A "Bob" Harris, P, Navy, Pacific; Chalmer L "Lum" Harris, P, Navy, Pacific; Charles "Bubba" Harris, P, Navy; Earl "Irish" Harrist, P, USAAF; Samuel "Sam" Harshany, C, Naval Reserve, Pacific; John E "Jack" Harshman, P, Navy; Christian H "Chris" Hartje, C, Coast Guard; Roy T "Spec" Hartsfield, 2B, Navy, USA; Clinton C "Clint" Hartung, P-OF, USAAF, USA; Donald I "Don" Hasenmayer, 2B-3B, Navy; John A "Buddy" Hassett, 1B, Navy, Pacific; Charles E "Gene" Hasson, 1B, Army; Fred J Hatfield, IF, Army; Ray W Hathaway, P, Navy; Joseph H "Joe" Hatten, P, Navy; Grady E Hatton, 3B-2B, USAAF, USA; Christopher F "Chris" Haughey, P, Army; Philip D "Phil" Haugstad, P ; James M "Jim" Hayes, P, Navy; Edward M "Ed" Head, P, Army, USA; Jehosie "Jay" Heard, P, Army; James T "Jim" Hearn, P, Army, Pacific; Thomas G "Tommy" Heath, C, Army; Wallace A "Wally" Hebert, P, Navy; Randolph R "Randy" Heflin, P, Navy; James E "Jim" Hegan, C, Coast Guard; Val R Heim, OF, Navy, USA; Kenneth A "Ken" Heintzelman, P, Army, ETO; Henry H "Hank" Helf, C, Navy; Ralston B "Rollie" Hemsley, C, Navy, Pacific; Thomas D "Tommy" Henrich, OF, Coast Guard, USA; Roy K Henshaw, P, Navy; William J B "Billy" Herman, 2B, Navy, Pacific; Eugene V "Gene" Hermanski, OF, Coast Guard, USA; Charles L "Buck" Herzog, IF, Army; John E "Johnny" Hetki, P, Army; James R "Jim" Hickey, P, Navy, USA; Clarence W "Buddy" Hicks, IF, Navy; Walter "Kirby" Higbe, P, Army, Pacific; Michael F "Pinky" Higgins, 3B, Navy, USA; Andrew A "Andy" High, 3B, Navy, Pacific; Walter F "Whitey" Hilcher, P, Army, ETO; Jesse T Hill, OF, Navy, USA; Avitus B "Vedie" Himsl, Manager, Navy; Harley P Hisner, P, Army; William C "Billy" Hitchcock, SS-3B, USAAF, Pacific; Jimmy Hitchcock Navy; Lloyd E Hittle, P, Army; Myril O

Hoag, OF, USAAF; Melvin A "Mel" Hoderlein, IF, USAAF; Gilbert R "Gil" Hodges (Hodge), 1B, Marine Corps, Pacific; Elmer R "Ralph" Hodgin, OF-3B, Army, USA; Aloysius J "Eli" Hodkey, P, Army; Frank J "Lefty" Hoerst, P, Navy, Atlantic/Pacific; Robert G "Bobby" Hofman, IF, Army; Robert C "Bobby" Hogue, P, Navy; G James "Jim" Honochick, Umpire, Navy, Atlantic/Pacific; Robert N "Bob" Hooper, P, USAAF; Richard L "Dick" Hoover, P, Navy; James M "Jim" Hopper, P, Army, USA; Vernard A "Vern" Hoscheit, Coach, USAAF, USA; Ralph G "Major" Houk, C, Army, ETO; Lee V "Lefty" Howard, P, Navy, Pacific; Calvin E Howe, P, Army; Homer E "Dixie" Howell, C, Army, ETO; Millard "Dixie" Howell, P, Army, ETO; Roland E "Tex" Hoyle, P, Army; Otto Huber, IF, Army; George W "Willis" Hudlin, P, USAAF; Sidney C "Sid" Hudson, P, USAAF, USA; Benjamin F "Ben" Huffman, C, Navy, Pacific; Thomas O "Tommy" Hughes, P, Army, USA; James R "Jim" Hughes, P, Marine Corps, Pacific; Cecil C "Tex" Hughson, P, USAAF, Pacific; Oliver J "Joel" Hunt, OF, USAAF; Herbert H "Herb" Hunter, IF, Navy; Frederick C "Fred" Hutchinson, P, Navy, Pacific.

I

Clarence E "Hooks" Iott, P, USAAF, USA; Monford "Monte" Irvin, OF, Army, ETO.

J

Ranson J "Randy" Jackson, 3B, Navy, USA; John L Jackson, P, Army; Anthony R "Tony" Jacobs, P, Marine Corps, Pacific; Sigmund "Sig" Jakucki, P, Army; Leroy G "Roy" Jarvis, C, Navy; Harold B "Hal" Jeffcoat, OF/P, Army, Mediterranean; Frank A Jelinich, OF, Navy; William L "Bill" Jennings, SS, Merchant Marine; Arthur H "Art" Johnson, P, Navy, Pacific; Earl D "Lefty" Johnson, P, Army, ETO; Adam R, Jr "Rankin" Johnson, P, Navy, Pacific; Silas K "Si"

Johnson, P, Navy, USA; William R "Billy" Johnson, 3B, Army, ETO; Kenneth W "Ken" Johnson, P, Army, Pacific; Clifford "Connie" Johnson, P, Army; Ernest T "Ernie" Johnson, P, Marine Corps, Pacific; Donald R "Don" Johnson, P, Army; Russell C "Jing" Johnson, P, Navy; Roy M "Pop" Joiner, P, Army; Stanley E "Stan" Jok, 3B-OF, Navy; David "Dave" Jolly, P, Army; Dale E "Nubs" Jones, P, Navy, Pacific; James M "Jake" Jones, 1B, Navy, Pacific; Vernal L "Nippy" Jones, 1B, Marine Corps, Pacific; Sheldon L "Available" Jones, P, USAAF, Canal Zone; Willie E "Puddin' Head" Jones, 3B, Navy; Niles C Jordan, P, Navy; John D "Spider" Jorgensen, 3B, USAAF; Walter F "Walt" Judnich, OF, USAAF, Pacific; Howard K "Howie" Judson, P, Navy; John S "Red" Juelich, IF, Army; Kenneth P "Ken" Jungels, P, Army, USA; Alvin J "Al" Jurisich, P, Coast Guard, USA.

K

Robert W "Bob" Kahle, Navy; Frank B "Fats" Kalin (Kalinkiewicz), OF, Army; Alexis W "Alex" Kampouris, 2B, USAAF; Martin G "Marty" Karow (Karowsky), IF, Navy; Herbert "Herb" Karpel, P, Army, ETO; Edward T "Eddie" Kazak (Tkaczuk), 3B, Army, ETO; Edward P "Eddie" Kearse, C, Army; Robert C "Bob" Keegan, P, Army, Mediterranean; Chester L "Chet" Kehn, P, USAAF, Pacific; Francis E "Frankie" Kelleher, OF, Army, USA; Charles "Charlie" or "King Kong" Keller, OF, Merchant Marine, USA; Alexander R "Alex" Kellner, P, Navy, USA; William H "Bill" Kelly, 1B, Army; Kenneth F "Ken" Keltner, 3B, Navy, Pacific; Robert D "Bob" Kennedy, 3B-OF, Marine Corps, Pacific; William G "Bill" Kennedy, P, Army, ETO; Montia C "Monte" Kennedy, P, Army, USA; Arthur J "Art" Kenney, P, USAAF, ETO; Wayman W "Bill" Kerksieck, P, Army; Russell E "Russ" Kerns, C, Army, ETO; Ellis R "Old Folks" Kinder, P, Army; Ralph M Kiner, OF, Navy Air Corps, Pacific; Lynn P King, OF, USAAF; Ernest A "Ernie" Kish,

OF, Coast Guard; George M Kissell, Coach, Navy, Pacific; Hubert M "Hub" Kittle, Coach, Army; Louis F "Lou" Klein, 2B, Coast Guard, USA; Theodore O "Ted" Kleinhans, P, Army, ETO; Robert H "Bob" Klinger, P, Navy, Pacific; Austin Knickerbocker, OF, Army; William H "Bill" Knickerbocker, SS, Army; John "Jack" Knott, P, Army, ETO; Donald M "Don" Kolloway, 2B, Army, ETO; Bruno B "Bruce" Konopka, 1B, Navy, Pacific; Casimir James "Jim" Konstanty, P, Navy, USA; Clement J "Clem" Koshorek, IF, Army; George B "Dave" Koslo (Koslowski), P, Army, ETO; Michael T "Mike" Kosman, Marine Corps; Ernest A "Ernie" Koy, OF, Navy; Albert K "Al" Kozar, 2B, Army; Joseph P "Joe" Kracher, C, Army; Joseph V L "Joe" Krakauskas, P, RCAF, CANADA; John H "Jack" Kramer, P, Navy, USA; John W "Jack" Kraus, P, Army; Lewis B "Lew" Krausse, P, Army; Albert J "Mickey" Kreitner, C, Army; Charles S "Charlie" Kress, 1B, Army; Louis H "Lou" Kretlow, P, USAAF, USA; Kurt F Krieger, P, Army; Howard W "Howie" Krist, P, Army, ETO; Richard D "Dick" Kryhoski, 1B, Navy, Pacific; John A "Johnny" Kucab, P, Army; Stanislaw L "Steve" Kuczek, PH, Army; Bernard C "Bert" Kuczynski, P, Navy, Pacific; Emil B Kush, P, Navy, USA; Robert L "Bob" Kuzava, P, Army, CBI; Alexander "Al" Kvasnak, OF, Army.

L

Clement W "Clem" Labine, P, Army; Doyle M "Porky" Lade, P, Coast Guard; Joseph J "Joe" Lafata, OF-1B, Army; Alfred A "Al" LaMacchia, P, Army; Frank "Hank" Lamanna, P, USAAF; Raymond S "Ray" Lamanno, C, Navy, Pacific; Eugene M "Gene" Lambert, P, Army; Clayton P Lambert, P, USAAF, USA; Stanley A "Stan" Landes, Umpire, Marine Corps; Walter O "Walt" Lanfranconi, P, Army; Donald C "Don" Lang, 3B, USAAF, Pacific; Hubert M "Max" Lanier, P, Army, USA; John Y "Johnny" Lanning, P, Army; Paul E LaPalme, P, Army; Andrew

"Andy" Lapihuska, P, Army, ETO; Raoul R "Ralph" LaPointe, SS, Army, USA; Harry A "Cookie" Lavagetto, 3B, Navy, Pacific; Garland F Lawing, OF, Army, ETO; Brooks U Lawrence, P, Army; Alfred V "Roxie" Lawson, P ; Peter J "Pete" Laydon, OF, USAAF; Ivoria H "Hillis" Layne, 3B, Army; Lester L "Les" Layton, OF, Navy; DeWitt W "Bevo" LeBourveau, OF, Navy; Roy E Lee, P, Navy; Wilfred H "Bill" LeFebvre, P-PH, Army; Paul E Lehner, OF, USAAF, Pacific; Edgar E "Ed" Leip, 2B, Army, Mediterranean; Robert G "Bob" Lemon, P, Navy, Pacific; Donald E "Don" Lenhardt, OF, Navy, Atlantic/Pacific; John J Leovich, C, Coast Guard; George E Lerchen, OF, Navy; Charlie Letchas, 2B, Army; James J "Jim" Levey, SS, Army; Edward C "Ed" Levy, OF, Coast Guard; John K "Buddy" Lewis, 3B-OF, USAAF, CBI; Robert E "Gene" Lillard, IF-P ; Louis "Lou" Limmer, 1B, USAAF; Lyman G Linde, P, USAAF; John H "Johnny" Lindell, OF-P, Army, USA; Walter C "Walt" Linden, C, Army; Royce J Lint, P, USAAF; John J "Johnny" Lipon, SS, USAAF; Daniel W "Danny" Litwhiler, OF, Army, USA; Everett A "Buddy" Lively, P, Army, ETO; Wesley A "Wes" Livengood, P, Navy, Pacific; Thompson O "Mickey" Livingston, C, Army, USA; Robert K "Bob" Loane, OF, Army; William C "Bill" Lobe, Coach, Army, ETO; Carroll W "Whitey" Lockman, OF, Merchant Marine; Dario A Lodigiani, 3B-2B, USAAF, Pacific; John "Johnny" Logan, SS, Army; Jack W "Lucky" Lohrke, 3B-2B, Army; Victor A "Vic" Lombardi, P, Navy; Stanley E "Stan" Lopata, C, Army, ETO; Omar J "Turk" Lown, P, Army; Harry L "Peanuts" Lowrey, OF, Army, USA; Samuel J "Sam" Lowry, P, Army; Hugh M "Hal" Luby, 3B, Navy; John "Johnny" Lucadello, 2B-3B, Navy, Pacific; Ray W Lucas, P, Navy, USA; Edward P "Eddie" Lukon, OF, Army; Ulysses J "Tony" Lupien, 1B, Navy, USA; Rollin J "Joe" Lutz, 1B, Marine Corps; Jerome E "Jerry" Lynn, 2B, Army, ETO; Theodore "Ted" Lyons, P, Marine Corps, Pacific; Albert H "Al"

Lyons, P, Navy, Pacific; Edward H "Eddie" Lyons, 2B, Navy; Herschel E "Hersh" Lyons, P, USAAF.

M

Raymond J "Ray" Mack (Mickovsky), 2B, Army; John J Mackinson, P, Army; Max C Macon, P, Army, USA; Harry W MacPherson, P, Navy, USA; Clarence J Maddern, OF, Army, ETO; Edward W "Ed" Madjeski, C ; Salvador "Sal" Madrid, SS, USAAF; Jack Maguire, OF, Army; Arthur L "Art" Mahan, 1B, Navy, USA; John W "Duster" Mails, P, Marine Corps; Forrest H "Woody" Main, P, Marine Corps; Henry "Hank" Majeski, 3B, Coast Guard, USA; Malcolm F "Mal" Mallette, P, USAAF; Leslie C "Les" Mallon, 2B, Navy; Robert P "Bob" Malloy, P, Army; Edward R "Eddie" Malone, C, Navy; Gordon R Maltzberger, P, Army; Francis O "Frank" Mancuso, C, Army, USA; Donald D Manno, IF, Navy, USA; Richard W "Dick" Manville, P, Navy; Clifford "Cliff" Mapes, OF, Navy, Pacific; Philip "Phil" Marchildon, P, RCAF, ETO; Cleneth E "Gene" Markland, 2B, Army; Harry S "Hal" Marnie, 2B, Army, USA; Robert "Bob" Marquis, OF, Navy; Fred F Marsh, IF, Navy; William Henry Marshall, 2B, Navy, USA; Charles A Marshall, C, Army; Milo M "Max" Marshall, OF, Navy, USA; Willard W Marshall, OF, Marine Corps, Pacific; Barnes R Martin, P, Navy; Raymond J "Ray" Martin, P, USAAF, ETO; Fred T Martin, P, Army, Pacific; Morris W "Morrie" Martin, P, Army, ETO; Stuart M "Stu" Martin, 2B, Navy; Boris M "Babe" Martin (Martinovich), OF-C, Navy, USA; Joe Marty, OF, USAAF, Pacific; Walter E "Walt" Masterson, P, Navy, Pacific; Gene W Mauch, 2B-SS, USAAF; Merrill G "Pinky" May, 3B, Navy, Pacific; James W "Buster" Maynard, OF, Army, USA; John L "Jack" Mayo, OF, Marine Corps; William G "Bill" McCahan, P, USAAF; John W "Windy" McCall, P, Marine Corps; John J "Johnny" McCarthy, 1B, Navy, Pacific; Myron W "Mike" McCormick, OF,

USAAF, Pacific; William B "Barney" McCosky, OF, Navy, Pacific; Benjamin J "Benny" McCoy, 2B, Navy, USA; Clyde E McCullough, C, Navy, USA; Pinson L "Phil" McCullough, P, Navy; Robert "Maje" McDonnell, Coach, Army, ETO; Frank McElyea, OF, Army; Edward J "Eddie" McGah, C, Navy, Pacific; Daniel A "Dan" McGee, SS, Navy, Pacific; Ezra M "Pat" McGlothin, P, Navy, USA; Tullis E "Mickey" McGowan, P, Navy, Pacific; John J McHale, 1B, Navy, USA; Rogers H McKee, P, Navy, USA; Wayne G McLeland, P, Army; Ralph A McLeod, OF, Army, ETO; Soule J "Jim" McLeod, 3B, Army; Calvin C J C T "Cal" McLish, P, Army, ETO; Carl M McNabb, 2B, Army, USA; Glenn R "Red" McQuillen, OF, Navy, Pacific; Irving J "Irv" Medlinger, P, Army; Russell H "Russ" Meers, P, Navy, Pacific; Sabath A "Sam" Mele, OF, Marine Corps, USA; Reuben F "Rube" Melton, P, Army; Lloyd A Merriman, OF, Marine Corps, USA; John W "Jack" Merson, 2B-3B, Army; James V "Jim" Mertz, P, Army; William A "Bill" Metzig, 2B, Army; Lambert D "Dutch" Meyer, 2B, USAAF; George F Meyer, 2B, Navy, USA; Russell C "Russ" Meyer, P, Army, USA; Edward A "Ed" Mickelson, 1B, USAAF, USA; Richard "Dick" Midkiff, P, USAAF, USA; Lawrence E "Larry" Miggins, OF, Merchant Marine; Edward T "Eddie" Miksis, 2B, Navy, USA; Wilson D "Dee" Miles, OF, Navy, Pacific; Robert J "Bob" Miller, P, Army, Pacific; Ronald A "Ronnie" Miller, P ; John A "Ox" Miller, P, Army, USA; Walter L "Wally" Millies, C, Navy, USA; Colonel B "Buster" Mills, OF, USAAF, Pacific; Howard R "Lefty" Mills, P, Army; Albert J "Al" Milnar, P, Army, Pacific; William J "Pete" Milne, OF, Navy; Paul E Minner, P, Army, USA; Loren D "Dale" Mitchell, OF, Army; John R "Johnny" Mize, 1B, Navy, Pacific; John H Mohardt, OF, Army; William J "Bill" Moisan, P, Army, ETO; Fenton L Mole, 1B, USAAF; Alex "Al" Monchak, SS-2B, Army; Rene Monteagudo, P–OF, Army; Jim I Mooney, P, Navy; Raymond L "Ray"

Moore, P, Army, USA; Anselm W "Anse" Moore, OF, Army, ETO; D C "Dee" Moore, C, Marine Corps, Pacific; Terry B Moore, OF, Army, Canal Zone; Lloyd A "Whitey" Moore, P, Army; Carlos W Moore, P, USAAF; William A "Cy" Moore, P, Army; Euel W Moore, P, Army; William A "Scrappy" Moore, 3B, USAAF; Robert M "Bobby" Morgan, IF, Army; Edward J "Ed" Moriarty, 2B, Navy, USA; Willard B "Bill" Morrell, P, USAAF, Mediterranean; Newell O "Bud" Morse, 2B, Army; Walter J "Walt" Moryn, OF, Navy; Arnold R "Arnie" Moser, Navy; Howard G "Howie" Moss, OF, Coast Guard, USA; John L "Les" Moss, C, Merchant Marine; Elisha M "Bitsy" Mott, IF, Navy; Glen H Moulder, P, USAAF; Maurice J "Mo" Mozzali, Coach, Navy, Pacific; Emmett J "Heinie" Mueller, 2B, Army, Pacific; Ray C Mueller, C, Army, USA; William L "Bill" Mueller, OF, Navy, USA; Leslie C "Les" Mueller, P, Army; Joseph G "Gordie" Mueller, P, Navy; Joseph A "Joe" Muir, P, Marine Corps; Hugh N "Losing Pitcher" Mulcahy, P, Army, Pacific; Ford P "Moon" Mullen, 2B, Army; Richard C "Dick" Mulligan, P, USAAF, USA; Patrick J "Pat" Mullin, OF, Army, USA; George D "Red" Munger, P, Army, ETO; Van Lingle Mungo, P, Army; Edward J "Ed" Murphy, 1B, Army; John J "Johnny" Murphy, P, Navy; Raymond L "Ray" Murray, C, USAAF; Joseph A "Joe" Murray, P, Navy; Daniel E "Danny" Murtagh, 2B, Army, USA; Stanley "Stan" Musial, OF, Navy, Pacific; Bernard J "Barney" Mussill, P, Army, USA.

N

Stephen "Steve" Nagy, P, Navy; Samuel R "Subway Sam" Nahem, P, Army, ETO; Earl E Naylor, OF-P, Navy; Robert O "Bob" Neighbors, SS, USAAF, USA; Glenn R "Rocky" Nelson, 1B, Army; Ernest A "Ernie" Nevers, P, Marine Corps, Pacific; Floyd E Newkirk, P, Army; Maurice M "Maury" Newlin, P, Naval Reserve, USA; Lamar A "Skeeter" News-ome, IF, Army; Constantine G "Gus" Niarhos, C, Navy, USA; Roy Nichols, IF, Army; Milton R "Milt" Nielsen, OF ; Jacob L "Jack" Niemes, P, Navy; Alfred J "Al" Niemiec, 2B, Navy, USA; Leo W "Red" Non-nenkamp, OF, Navy, USA; Irving A "Irv" Noren, OF, Army; Ronald J "Ron" Northey, OF, Army, USA; Louis A "Lou" Novikoff, OF, USAAF.

O

Frank J Oceak, Coach, Navy; Walter A Ockey (Okpych), P, Army; Paul O'Dea, OF, Army; James D "Jim" Oglesby, 1B, Army, USA; Leonard J "Len" Okrie, C, Navy; Thomas N "Tom" Oliver, OF, Navy, Pacific; Vern J Olsen, P, Navy, Pacific; Bernard C "Barney" Olsen, OF, Navy; Harry M O'Neill, C, Marine Corps, Pacific; John J "Buck" O'Neill, Coach, Navy, Pacific; Frederick R "Fritz" Ostermueller, P, Navy; Joseph P "Joe" Ostrowski, P, USAAF; Arnold M "Mickey" Owen, C, Navy; Paul F Owens, Man-ager, Army; Daniel L "Danny" Ozark (Orzechowski), Manager, Army.

P

Don W Padgett, OF-C, Navy, USA; Jack Paepke, Coach, Navy, Pacific; Michael R "Mike" Palagyi, P, Army; Richard P "Mike" Palm, P, USAAF; Alfred T "Al" Papai, P, Army; Clarence M "Ace" Parker, SS, Navy, USA; Francis J "Salty" Parker, IF; Artie W "Art" Parks, OF, Army; Melvin L "Mel" Parnell, P, USAAF, USA; Edward D "Dixie" Parsons, C, Navy; Roy R Partee, C, Army; Stanwood W "Stan" Partenheimer, P, Army; Arthur M "Art" Passarella, Umpire, Army, USA; Robert L "Bob" Patrick, OF, Army; George W "Bill" Patton, C, Army; Gene T Patton, Unknown, Army; Theodore J "Ted" Pawelek, C, Marine Corps, USA; Franklin T "Frank" Pearce, P, Navy; Isssac O "Ike" Pearson, P, Marine Corps, USA; Leslie E "Les" Peden, C, Army, ETO; Stephen G "Steve" Peek, P, Army, ETO; Homer H Peel, OF,

Navy, USA; Edward C "Eddie" Pellagrini, SS-2B, Navy, Pacific; James E "Jim" Pendleton, OF-3B; John J Perkovich, P, Army; Harry W Perkowski, P, Navy, Pacific/ETO; Leonard J "Len" Perme, P, Navy; John M "Johnny" Pesky (Paveskovich), SS, Navy, Pacific; William D "Bill" Peterman, C, Army, USA; Russel D "Rusty" Peters, IF, Army; Kent F Peterson, P, Army, Pacific; Carl F "Buddy" Peterson, SS, Navy; George E Pfister, C, USAAF; Raymond W "Bill" Phebus, P, Army; David E "Dave" Philley, OF, Army; Damon R Phillips, SS, Army; Jack D Phillips, 1B, Navy, Pacific; Nicholas T "Nick" Picciuto, 3B, Army; Aloysius E "Al" Piechota, P, Army; Raymond L "Ray" Pierce, P, Navy; Jess W Pike, OF, Navy; Antone J "Andy" Pilney, OF, Navy, USA; Henry H "Cotton" Pippen, P, Navy; Alexander "Alex" Pitko, OF, Army; Mizell G "Whitey" Platt, OF, Navy, Pacific; Cletus E "Boots" Poffenberger, P, Marine Corps, Pacific; Hugh R Poland, C, Army, USA; Kenneth L "Ken" Polivka, P, Navy; Howard J "Howie" Pollett, P, USAAF, Pacific; Raymond H "Ray" Poole, OF, Army, CANAL ZONE; David "Dave" Pope, OF, Army, USA; Edward J "Eddie" Popowski, Coach, Army; Richard T "Dick" Porter, OF, Coast Guard, USA; Edwin C "Bob" Porterfield, P, Army, ETO; William "Barnacle Bill" Posedel, P, Navy; John S "Jack" Pramesa, C, Marine Corps, USA; Melvin A "Mel" Preibisch, OF, Navy, USA; James B "Jim" Prendergast, P, Army, ETO; Gerald E "Jerry" Priddy, SS, USAAF, Pacific; Everett V "Pid" Purdy, OF, Navy; Frank A "Frankie" Pytlak, C, Navy, USA.

Q

Melvin D "Mel" Queen, P, Army; James H "Hal" Quick, SS, USAAF; Wellington H "Wimpy" Quinn, P, Marine Corps, Pacific.

R

Stephen S "Steve" Rachunok, P, Army, ETO; Marvin E "Marv" Rackley, OF, USAAF; Raymond A "Rip" Radcliff, OF, Navy, USA; Kenneth D "Ken" Raffensberger, P, Navy, USA; Robert L "Bob" Ramazzotti, IF, Army, ETO; Frank R D "Ribs" Raney (Raniszewski), P, Navy; Earl W Rapp, OF, Army, ETO; Joseph A "Goldie" Rapp, 3B, Navy; Victor J A "Vic" Raschi, P, USAAF; George H "Buck" Redfern, IF, Navy; Ed Redys, Coach, Army; William J "Billy" Reed, 2B, Army; William E "Bill" Reeder, P, Army, Pacific; Harold H "Pee Wee" Reese, SS, Navy, Pacific; James H "Jimmie" Reese (Soloman), 2B, Army, USA; Robert E "Bobby" Reeves, IF, Army; Herman C Reich, OF, Army; Earl P Reid, P, Army; Thomas E "Tommy" Reis, P, Army; Harold P "Pete" Reiser, OF, Army, USA; James D "Jim" Reninger, P, Navy, USA; William B "Bill" Renna, OF, Marine Corps, USA; Dino P Restelli, OF, Army; Robert J "Rocky" Rhawn, IF, Army, USA; John G "Gordon" Rhodes, P, Army, N Africa; John L Rice, Umpire, Marine Corps; Harold H "Hal" Rice, OF, Army; Woodrow E "Woody" Rich, P, Marine Corps; Donald L "Don" Richmond, 3B, Army, Pacific; Allen G "Al" Richter, SS, Army; Marvin A "Marv" Rickert, OF, Coast Guard, Pacific; Harvey D "Hank" Riebe, C, Army, ETO; Lewis S "Lew" Riggs, 3B, USAAF; John D "Johnny" Rigney, P, Navy, Pacific; William J "Bill" Rigney, 2B-3B, Coast Guard; Culley Rikard, OF, USAAF, USA; Walter F "Walt" Ripley, P, USAAF; Arthur B "Tink" Riviere, P, Army; John C "Johnny" Rizzo, OF, Navy, USA; Philip "Phil" Rizzuto, SS, Navy, Pacific; Douglas W "Scotty" Robb, Umpire, Navy, ETO; Thomas V "Tommy" Robello, 2B-3B, Navy; J Albert A "Skippy" Roberge, IF, Army, ETO; Robin E Roberts, P, USAAF, USA; Charles E "Red" Roberts, IF, Army; Sherrard A "Sherry" Robertson, IF-OF, Navy, Pacific; William E "Eddie" Robinson, 1B, Navy, USA; Aaron A Robinson, C, Coast Guard; John E "Jack" Robinson, P, Navy, USA;

Jack R "Jackie" Robinson, IF, Army, USA; Warren G "Sheriff" Robinson, Coach, Navy, Pacific; Louis J "Lou" Rochelli, 2B, Navy; William S "Bill" Rodgers, OF, Army; Oscar F L Roettger, P–1B, Army; Stanley F "Packy" Rogers (Hazinski), IF, Navy, Pacific; Stanley A "Stan" Rojek, SS, USAAF; James K "Jim" Romano, P, Navy; Albert L "Al" Rosen, 3B, Navy, USA; Simon "Si" Rosenthal, OF, Navy, ETO; Chester J "Chet" Ross, OF, Navy, USA; Joe Rossi, C, Army; John H "Jack" Rothrock, OF, Army, USA; Lynwood T "Schoolboy" Rowe, P, Navy, Pacific; Ralph E Rowe, Coach; Carvel W "Bama" Rowell, 2B, Army, USA; Richard L "Dick" Rozek, P, Navy; Charles H "Red" Ruffing, P, USAAF, USA; Robert R "Bob" Rush, P, Army; Marius U "Lefty" Russo, P, Army; Henry A "Hank" Ruszkowski, C, Army; Milton "Mickey" Rutner, 3B, Army; Cornelius J "Connie" Ryan, 2B, Navy, Pacific; John C "Blondy" Ryan, IF, Navy.

S

Alexander "Alex" Sabo (Szabo), C, Navy, N Africa; Thomas J "Tom" Saffell, OF, USAAF; John F "Johnny" Sain, P, Navy Air Corps, USA; Manuel "Manny" Salvo, P, Army, USA; Edward W "Ed" Samcoff, 2B, Marine Corps; John F "Fred" Sanford, P, Army, Pacific; John D "Jack" Sanford, 1B, USAAF; Edward R "Ed" Sanicki, OF, Navy; Francis F "Frank" Saucier, OF, Navy, Pacific; Henry J "Hank" Sauer, OF, Coast Guard, USA; John "Bob" Savage, P, Army, ETO; William N "Bill" Sayles, P, Army; Frank J "Skeeter" Scalzi, IF, Navy, USA; Rae W "Ray" Scarborough, P, Navy, USA; Harold "Hal" Schacker, P, Army; LeRoy J "Roy" Schalk, 2B, Army; George A Scharein, SS, Army, ETO; Robert B "Bob" Scheffing, C, Navy, Pacific; Carl A Scheib, P, Army; Michael "Mike" Schemer, 1B, Army; Henry L "Hank" Schenz, 2B, Navy, Pacific; Robert E "Bob" Scherbarth, C, Navy; George E Schmees, OF, Navy; Frederick A "Freddy" Schmidt, P, Army; John A "Johnny" Schmitz, P, Navy,

Pacific; Henry A "Hank" Schmulbach USAAF; Albert F "Red" Schoendienst, 2B, Army, USA; Edward W "Wes" Schulmerich, OF, Navy, Pacific; Herman J "Ham" Schulte (Schultehenrich), 2B, Army; Robert D "Bob" Schultz, P, USAAF, USA; William M "Mike" Schultz, P, Army; Harold H "Hal" Schumacher, P, Navy, Pacific; Ralph R "Blackie" Schwamb, P, Navy; Kenneth E "Ken" Sears, C, Navy, Pacific; George A Selkirk, OF, Navy; Theodore W "Ted" Sepkowski (Sczepkowski), OF-3B, Coast Guard; Walter A Sessi, OF, Army; Robert C "Bobby" Shantz, P, Army, Pacific; Wilmer E "Billy" Shantz, C, Navy; Francis J "Spec" Shea (O'Shea), P, Navy, Pacific; Hollis K "Bud" Sheely, C, Army; Robert E "Bert" Shepard, P, USAAF, ETO; Neill R Sheridan, OF, Marine Corps; James R "Jim" Shilling, IF, Coast Guard; Milburn J "Milt" Shoffner, P, USAAF, ETO; Edward C "Eddie" Shokes, 1B, Navy, Pacific; Raymond E "Ray" Shore, P, USAAF; David O "Dave" Short, OF, USAAF; Clyde M Shoun, P, Navy, Pacific; Charles A R "Charlie" Silvera, C, USAAF, Pacific; Kenneth J "Ken" Silvestri, C, Army, USA; Albert "Al" Sima, P, Navy; John E Simmons, OF, Marine Corps, Pacific; Harry L Simpson, OF/1B, Army; Frederic W "Fred" Sington, OF, Navy, USA; Richard A "Dick" Sisler, 1B-OF, Navy, USA; Sebastian D "Sibby" Sisti, 2B-SS, Coast Guard; Peter "Pete" Sivess, P, Navy, ETO; Enos "Country" Slaughter, OF, USAAF, Pacific; Louis M "Lou" Sleater, P, Navy, USA; Bruce A Sloan, OF, Army; Dwain C "Lefty" Sloat, P, Army; Roy F Smalley, SS, Navy, USA; Joseph P "Joe" Smaza, OF, Navy; Vincent A "Vinnie" Smith, C/Umpire, Navy, Pacific; Edgar "Eddie" Smith, P, Army, Mediterranean; John M Smith, 1B ; Edwin D "Duke" Snider, OF, Navy, Pacific; Albert Henry "Hank" Soar, Umpire, Army, USA; William D "Bill" Sommers, 3B-2B, Army; Victor G "Vic" Sorrell, P, Navy; Stephen "Steve" Souchock, 1B-OF, Army, ETO; Warren E Spahn, P, Army, ETO; Stanley O "Stan" Spence, OF,

Navy, USA; Glenn Edward Spencer, P, Navy, USA; Robert O "Bob" Spicer, P, Army; Homer F Spragins, P, USAAF; Edward J "Ebba" St Claire, C, Army; Gerald L "Jerry" Staley, P, Army, Pacific; Thomas V "Virgil" Stallcup, SS, Navy; George W Staller, OF, Marine Corps, Pacific; Charles "Charley" Stanceu, P, Army; Richard E "Dick" Starr, P, Army; Henry J "Hank" Steinbacher, OF, Army; Bryan M Stephens, P, Army; Joseph C "Joe" Stephenson, C, Army; Charles A "Chuck" Stevens, 1B, USAAF, Pacific; Edward P "Bud" Stewart, OF, Army; Lee E Stine, P, Navy; Raymond T "Ray" Stoviak, OF, Navy, USA; Alan C Strange, SS, Army; George B Strickland, IF, Navy; Louis B "Lou" Stringer, 2B, USAAF, USA; Paul H Stuffel, P, Army; Robert H "Bobby" Sturgeon, SS, Navy; John P J "Johnny" Sturm, 1B, Army, USA; Charles M "Charley" Suche, P, Army; James J "Jim" Suchecki, P, Navy; Peter "Pete" Suder, 2B, Army; William J, Jr "Billy" Sullivan, C, Navy, USA; John P Sullivan, SS, Army, Pacific; Stephen R "Steve" Sundra, P, Army, USA; Matthew C "Max" Surkont, P, Navy, Pacific; Charles I "Butch" Sutcliffe, C, Army; Howard A "Dizzy" Sutherland, P, Army, Mediterranean; Oadis V "Oad" Swigart, P, Army.

T

James R "Jim" Tabor, 3B, Army; Leroy E Talcott, P, Navy; Vitautis C "Vito" Tamulis, P, USAAF, USA; Elvin W "El" Tappe, C, Navy; Alvin W "Al" Tate, P, Army; V T "Tommy" Tatum, OF, USAAF; Fred J Tauby (Taubensee), OF, Navy, USA; James H "Harry" Taylor, P, Navy; Edward J "Ed" Taylor, 3B-SS, Navy; Frederick R "Fred" Taylor, 1B, USAAF; George R "Birdie" Tebbetts, C, USAAF, Pacific; Richard L Teed, PH, Marine Corps; Joseph J "Joe" Tepsic, OF, Marine Corps, Pacific; Willard W "Wayne" Terwilliger, 2B, Marine Corps, Pacific; Leo R Thomas, IF, Navy; Jon S "Jocko" Thompson, P, Army, ETO; Eugene E "Junior" Thompson, P, Navy,

USA; Henry C "Hank" Thompson, 2B, Navy, ETO; Robert B "Bobby" Thomson, OF, USAAF, USA; Benjamin R "Bob" Thorpe, OF, Navy, Pacific; Louis C F "Lou" Thuman, P, Army, ETO; Robert "Bob" Thurman, OF, Navy; Joe H Tipton, C, Navy; John P "Johnny" Tobin, 3B, Navy; William H "Hal" Toenes, P, USAAF; Clifford E "Earl" Torgeson, 1B, Army, ETO; Louis E "Lou" Tost, P, Navy, Pacific; Stephen J "Red" Tramback, OF, Navy, Pacific; Cecil H Travis, SS-3B, Army, ETO; Frank A Trechock, SS, Army; Nicholas J "Nick" Tremark, OF, Navy, USA; Kenneth W "Ken" Trinkle, P, Army, ETO; Virgil O Trucks, P, Navy, Pacific; Thurman L Tucker, OF, Navy, USA; George E Turbeville, P, USAAF, USA; Edward L Turchin, IF, Navy, USA; Thomas R "Tom" Turner, C, Army; Earl E Turner, C, Army.

U

Robert E "Bob" Uhle, P, Army; Michael E "Mike" Ulisney, C, Army; R T "Dixie" Upright, Army; Thomas H "Tom" Upton, SS, Navy, USA; Robert R "Bob" Usher, OF, Navy, Pacific.

V

Elmer W Valo, OF, Army, USA; Christian G "Chris" Van Cuyk, P, Navy, Pacific; John H "Johnny" Van Cuyk, P, Army; Maurice R Van Robays, OF, Army, ETO; Joseph A "Joe" Vance, P, Navy; John S "Johnny" Vander Meer, P, Navy, Pacific; Cecil P "Porter" Vaughan, P, Army; Allen F "Al" Veigel, P, USAAF; Vincent "Vince" Ventura, OF, USAAF; James B "Mickey" Vernon, 1B, Navy, Pacific; Clyde F Vollmer, OF, Army.

W

Jacob F "Jake" Wade, P, Navy, USA; Benjamin S "Ben" Wade, P, Army; Charles T "Charlie" Wagner, P, Navy, Pacific; Harold E "Hal" Wagner, C, Army; Edward S

"Eddie" Waitkus, 1B, Army, Pacific; Richard C "Dick" Wakefield, OF, Navy Air Corps, Pacific; Edwin J "Ed" Walczak, 2B, Army; Harry W "Harry the Hat" Walker, OF, Army, ETO; Harvey W "Hub" Walker, OF, Navy, USA; James E "Jim" Walkup, P, USAAF; James H "Lefty" Wallace, P, Army; John "Jack" Wallaesa, SS, Army, Mediterranean; James G "Junior" Walsh, P, Army; Joseph P "Joe" Walsh, SS, Navy; Lonnie "Lon" Warneke, P, Army; Bennie L Warren, C, Navy, USA; Thomas G "Tommy" Warren, P, Navy, N Africa; Harold "Hal" Weafer, Umpire, Navy; Kenneth A "Ken" Weafer, P, Navy; Cyril R "Roy" Weatherly, OF, Army; Montie "Monte" Weaver, P, USAAF, ETO; Samuel H "Red" Webb, P, Coast Guard; Ralph R "Wig" Weigel, C, Coast Guard, USA; Richard H "Dick" Weik, P, Navy; Edwin N "Ed" Weiland, P, Navy, Pacific; William F "Roy" Weir, P, Navy; John L "Johnny" Welaj, OF, Army; Leo D Wells, SS-3B, Coast Guard, Pacific; Charles W "Butch" Wensloff, P, Army; William G "Bill" Werle, P, Army; Victor W "Vic" Wertz, OF, Army, Pacific; Richard T "Dick" West, C, Navy, Pacific; Max E West, OF, USAAF, USA; Samuel F "Sam" West, OF, Army; Waldon T "Wally" Westlake, OF, Coast Guard; Wesley N "Wes" Westrum, C, Army, USA; Donald W "Don" Wheeler, C, Army; Ernest D "Ernie" White, P, Army, ETO; Harold G "Hal" White, P, Navy, Pacific; Albert E "Fuzz" White, OF, Army, USA; Donald W "Don" White, OF, Navy; Burgess U "Whitey" Whitehead, 2B, USAAF; Dick C Whitman, OF, Army, ETO; Walter F "Frank" Whitman, SS, Army; William R "Bill" Wight, P, Navy, USA; Delbert Q "Del" Wilber, C, USAAF, USA; James H "Hoyt" Wilhelm, P, Army, ETO; Aldon J "Lefty" Wilkie, P, Army, ETO; Robert F "Ace" Williams, P, Navy, USA; Theodore S "Ted" Williams, OF, Navy/Marine Corps, Pacific; Edwin D "Dib" Williams, IF, Army; Vernon S "Whitey" Wilshere, P, Navy; Max Wilson, P, Navy, Pacific; George W Wilson, OF, Army, ETO; Grady H Wilson, SS, Army; Walter W "Walt" Wilson, P, Army; Lester W "Les" Wilson, OF, USAAF; John T "Tom" Winsett, OF, USAAF, Pacific; Francis M "Whitey" Wistert, P, Navy; Nicholas J "Mickey" Witek, 2B, Coast Guard, USA; Jerome C "Jerry" Witte, 1B, Army; Joseph F "Joe" Wood, P, Navy; Kenneth L "Ken" Wood, OF, Coast Guard; Eugene R "Gene" Woodling, OF, Navy, Pacific; Taft S "Taffy" Wright, OF, USAAF, Pacific; Albert E "Al" Wright, 2B, Navy; Forrest G "Glenn" Wright, SS, Navy, USA; Frank J Wurm, P, Army; Early Wynn, P, Army, Pacific; John B "Johnny" Wyrostek, OF, Army, ETO.

Y

George E Yankowski, C, Army; Waldo W "Rusty" Yarnall, P, Navy; Raymond A A "Ray" Yochim, P, Marine Corps, Pacific; Anthony B "Tony" York, IF, Army; Edward F J "Eddie" Yost, 3B, Navy, USA; Norman R "Babe" Young, 1B, Coast Guard; Ralph S Young, 2B, Navy; Floyd E "Eddie" Yount, OF, Army; John E "Eddie" Yuhas, P, Army, ETO; Salvador A "Sal" Yvars, C, USAAF.

Z

Adrian Zabala, P, Cuban Army; Frank T "Frankie" Zak, SS, Army; Allen L "Al" Zarilla, OF, Army, USA; Gus E Zernial, OF, Navy; Benedict J "Benny" Zientara, 2B, Army, ETO; George Zuverink, P, USAAF, Pacific.

Major and Minor Leaguers Killed During World War II

MAJOR LEAGUE

NAME	EXPERIENCE	SERVICE	CAUSE OF DEATH	LOCATION	DATE
Elmer Gedeon	Major League	USAAF	Killed in Action	ETO	April 20, 1944
Harry O'Neill	Major League	USMC	Killed in Action	PACIFIC	March 6, 1945

MINOR LEAGUE

NAME	EXPERIENCE	SERVICE	CAUSE OF DEATH	LOCATION	DATE
Herman Bauer	Minor League	US Army	Died From Wounds	ETO	July 12, 1944
Fred Beal	Minor League	US Army	Died in Hospital	USA	February 11, 1944
Leonard Berry	Minor League	US Army	Killed in Action	ETO	December 24, 1944
Keith Bissonette	Minor League	USAAF	Killed in Action	CBI	1944
Dave Blewster	Minor League	Unknown	Unknown	Unknown	Unknown
Charles Bowers	Minor League	US Army	Died From Wounds	ETO	April 15, 1945
Lefty Brewer	Minor League	US Army	Killed in Action	ETO	June 6, 1944
Ed Brock	Minor League	US Navy	Killed in Action	PACIFIC	February 26, 1945
Murrill Brown	Minor League	US Navy	Plane Crash	USA	September 1944
Whitey Burch	Minor League	US Army	Military Accident	USA	November 29, 1941
George Chandler	Minor League	USAAF	Plane Crash	USA	September 28, 1942
Floyd Christiansen	Minor League	USAAF	Plane Crash	USA	July 10, 1945
Ordway Cisgen	Minor League	US Army	Killed in Action	ETO	July 11, 1944
Edward Dalton	Minor League	US Army	Killed in Action	ETO	March 30, 1945

Howard DeMartini	Minor League	US Army	Killed in Action	ETO	December 24, 1944
Hal Dobson	Minor League	USAAF	Plane Crash	USA	May 23, 1943
Norman Duncan	Minor League	US Navy	Killed in Action	PACIFIC	April 12, 1945
Louis Elko	Pro Contract	US Army	Military Accident	UNKNOWN	UNKNOWN
Charles Etherton	Minor League	USMC	Suicide	USA	December 27, 1945
Herb Fash	Minor League	US Navy	Explosion	PACIFIC	February 21, 1945
Frank Faudem	Minor League	US Army	Killed in Action	PACIFIC	January 1945
Ernest Ford	Minor League	USMC	Military Accident	USA	May 1945
George Gamble	Minor League	USAAF	Killed in Action	CBI	December 4, 1944
Bob Gary	Minor League	USAAF	Plane Crash	USA	February 4, 1944
Conrad Graff	Minor League	US Army	Killed in Action	ETO	July 8, 1944
Alan Grant	Minor League	USAAF	Plane Crash	ETO	December 29, 1943
Jim Grilk	Minor League	USAAF	Auto Accident	USA	July 16, 1942
Frank Haggerty	Pro Contract	USAAF	Plane Crash	USA	September 23, 1943
Bill Hansen	Minor League	US Army	Died From Wounds	ETO	1944
Billy Hebert	Minor League	US Navy	Killed in Action	PACIFIC	October 21, 1942
Nay Hernandez	Minor League	US Army	Killed in Action	ETO	March 22, 1945
Bob Hershey	Minor League	US Navy	Killed in Action	PACIFIC	September 1943
Roswell Higgin-botham	Minor League	US Navy	Died After Operation	USA	May 23, 1943
Ernie Holbrook	Minor League	US Army	Killed in Action	ETO	December 16, 1944
Bob Holmes	Minor League	USMC	Died From Wounds	PACIFIC	February 22, 1945
Gordon Houston	Minor League	USAAF	Plane Crash	USA	February 10, 1942
Ernie Hrovatic	Minor League	US Army	Killed in Action	ETO	January 14, 1945
Harry Imhoff	Minor League	USMC	Killed in Action	PACIFIC	1945
Frank Janik	Minor League	US Army	Killed in Action	PACIFIC	April 29, 1945
Tony Janis	Minor League	Unknown	Unknown	Unknown	Unknown
Art Keller	Minor League	US Army	Killed in Action	ETO	September 29, 1944
Stan Klores	Minor League	US Navy	Killed in Action	PACIFIC	December 3, 1944
Curly Kopp	Minor League	USAAF	Plane Crash	USA	1944
Harry Ladner	Umpire	US Army	Killed in Action	PACIFIC	April 18, 1945
Walter Lake	Minor League	US Army	Died from Wounds	ETO	July 26, 1944
Whitey Loos	Minor League	USAAF	Plane Crash	PACIFIC	January 16, 1944

Jack Lummus	Minor League	USMC	Died From Wounds	PACIFIC	March 9, 1945
Ted Maillet	Minor League	US Army	Killed in Action	ETO	April 7, 1945
William Marszalek	Minor League	US Army	Unknown	USA	October 7, 1942
Henry Martinez	Minor League	US Navy	Killed in Action	PACIFIC	January 5, 1945
Duke McKee	Minor League	US Army	Killed in Action	ETO	1945
Paul Mellblom	Minor League	US Army	Killed in Action	ETO	January 14, 1945
Lou Miller	Minor League	Unknown	Unknown	Unknown	Unknown
Joe Moceri	Minor League	US Army	Killed in Action	ETO	June 30, 1944
John Moller	Minor League	USAAF	Killed in Action	PACIFIC	August 8, 1943
John Munro	Minor League	Unknown	Unknown	Unknown	Unknown
George Myers	Minor League	US Army	Killed in Action	ETO	1945
Walter Navie	Minor League	US Army	Suicide	USA	October 9, 1945
Ed Neusel	Minor League	US Navy	Died From Illness	USA	July 31, 1944
William Niemeyer	Minor League	US Army	Killed in Action	ETO	March 4, 1945
Hank Nowak	Minor League	US Army	Killed in Action	ETO	January 1, 1945
Joe Palatas	Minor League	USAAF	Died as POW	ETO	April 11, 1944
Jack Patterson	Minor League	USMC	Killed in Action	PACIFIC	November 2, 1944
Metro Persoskie	Minor League	USAAF	Flying Accident	ETO	February 22, 1944
Charlie Pescod	Minor League	US Army	Killed in Action	ETO	December 2, 1944
Harold Phillips	Minor League	USAAF	Plane Crash	USA	August 9, 1945
Joe Pinder	Minor League	US Army	Killed in Action	ETO	June 6, 1944
Ernie Raimondi	Minor League	US Army	Died From Wounds	ETO	January 26, 1945
John Regan	Minor League	USAAF	Plane Crash	CBI	May 25, 1944
Pete Rehkamp	Minor League	USAAF	Auto Accident	USA	September 9, 1942
Joseph Rodgers	Minor League	US Navy	Killed in Action	MTO	October 10, 1943
Michael Sambolich	Minor League	US Army	Killed in Action	ETO	November 4, 1944
Glenn Sanford	Minor League	USAAF	Plane Crash	USA	November 6, 1943
Bill Sarver	Minor League	US Army	Killed in Action	ETO	April 6, 1945
Charles Schaube	Minor League	US Army	Killed in Action	ETO	April 16, 1945
Walt Schmisseur	Minor League	US Navy	Killed in Action	PACIFIC	February 20, 1945
Bob Schmukal	Minor League	US Army	Killed in Action	ETO	October 3, 1944
Eddie Schohl	Minor League	US Army	Died from Wounds	MTO	November 1, 1943

Frank Schulz	Minor League	USAAF	Killed in Action	PACIFIC	June 17, 1945
Carl Scott	Minor League	US Army	Killed in Action	ETO	July 26, 1944
Marcel Serventi	Minor League	US Army	Auto Accident	USA	July 5, 1941
Harold Sherman	Minor League	USAAF	Plane Crash	CBI	July 7, 1945
Jack Siens	Minor League	US Navy	Plane Crash	ETO	September 10, 1943
Art Sinclair	Minor League	US Army	Killed in Action	MTO	January 26, 1944
John Smith	Minor League	US Army	Killed in Action	ETO	November 4, 1944
Norman Smith	Minor League	US Navy	Missing in Action	PACIFIC	August 9, 1942
Marshall Sneed	Minor League	USAAF	Killed in Action	MTO	February 22, 1943
Billy Southworth Jr	Minor League	USAAF	Plane Crash	USA	February 15, 1945
Earl Springer	Minor League	US Army	Killed in Action	ETO	January 25, 1945
Gene Stack	Minor League	US Army	Natural Causes	USA	June 26, 1942
Don Stewart	Umpire	Canadian Army	Killed in Bombing Raid	ETO	March 13, 1941
Al Stiewe	Minor League	US Army	Killed in Action	MTO	February 15, 1945
Sylvester Sturges	Minor League	USAAF	Killed in Action	ETO	June 7, 1944
Fred Swift	Minor League	USAAF	Plane Crash	USA	April 23, 1944
Johnny Taylor	Minor League	USMC	Killed in Action	PACIFIC	July 26, 1944
Steve Tonsick	Minor League	US Army	Killed in Action	MTO	March 28, 1943
James Trimble	Pro Contract	USMC	Killed in Action	PACIFIC	March 1, 1945
Wirt Twitchell	Minor League	US Army	Killed in Action	PACIFIC	July 1944
Lou Vann	Minor League	USMC	Killed in Action	PACIFIC	May 18, 1944
Art Vivian	Minor League	USMC	Killed in Action	ETO	August 1, 1944
Elmer Wachtler	Minor League	US Army	Killed in Action	ETO	January 5, 1945
Leo Walker	Minor League	USAAF	Plane Crash	USA	November 2, 1941
Roman Wantuck	Minor League	US Army	Killed in Action	PACIFIC	June 16, 1944
Jim Whitfield	Minor League	US Army	Killed in Action	PACIFIC	September 22, 1944
Dick Williams	Minor League	US Army	Killed in Action	PACIFIC	February 21, 1945
Les Wirkkala	Minor League	US Army	Killed in Action	ETO	September 7, 1944
Stanford Wolfson	Minor League	USAAF	Killed in Action	ETO	November 5, 1944
Elmer Wright	Minor League	US Army	Killed in Action	ETO	June 6, 1944
Fred Yeske	Minor League	US Army	Killed in Action	MTO	December 21, 1944
Marion Young	Minor League	USMC	Killed in Action	PACIFIC	December 13, 1944
Peter Zarilla	Minor League	USAAF	Plane Crash	USA	August 9, 1945
Lamar Zimmerman	Minor League	US Army	Killed in Action	PACIFIC	January 24, 1945

| John Zulberti | Minor League | US Army | Killed in Action | MTO | January 1944 |
| George Zwilling | Minor League | US Army | Killed in Action | MTO | March 31, 1943 |

This listing of players who served in World War II is as complete as could be at the time this book went to press. However, ongoing research continues and changes are being made from time to time. For the most current up-to-date listing, please consult Gary Bedingfield's Baseball in Wartime Web site at www.baseballinwartime.com. Baseball in Wartime is the only online resource dedicated to baseball during World War II, with more than 400 biographies, team rosters, photos, and much more.

Contributors

TERRY ALLVORD

Terrence Allvord is a combat veteran and Santa Monica, California, native with a degree in education, training, and development. He recently retired from his position as defense/acquisition program manager for the Chairman of the Joint Chiefs of Staff's Coalition Warrior Interoperability Demonstration after 23 years of service in the U.S. Navy. He logged over 5,000 flight hours as a crew chief, rescue swimmer, and naval aviator while completing seven tours of duty in the Middle East.

During Operation Iraqi Freedom, Allvord served on the USS *Tarawa*, USS *Essex*, and Commander Task Force 76. He managed the President of the United States' visit to Southeast Asia. He served in the aftermath of numerous disasters including Hurricane Katrina and the World Trade Center in New York City assisting in the recovery of personnel lost in the 9/11 tragedy. His experiences led him to establish the So Others May Live Foundation and publish his story, *Back from Ground Zero*. He has written two books for use by military recruiters: *The Mustang Handbook: Guide to Becoming a Military Officer* and *Goal Setting: Formula for Success*. His third book, *Home and Away: An American Life in the 9/11 Generation* is due for release in the summer of 2009. He resides in San Diego with his wife and their three children.

TODD W. ANTON

Todd Anton, a U.S. history teacher in the Snowline Unified School District, author, and member of the National World War II Museum's Board of Trustees, was instrumental in the concept and planning of the national conference and exhibition on Baseball in World War II for the museum along with author Bill Nowlin. Museum co-founder and famed historian, the late Stephen Ambrose, took Anton under his wing after he was nominated as "Teacher of the Year" by the Veterans of Foreign Wars as a result of his and his student's nearly 2,000 interviews with veterans of WWII. Along with the influence of his late father, WWII/Korean veteran and avid Dodger fan Wally Anton, Todd's association with Ambrose led him toward his life's work: preserving the stories of the men who served their country during WWII and also played Major League Baseball. His book, *No Greater Love: Life Stories from the Men Who Saved Baseball* fulfilled his quest. Anton, along with author Bill Nowlin and Red Sox ace Curt Schilling, collaborated on Fox TV's "War Stories" epi-

234

sode devoted to World War II and baseball called "From the Ballpark to the Battlefield: Baseball and World War II"—the concept largely drawn from Anton's book. Today, Anton continues to teach and write and shares a home with his wife, Susan, and their two children, Jamie and Jason.

Gary Bedingfield

How does an Englishman now living in Scotland develop a love for baseball? It is a question often pitched to Gary Bedingfield. As his father toured U.S. Air Force bases in Britain as a musician, he brought back a ball and glove. Some years later his young son discovered them, and, soon, Gary was hooked! As a youth, he played on the British Championship team four times, the British National and Olympic teams, and coached varsity baseball at the American School in London. Through all of this, he developed a passion for the game and its history, especially as it was played in his native land. That passion led him to research, write, and publish *Baseball in World War II Europe* in 2000. Since then Bedingfield has written numerous magazine and newspaper articles on WWII baseball, and contributed his knowledge to many other projects. His website, www.baseballinwartime.com, is recognized as the world's leading source on the subject. The Dodgers fan has four children and lives with his wife, Lainy, in Glasgow, Scotland.

Frank Ceresi

Ceresi is an attorney, museum consultant, and professional appraiser specializing in valuing sports memorabilia and vintage photographs (http://www.fcassociates. com). He has written widely and is currently co-authoring a book on baseball treasures at the Library of Congress. Ceresi grew up in the U.S. and abroad as an Army brat. His father was a lifelong member of the United States Army who fought in Europe in the trenches during World War II, was wounded at Normandy, and was present at the fall of Paris. Col. Ceresi also served his country in the infantry during Korea. After his retirement from the service, the Ceresi family settled in Alexandria, Virginia, where Frank practices law to this day. Frank's lifelong interest in baseball and admiration for the men and women who serve in the armed forces is due to Frank's love of his father and for everything he taught him.

Merrie A. Fidler

In 1976, it was beyond Merrie Fidler's wildest imagination to conceive that her 1976 Sports Studies master's thesis about "The Development and Decline of the All-American Girls Baseball League" for UMass Amherst would play a role in the production of a major motion picture, *A League of Their Own*. As a lifetime softball participant and baseball enthused graduate student, she was captivated when she discovered Philip K.

Wrigley's creation of the All-American Girls Soft Ball/Base Ball League during World War II. In the early 1980s, Fidler's thesis helped motivate ex-All-American players to organize a national reunion, which ultimately led to the premiere of *A League of Their Own* in 1992. In the meantime, Fidler enjoyed a career as a northern California high school English and physical education teacher who also coached volleyball, basketball, and softball. It wasn't until she retired in 2003 that All-American Players' Association Board Members approached her to update and publish her thesis as *The Origins and History of the All-American Girls Professional Baseball League* (McFarland, 2006). Fidler now lives with her foster mother near the seaside village of Trinidad in northern California, serves as secretary for the AAGPBL Players' Association, and continues to study and write about the professional girls' baseball league fostered by World War II.

Linda McCarthy

One might not expect to hear from a former spokesperson for the Central Intelligence Agency at a conference on baseball, but Linda McCarthy is known for delivering the unexpected. Through the creation of the CIA Museum, McCarthy gained a wealth of knowledge on the espionage game. She molded that knowledge into a public speaking business called History is a Hoot, Inc.

Using rare spy artifacts from her private collection, McCarthy now delights audiences with fascinating stories gleaned from her research and experiences. As author of the book *Spies, Pop Flies, and French Fries: Stories I Told My Favorite Visitors to the CIA Exhibit Center*, McCarthy entertains a variety of audiences nationwide. For her contributions to a two-part story on World War II-era baseball player turned spy, Moe Berg, she was awarded an Emmy for "outstanding research" for NBC News. She is the only intelligence official so honored.

William B. Mead

William B. Mead is the author of six baseball history books and co-author of a seventh. His first book, *Even the Browns* (now in a new edition under the title of *Baseball Goes to War*) is an anecdotal history of baseball's role in World War II. It was praised by reviewers in the *New York Times*, *Time* magazine, the *Philadelphia Inquirer*, and many other newspapers and magazines. Mead's attachment to the subject came naturally: He grew up in St. Louis and was 10 years old when his hometown Browns and Cardinals met in the 1944 World Series.

Bill Nowlin

Bill Nowlin's interest in baseball and war-time began as a child aware of Ted Williams' time as a Marine Corps pilot during the Korean War. A former professor of political science, he founded Rounder Records with two friends in 1970 and the company has produced over 3,000 record albums of American roots and other music. In the mid-1990s, Nowlin began to work on another passion: writing about the Boston Red Sox. To date, he's authored or edited over 20 books on the team and its tribulations, including *Red Sox Threads* and *Day by Day with the Boston Red Sox*. He wrote Johnny Pesky's biography, *Mr. Red Sox*, and a full book dedicated to Ted Williams' military service, *Ted Williams At War*. Nowlin collaborated with Todd Anton on Fox TV's "War Stories" episode devoted to World War II and baseball. Anton and Nowlin helped inspire the "When Baseball Went to War" conference and exhibition at the National World War II Museum. Nowlin has been vice president of the Society for American Baseball Research since 2004.

Bill Swank

In 1994, following his retirement from a 31-year career with the San Diego County Probation Department, Bill Swank used his investigative skills to track down over 150 of the most notorious San Diego Padres from the Pacific Coast League era. He told their stories in *Echoes from Lane Field* and later wrote a two volume book set titled, *Baseball in San Diego: From the Plaza to Petco*. Most recently, he co-authored Bob Chandler's *Tales from the San Diego Padres*. For more

than 30 years, Bob Chandler was a Padres radio and television partner of Jerry Coleman. Swank maintains the ongoing Whitey Wietelmann San Diego Padres Box Score Scrapbook collection, now in its 40th year, for the San Diego Public Library and has written a quarterly newsletter for old Padres players for the last 14 years. His scale model of Lane Field is on display at the San Diego Hall of Champions Sports Museum. He is also known as "Baseball Santa" and played as Santa Claus for the original House of David baseball team in 2003-2006. Swank, a former Marine, and his wife, Jeri Lynne, are the parents of five grown children. His advice to them, their grandchildren—and others: "Learn to hit the curve ball. You'll see lots of them in your lifetime."

Kerry Yo Nakagawa

Curator, filmmaker, author, educator, producer—Yo Nakagawa describes himself as a multimedia person and takes tremendous pride in his five tools of passion. He is the founding curator of the "Diamonds in the Rough" exhibit that has been displayed at the baseball hall of fame in Cooperstown, Tokyo, and museums around the country. To make the exhibit more multimedia and interactive, he produced and directed the *Diamonds in the Rough* documentary with his Godpapa Pat Morita. He authored *Through A Diamond: 100 Years of Japanese American Baseball* in 2001 and co-produced a curriculum guide with Stanford Universities SPICE organization titled *Diamonds in the Rough: Baseball and Japanese American Internment*. His fifth project is a five-year labor of love as a feature film, *American Pastime*. The independent film won the "Audience Favorite" award in San Francisco and has been entertaining and educating audiences around the country. He was the associate producer, actor, behind-the-scenes filmmaker, and human ball machine.

Baseball and War

by Terry Allvord and Todd Anton

Arguably one of the first victims in a war is a person's humanity, the memory of the person he was before the nightmare of war, before the sacrifice began and the long and tired feeling of war and regret set in as young boys became men much too early and much too fast. This was true in World War II and is still true today.

In the Korean War, in Vietnam, in Desert Storm, and even today in Iraq, soldiers would burn off a little energy when they could and play baseball to regain a sense of the person they once were and hoped to become again.

During the Korean War, one baseball veteran was lost in action—Bob Neighbors, who had played with the Browns in 1939—but became a career officer in the Air Force. Others were called to serve. Ted Williams and Jerry Coleman were both recalled as Marine pilots, and both saw combat. Willie Mays of the Giants was called to duty in the U.S. Army after establishing himself as an upcoming star. We can only wonder what Mays would have done with two more years

in his prime playing years. Braves catcher Del Crandall was drafted into the Army right after making it with the Braves. He served in Japan during the Korean War, but neither Mays nor Crandall regretted their service. It maybe didn't always seem fair, but that was what Americans did.

Star pitcher Don Newcombe of the Brooklyn Dodgers was just eight months away from being too old for the draft. When he got the call, he knew that many much younger men were not being summoned, but he knew that a challenge would be misunderstood. He reported for duty and to this day considers it his highest honor. When asked why he served, "Newk" simply says, "When your country calls, you go. I was an American." Sgt. Newcombe eventually was in charge of physically training recruit Army doctors at Camp Pickett, Texas. He loved the irony of his position of authority observing, "It shows you where America was going with Jackie breaking the color line. Now there was an integrated Army and me in charge of hundreds of white doctors, and me training them at a base named after a

November 6, 2004 (all photos in this section): Only one day before the battle of Fallujah, Marines with 1st Battalion, 8th Marine Regiment take a break from round-the-clock training with a few innings of the national pastime. On a diamond of sand and rocks, the Marines used their resourcefulness and played with sandbag bases, a hollow plastic ball, and a tape-wrapped broomstick for a bat. Twenty-four hours later these same Marines would be fighting in one of the largest and deadliest battles of the Iraq war.
Photos by Cpl. Joel A. Chaverri

Confederate general. I am glad I got to live to see it."

In Vietnam, Los Angeles Dodgers slugger Roy Gleason gave a great deal in a war many questioned. But nobody can question Gleason's character, his honor and commitment to America. Gleason had been touted as the "next Frank Howard," meaning he was a big and strong man. He was called up from the minors in September 1963 and played

eight games late in the season, used primarily as a pinch runner. He stayed with the club all the way through the World Series as the Dodgers swept the Yankees, earning him a highly prized World Series ring.

Not long afterwards, it all changed and Gleason went in to combat in the jungles of Vietnam. Doing his duty seemed natural to Gleason, who hoped to rejoin the Dodgers upon his return. But those future plate

appearances were not to be. He served in the U.S. Army for 21 months during the Vietnam War. He was wounded in combat, shot in the left arm and in both legs, and was one of only two survivors of battle in his 45-man platoon. Through his struggles to survive and protect his men, his treasured World Series ring was lost in the mud—forever. That one coveted representation of

the baseball player he once was, but would never be again, was now replaced by a new medal—a Purple Heart.

In recognition of his service to the nation, the Dodgers presented Gleason with a replacement 1963 World Series ring at a pregame ceremony in 2003, noting at the time that Roy Gleason holds the highest batting average in Dodgers history—a

perfect 1.000. Emotional and deeply honored, one could sense that Ray Gleason was indeed at ease—at last.

Veterans of America's current conflicts such as Desert Storm and Iraq also serve and play baseball with passion in their spare time. Navy pilot Lt. Commander Terry Allvord saw the importance of baseball as an essential element to morale, discipline, and hope. The U.S. Military All-Stars are servicemen and women from all branches who give up their leave time to play baseball, paying the cost out of their own pockets. Unlike World War II, where the players were flown from event to event by the government, the U.S. Military All Stars choose not to accept government money; they want the government to spend all funds for those serving in the War on Terror.

In 1990, then–Aviation Candidate Allvord had the honor of escorting President George H. W. Bush in Pensacola, Florida, and the conversation quickly turned to baseball. It was a subject for which both naval aviators held a deep passion. Bush mentioned how in his day, "Military base-

ball helped them pass the time, feel a sense of home, and gave them hope." Then the president asked how the current Navy team was doing.

"We don't have a (base) team, Mr. President," Allvord answered. The president was disappointed. "Someone should start a team," answered the former Yale baseball captain. Allvord agreed, and the U.S. Military All-Stars were born. In nearly two decades, those original teams grew to more than 35 single-service teams worldwide. Allvord selected players from those teams and the best players from worldwide tryouts to create the first and only combined armed forces team, U.S. Military All-Stars.

Players from the U.S. Military All-Stars were among those who pulled Saddam Hussein from the depths of a spider hole in Iraq. Allvord notes, "There is something unique, something special, when an evil dictator is pulled out of his hole by a liberator, but the fact it was also one of our players makes it even better." These men are more than willing to give up their cherished free time to represent their country on and off the field. Former Dodgers farm hand and U.S. Military All-Star second baseman Ray Judy USN has a simple answer about playing baseball in the armed forces: "We love baseball, but we love our country more."

This uniquely American legacy continues.

LIFE DURING THE
GREAT CIVILIZATIONS

Ancient Persia

Don Nardo

**BLACKBIRCH®
PRESS**

San Diego • Detroit • New York • San Francisco • Cleveland • New Haven, Conn. • Waterville, Maine • London • Munich

© 2003 by Blackbirch Press™. Blackbirch Press™ is an imprint of The Gale Group, Inc.,
a division of Thomson Learning, Inc.

Blackbirch Press™ and Thomson Learning™ are trademarks used herein under license.

For more information, contact
The Gale Group, Inc.
27500 Drake Rd.
Farmington Hills, MI 48331-3535
Or you can visit our Internet site at http://www.gale.com

Photo credits on page 47

LIBRARY OF CONGRESS CATALOGING-IN-PUBLICATION DATA

Nardo, Don, 1947-
  Ancient Persia / by Don Nardo.
     p. cm. — (Life during the great civilizations)
Includes bibliographical references and index.
Contents: A short-lived but influential empire — Society dominated by a privileged
few — Lifestyles of the rich and poor — Religious beliefs and practices — Large-scale
engineering projects.
  ISBN 1-56711-740-6
  1. Iran—Juvenile literature. [1. Iran—Civilization—To 640.] I. Title. II. Series.

DS254.75.N37 2004
935—dc21   2003009286

Printed in United States
10 9 8 7 6 5 4 3 2 1

Contents

INTRODUCTION

A Short-Lived but Influential Empire

The heartland of ancient Persia was the region today occupied by Iran and Iraq. It included the Plateau of Iran, a large area of rugged hills and valleys northeast of the Persian Gulf. The Persians also controlled Mesopotamia. Lying northwest of the gulf, this mainly flat region contains the Tigris and Euphrates Rivers. It was in Mesopotamia that the world's first cities rose in the fourth millennium B.C. (more than five thousand years ago). A series of peoples and cultures rose and fell in the area over the course of many centuries. These included the Sumerians, Babylonians, Assyrians, and others.

In the sixth century B.C., still another people rose to prominence in the region—the Persians. Led by a vigorous and ambitious king, Cyrus II, they quickly built a mighty empire. It stretched from the Mediterranean coast in the west to the borders of India in the east. Under

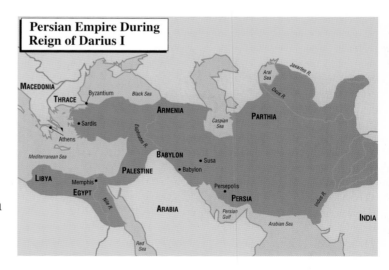

Persian Empire During Reign of Darius I

Opposite Page: Mount Zagros is one of many low peaks in Iran's rugged uplands.

Cyrus's successors, the realm continued to expand. Egypt fell under Persian domination. So did a number of Greek cities in western Asia Minor (the area occupied by modern Turkey).

Contact with the Greeks ultimately proved to be Persia's undoing, however. Persian armies under King Darius I and his son, Xerxes, invaded mainland Greece in the early 400s B.C. The Greeks delivered them one crushing defeat after another. The Persians suffered more

Cyrus the Great, founder of the Persian Empire, ruled from 550 to 530 B.C.

defeats in the century that followed, when Alexander the Great led a Greek army into Persia. In 330 B.C., the last Persian king, Darius III, died while fleeing the invaders. At that moment, the Persian Empire founded by Cyrus ceased to exist, and its lands became part of Alexander's own empire.

The Persian Empire did not last long—only a little more than two centuries. Its cultural influence remained strong in the ages that followed, however. In A.D. 224, a local Iranian leader named Ardas founded the Sassanian dynasty in the region. The Sassanians emphasized old Persian customs and made the old Persian religion supreme. In the 600s, Arab armies defeated the Sassanians and introduced a new religion, Islam. Yet Islamic culture, which still dominates the area, retained strong elements of Sassanian art, architecture, and laws. In this way, some aspects of ancient Persian culture survived into the modern era.

This ancient mosaic shows a battle between the forces of Alexander and Darius III.

CHAPTER ONE

Society Dominated by a Privileged Few

The study of ancient Persian society has been a challenge for historians because little information has survived about Persian social customs and everyday life. Scholars do, however, know that there were actually two Persian societies. The first was made up of the few thousand well-to-do nobles who ruled the empire. More than 90 percent of the surviving information concerns their lives and customs. This is because Persian writings were compiled mainly by and for members of the upper classes.

Another major source of information consists of descriptions of Persian society in the works of ancient Greek writers. In particular, the fifth-century B.C. historian Herodotus provided some useful information about Persian social classes and customs. Yet he, too, concentrated primarily on the upper classes.

The other Persian society was made up of the millions of people in the lower classes. Whether free or slave, with only a few exceptions, they were extremely poor. Farmhands, animal herders, servants, and laborers, they worked from sunup to sundown for few material rewards. Most died before they were forty and left behind no traces of their existence, not even their names.

Moreover, their lives were no different from those of their parents, grandparents, and earlier ancestors. Indeed, the same way of life had existed in the region of Mesopotamia (centered in what is now Iraq) for thousands of years. During those many centuries, various ruling classes had come and gone. The Sumerians, Akkadians,

Opposite Page: This modern drawing depicts ancient Persian noblemen displaying their weapons.

Babylonians, Assyrians, Medes, and their empires had risen and fallen in and around Mesopotamia. Yet life for most people, often including the rulers themselves, had changed little. Therefore, Persian society was in many ways a continuation of traditional Mesopotamian society.

In fact, Herodotus claimed that the Persian upper classes borrowed much of their culture from older Middle Eastern peoples. "No race is so ready to adopt foreign ways as the Persian," he wrote.[1] Persian nobles adopted the clothing styles of the Medes, for example. The military and political ideas of the Persians were based closely on those of the Assyrians. Also, rich Persians ran their large farming estates the same way Babylonian nobles had.

The King and His Court

Such borrowings can readily be seen in the social customs and rankings of the Persian royal court and privileged upper classes. At the top of the social ladder was the king. He, his family, and his close advisers lived in splendor in magnificent palaces and mansions. When he held court, the king wore a long purple robe and a crown filled with priceless jewels. He also wore golden chains, earrings, and bracelets. Another luxury was a special purple carpet that only he was allowed to walk on. Furthermore, when

This golden drinking cup decorated with a winged lion belonged to a Persian noble.

anyone, even a noble, approached the king, that person had to lie face-down on the floor and avoid eye contact. The Greeks who witnessed this act viewed it as degrading.

The king also kept his distance from social inferiors during dinners and parties given in the palace. According to a Greek eyewitness:

> Of the king's guests, some dine outside in full view of the public, others indoors with the king. But even the latter do not dine with the king. There

Male Persian Vanity

The fourth-century B.C. Greek writer Xenophon wrote a treatise about the Persian king Cyrus II. The work includes some information about the social customs of the upper classes. This excerpt tells some of the ways that vain rich men tried to enhance their appearance.

"He [Cyrus] chose to wear the Median dress himself and persuaded his associates also to adopt it; for he thought that if anyone had any personal defect, that dress would help to conceal it, and that it made the wearer look very tall and very handsome. For they have shoes of such a form that without being detected the wearer can easily put something into the soles so as to make him look taller than he is. He encouraged also the fashion of penciling the

This detail of an enameled brick panel shows a fashionable Persian noble who penciled his eyes.

eyes, that they might seem more lustrous [gleaming] than they are, and of using cosmetics to make the complexion look better than nature made it."

are two apartments opposite one another, and the king breakfasts in one while his fellow diners are in another. The king can see them through the curtain in the doorway, but they cannot see him. Occasionally, however, on a feast day, they all dine in one room with the king.... If, as often happens, the king has a drinking party, up to a dozen guests may be called into his presence.... They drink with him, but not the same wine, and they sit on the floor while he reclines on a couch with gold feet.[2]

The Nobles

Occupying the rung directly below that of the king on the social ladder were Persia's chief nobles. Each had a large country estate. By law, all land in the empire belonged to the king; but by custom, he gave parcels to the nobles who served as officers in his armies. In return, each estate owner was obligated to supply a certain number

This relief sculpture shows two Persian nobles greeting each other. Nearly all Persian men wore full beards.

of men and weapons for the military. The lord of a "bow land" supplied one or more archers. Similarly, a noble who lived on a "chariot land" contributed one or more chariots, along with drivers.

Thanks to their money and high social status, these nobles enjoyed lives of comfort and privilege. They saw themselves as better than others (with the exception of the king). According to Herodotus, "Themselves they consider in every way superior to everyone else in the world."[3] The nobles usually viewed one another as equals, however. This could be seen in their customary greetings. "When Persians meet in the streets," said Herodotus, "one can always tell by their mode of greeting whether or not they are of the same rank. For they do not speak, but kiss their equals upon the mouth."[4]

Not surprisingly, both the nobles and king desired to keep the privileged class from growing smaller and weaker. The solution was to have as many babies as possible, especially boys, since society was male dominated. Herodotus explained:

> Every [upper-class] man has a number of wives.... After prowess in fighting, the chief proof of manliness is to be the father of a large family of boys. Those who have the most sons receive an annual present from the king—on the principle that there is strength in numbers.[5]

Women and the Lower Classes

Much less is known about the other Persian social classes than about the nobles. Because of the social prominence of boys and men, for example, little information survives about Persian women. That men could have multiple wives indicates that women were considered inferior to men. Also, the Greek sources claim that Persian wives spent most of their time secluded in the home. Yet evidence from Persian sources suggests that women were allowed to keep their personal property after a divorce. (It is unclear, however, whether a wife could

In this ancient mosaic, a women plays the harp, probably to entertain some nobles.

sue her husband for divorce.) Also, royal and other upper-class women could own land.

In contrast, lower-class women, and most lower-class men as well, could not own land. Many toiled as field workers, maids, and cooks on the nobles' wealthy estates. A few of these laborers were free people who received small wages. Most, however, were either slaves or serfs. A Persian serf was a free person who was allowed to live and work on a small plot of a nobleman's land in exchange for giving the nobleman a large portion of the harvest. Always in debt, serfs became almost totally dependent on their landlords and often had worse lives than many slaves. Household slaves, for instance, were generally well fed and treated humanely. On occasion, a master would even free a slave. The downside was that the slave remained poor and could not own land. Clearly, the Persian social system kept the poor masses in their place and allowed a select few to possess nearly all the power, prestige, and privilege.

CHAPTER TWO

Lifestyles of the Rich and Poor

The huge difference in wealth between Persia's nobles and peasants created markedly contrasting lifestyles. The poor lived in small homes with no luxuries. For them, life was a constant struggle simply to keep clothed and fed. In contrast, the rich dwelled in large, comfortable houses with fine furniture and decorations, and they had servants who waited on them hand and foot.

The King's Residence

Most comfortable of all was the Persian king. He had several palaces to choose from; one of the finest was located in the capital of Persepolis, northeast of the Persian Gulf. The structure rested on a flat stone terrace 1,400 feet long and 1,000 feet wide. Two grand staircases led from ground level to the terrace. Each was 23 feet wide and had 111 steps. On the great terrace were many splendid buildings, among them the vast audience hall, or *apadana*, where the king greeted his subjects and guests. The palace walls were highly decorated. Everywhere could be seen carved figures and scenes painted in bright colors in imitation of Assyrian and Babylonian art.

The king could stroll from building to building in complete safety. This was because a regiment of specially trained soldiers, called the Immortals, lived right on the premises. In an inscription, King Darius I recognized the importance of his soldiers. "From no

Opposite Page: This stairway (lower right) is one of two that led to the audience hall of the palace at Persepolis.

enemy let me fear," he said. As long as his army remained strong, prosperity "shall descend upon this house."[6]

This grand palace may have been created mainly for the king to conduct state business. His actual residence was probably situated in the town that once surrounded the great terrace. Archaeologists have discovered the foundations of a large house near the palace. The house had many rooms, a large garden, and a small artificial lake. Some experts think this was the private mansion of King Xerxes, who led Persia's second invasion of Greece.

Houses of the Well-to-Do

Other large town houses existed near the king's residence. These belonged to the king's leading nobles. Some were high palace officials, military generals, and royal ambassadors. Others had no profession, since they did not need a job to make money. All of the nobles made substantial livings from the revenues produced by the large farming estates they owned.

Their town houses were usually constructed of the best bricks available. These were made by combining mud and clay with straw and then baking the mixture in a kiln until it hardened. Such houses usually followed a plan in which most of the rooms surrounded a roofless central courtyard. Inside the front door was a roofed foyer. From there, one stepped down into the open courtyard. It was paved, with the stones slanted very slightly to make rainwater flow away into a drain.

Among the rooms clustered around the courtyard on the ground floor was a kitchen. It had one or more wood-burning hearths for cooking. The pots and pans were made of copper, the plates and cups of ceramics. Other ground-floor rooms included a dining room, bathroom, one

These walls, constructed of baked bricks, were found in the Persian city of Susa.

or more guest rooms, storage space, and servants' quarters. A flight of stairs led to the second story. There, a corridor led to the family bedrooms. The house was well furnished, with couches, tables, chairs, carpets, and draperies on walls, around doorways, and on window frames.

Houses and Jobs of Poor City Folk

Each of these spacious, comfortable houses was surrounded by a high wall made of baked bricks. Such walls provided privacy for the well-to-do people who dwelled in these houses. The walls also separated the rich from the poor. The houses of poorer city families, which crowded around the nicer homes, were much smaller, less private, and less comfortable. The average city house consisted of three or four tiny, windowless, and sparsely furnished chambers. These rooms often surrounded a small inner courtyard. It was also common for a house to share one or more walls with neighboring homes.

The people who lived in these modest city homes worked in a variety of jobs. Some walked outside the town each morning and toiled in the surrounding fields. Others worked inside the city walls. A few were shopkeepers and potters. Many others worked in small factories, essentially large workrooms, where they made carpets, clothes, and other items by hand.

Farmers and Their Huts

The dwellings of poor country folk were even less substantial than those of poor townspeople. Most farmers lived in small huts. Some of these structures were made from sun-dried mud bricks. The sun-dried bricks were less expensive and considerably less sturdy and durable than the baked variety. The result was that houses made of sun-dried bricks rapidly began to crumble and needed constant repairs.

Darius Brags About His Palace

This is part of an inscription found at another of Darius's palaces, in Susa, not far north of the Persian Gulf. In it the king bragged about the structure and the many foreign materials and workers he gathered to erect it.

"This is the palace I built at Susa. From afar, its ornamentation [decorations] was brought. Deep down the earth was dug, until rock bottom I reached. When the excavation was made, gravel was packed down, one part sixty . . . feet in depth. On that gravel a palace I built. . . . The cedar timber was brought from a mountain named Lebanon. The Assyrians brought it to Babylon, and from Babylon the Carians . . . brought it to Susa. Teakwood was brought from Gandara. . . . The gold which was used here was brought from Sardis and from Bactria. . . . The silver and copper were brought from Egypt. . . . The ivory was brought from Ethiopia. . . . The artisans who dressed the stone were Ionians and Sardians. The goldsmiths . . . were Medes and Egyptians. . . . Those who worked the baked brick were Babylonians."

The farmers who lived in these huts grew a variety of crops. The most important was barley, a type of wheat. Part of an old Mesopotamian almanac, which gives tips on growing barley, has survived. It advises the farmer:

> Keep your eye on the man who puts in the barley seed. Let him drop the grain uniformly two inches deep. . . . If the barley seed does not sink in properly, [adjust the front of the] plow. . . . [Do not] let the barley bend over on itself. Harvest it at the moment [of its full] strength.[7]

People crushed the barley grains into flour, from which they made a flat bread, one of the staple foods of the Middle East. They also made a thick porridge from barley grains. Other common food crops included beans, peas, lentils, lettuce, figs, and grapes.

Hunters of the Marshlands

As poor as they were, those farmers who lived in brick houses were fortunate compared to their even poorer neighbors. Many peasants, especially in the marshy areas near the rivers, had one-room huts made from plant stems. They collected the stems into bundles. Then they stuck the bottoms of the bundles into holes dug in the ground. After bending the bundles

The farmers' most important crop was barley (pictured), from which a popular flat bread was made.

over and tying them together at the top, they filled in the spaces with mats made of reeds or with packed mud.

Most of the people who lived in such huts made their living by hunting in the marshes. Mostly, they caught fish and waterbirds, such as herons and ducks. The hunters constructed their boats with the same river reeds that they used to make their houses. When stalking prey, a hunter stood up in his boat. His weapon was a bamboo pole with a metal tip.

Little else is known about the poor farmers and hunters who made up the bulk of the population of the Persian Empire. This is hardly surprising. Their houses and few belongings were highly perishable, and over time almost all traces of them disappeared. Meanwhile, the nobles left behind more substantial remains, as well as writings, which later revealed at least a small glimpse of their lifestyle to future generations.

These modern-day Arab boys, who live in the marshlands along the Iran-Iraq border, live much like the peasants of ancient Persia did.

CHAPTER THREE

Religious Beliefs and Practices

The Persian Empire had no single religion followed by all or most of its inhabitants because the realm was huge and diverse. It was made up of Medes, Babylonians, Jews, Egyptians, and dozens of other subject peoples conquered by the Persian king and his army. Each of these peoples worshipped one or more of their own gods. The Egyptians, for example, were polytheistic, which means that they worshipped multiple gods. They had a pantheon, or group of gods, that included Ra, Osiris, and Isis. The Jews, by contrast, were monotheists. They worshipped a single god, named Jehovah. Persian leaders did not try to overturn these deities or impose their own beliefs on the subject peoples.

These native Persian beliefs came from Iran. Once a subject people of the Medes, the Persians had originated in Fars, a small region of southern Iran. They adopted the prevailing religious beliefs of central and southern Iran. At first, the Iranians were polytheistic. They worshipped a series of nature gods called *daevas*. Eventually, however, they began to follow the teachings of a great prophet named Zarathushtra. He later became better known by the name the Greeks gave him—Zoroaster. The new faith was essentially monotheistic. All of Persia's kings, their nobles, and an unknown number of their subjects followed it devoutly.

Opposite Page: A modern drawing depicts the religious prophet Zoroaster, founder of Persia's main religion.

The Battle Between Good and Evil

The Zoroastrian god was Ahura-Mazda, the "wide lord." He had originally been a sky god, one of several *daevas* worshipped in early Iran. Zoroaster preached that Ahura-Mazda was the one true god. Persian artists almost always depicted the deity the same way—as a bearded man perched inside a large ring that floated in the sky with the aid of outstretched wings. In his left hand, he held a smaller ring that signified his authority over earthly kings. Meanwhile, he held his right hand palm up, to bless his followers. Two lightning bolts shot downward from the ring to demonstrate the god's great power. (The Greeks

In this ancient rock carving, the chief Persian god, Ahura-Mazda, floats in the sky.

identified Ahura-Mazda with their own god Zeus, who also wielded lightning bolts.)

One of the central tenets of the faith was that Ahura-Mazda represented goodness, truth, and light. His followers believed he could bestow peace, prosperity, and good behavior on humans. Part of a surviving prayer to the god asks him to grant the lowly and weak person "strength, righteousness, and . . . good thought, whereby he may establish pleasant dwellings and peace. I [believe], Mazda, that you can bring this to pass."[8]

Another chief concept of the Zoroastrian faith was that Ahura-Mazda was engaged in an eternal struggle with evil. That evil took the form of a dark force or being called Ahriman. The evil one's chief followers were the old *daevas*, now seen as wicked demons and spirits. Ahura-Mazda's forces of truth (or order) were always at war with Ahriman's forces of untruth, called the lie (or disorder). Good, worthy people who followed the way of truth were known as *ashavans*, while corrupt people who followed the lie were called *drugvans*.

Animals Killed in God's Name

Very little is known about the actual rituals of Zoroastrian worship in ancient Persia. Of the few surviving sources that describe these rituals, that of Herodotus is the most important. He got some of his facts secondhand, so his account is probably not totally accurate. Still, for the most part, it is informative and illuminating.

According to Herodotus, some Zoroastrian priests (there may have been others) were called Magi. Apparently, a Magus always performed or was present during the important ritual of sacrifice. This was an offering made to Ahura-Mazda, usually an animal that was killed to give a god extra nourishment. Herodotus does not say how the animal, called the victim, was killed. Probably the manner was similar to that

In this illustration, a group of Zoro-astrian priests, called Magi, examine some written records.

of the Greeks, who used a club to stun the beast, then slit its throat with a knife. Before the start of a Persian sacrifice, Herodotus wrote,

> a man sticks a spray of leaves, usually myrtle leaves, into his headdress, takes his victim to some open place and invokes [calls upon] the deity. . . . The actual worshiper is not permitted to pray for any personal or private blessing, but only for the king and the general good of the community. . . . When he has cut up the animal and cooked it, he makes a little heap of the softest green-stuff he can find, preferably clover, and lays all the meat upon it. This done, a Magus . . . utters an incantation [magic spell] over it. . . . Then, after a short interval, the worshiper removes the flesh and does what he pleases with it.[9]

In addition to performing sacrifice and other rituals, the Magi indulged in some beliefs and practices that the Greeks and others viewed as odd or extreme. For example, the Magi preached that cattle and dogs were good. In contrast, they insisted, many other animals were vile followers of Ahriman and therefore must be killed. "The Magi are a peculiar caste [group]," Herodotus pointed out,

> quite different from the Egyptian priests and indeed from any other sort of person. The Egyptian priests make it an article of religion to kill no living creature except for sacrifice, but the Magi not only kill anything . . . with their own hands, but make a special point of doing so. Ants, snakes, animals, birds—no matter what, they kill them.[10]

Burial Customs

Another unusual custom practiced by the Magi was the gruesome way they dealt with dead bodies. When a Magus died, his companions left his corpse outside to be eaten by dogs, birds, and other animals. The reason for this is unclear. According to Herodotus, the custom "is not spoken of openly and is something of a mystery."[11]

What is more certain is that not all Zoroastrian Persians followed this practice. Preferring to keep the body intact after death, most people covered it in wax to preserve it, and then buried it. The well-to-do could afford to place the waxed body in a stone tomb. King Darius I,

The bodies of Persian priests were left outside, exposed to the elements and animals.

Reverence for Ahura-Mazda

According to tradition, the great god Ahura-Mazda appeared to the prophet Zoroaster in a dream. Overcome with awe and reverence, the prophet said in part:

"Let me arise and drive away the scorners of your doctrine, with all who bear in mind your holy words. As the Holy One, then I acknowledged you, Ahura-Mazda, when good thought once came to me, best silent thought made me proclaim: Let not man seek to please the many Liars, for they make all the righteous foes to you [i.e., liars are your enemies]…. May piety being the Kingdom that beholds the sun [i.e., Ahura-Mazda's realm of light and truth], with good thought may he assign Destiny to men for their deeds."

Ahura-Mazda floats above winged guardians in this image on a palace wall.

The tomb of King Darius I was decorated with a carving of Ahura-Mazda (near top).

for example, was placed in a stone coffin inside a chamber carved into the face of a great vertical cliff. In an inscription, the dead monarch bragged about his widespread conquests: "The spear of a Persian man has gone forth afar."[12]

The fact that the Magi had one burial ritual and other Persians another suggests that different versions of the Zoroastrian faith existed. Perhaps the Magi practiced the orthodox, or strict and conservative, version, while the king and nobles followed a less strict version. Any peasants who adhered to the faith may well have followed a third version. Until further evidence is unearthed, Persian religious practices will remain somewhat mysterious.

CHAPTER FOUR

Large-Scale Engineering Projects

Like other ancient peoples, the Persians inherited a way of life that lacked modern technology. People had no electricity and no complex machines, so everyday life was very labor intensive. All work had to be done by the muscle power of humans or animals. Messages and news had to be carried by hand and word of mouth, for instance. Also, messengers, traders, and other travelers moved through the countryside by foot, donkey, horse, or wagon. Before the Persian Empire, roads in the Middle East were few and mostly made of dirt. When it rained, they turned to mud, which impeded travel. The result was that both information and people took weeks and sometimes months to reach distant cities.

Obtaining water was another challenge. People in the ancient Middle East possessed no advanced knowledge of pipes and plumbing. This forced them to carry water for drinking, cooking, and bathing by hand from nearby rivers, wells, and other natural sources.

Fortunately for the Persians, some of the peoples they conquered had already partially overcome some of these problems. The Assyrians and Babylonians had built a few short paved roads, for example. These peoples and other Mesopotamians had also dug long water channels to irrigate crops. The imitative Persians built on these achievements. Their engineers expanded and improved the older water channels and constructed new

*Opposite Page: Donkey-drawn
carts like the one in this relief were
common in ancient Persia.*

ones. The Persian road system was even more impressive. Thousands of miles of well-made roads linked key points in the empire, which made the movement of news, mail, armies, and traders much faster and easier.

The Royal Roads

Of the many uses for the roads, carrying troops and military dispatches were most important to the Persian kings. Early on, they realized that it was imperative for armies and royal messages to move swiftly. Otherwise, it would be impossible to maintain order in and control over the many and widely spaced regions of their vast empire. Another obvious benefit of a good road system was economic in nature. Trade goods moved faster and more cheaply from one Persian province to another.

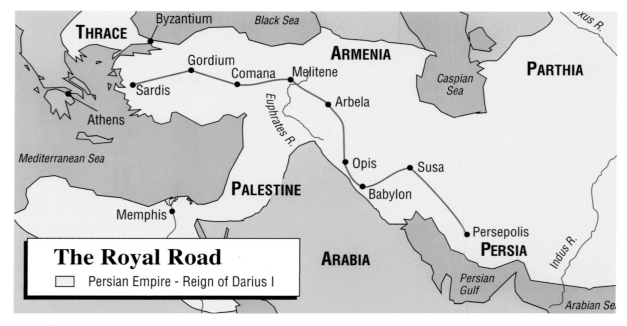

The Royal Road

☐ Persian Empire - Reign of Darius I

The roads built by the Persian kings became known appropriately as the "Royal Roads." Most of them have long since disappeared. Therefore, it is difficult to tell exactly how many there were and where they all began and ended. Luckily for modern researchers, a fair amount of information has survived about two of these roads. One stretched westward from Persepolis to Susa.

The other and longer Royal Road, built by Darius I, continued westward from Susa and went all the way to Sardis, in western Asia Minor, not far from Greece. Some sixteen hundred miles in length, it was the longest road in the world at the time. Archaeologists have studied some of the surviving sections of the road. They found that it was about twenty feet wide and had a surface made of hard-packed gravel. Uniform paving stones lined each side of the highway.

In addition to the length and high quality of the road itself, travelers benefited from many conveniences. Herodotus traveled on this road on his way to Babylon in the fifth century b.c. He later wrote

that posting stations existed every few miles along the way. Such a station had stables to care for horses and donkeys, along with fresh mounts for mail carriers. There were also places for travelers to eat and sleep, and guard posts for security. "At intervals all along the road," Herodotus said,

> are recognized stations, with excellent inns, and the road itself is safe to travel by, as it never leaves inhabited country. In Lydia and Phrygia [in Asia Minor], over a distance of ... about 330 miles—there are 20 stations. On the far side of Phrygia, one comes to the river Halys. There are gates here, which have to be passed before one crosses the river, and a strong guard-post.... The total number of stations, or post-houses, on the road from Sardis to Susa is 111.... Traveling at the rate of 150 furlongs [eighteen miles] a day, a man will take just ninety days to make the journey.[13]

Darius's Couriers

Although ordinary travelers like Herodotus took ninety days to go from Sardis to Susa, royal couriers could make it much faster. These were special horsemen established by Darius. Their job was to carry military and political dispatches from one section of the empire to another. They rode in relays and refused to stop for anything or anyone. As a result, they sped from Susa to Sardis or vice versa in only fifteen days, then seen as an incredible feat. In Herodotus's words:

> There is nothing in the world which travels faster than these Persian couriers. The whole idea is a Persian invention and works like this: Riders are stationed along the road, equal in number to the number of days the journey takes—a man and a horse for each day. Nothing keeps these riders from covering their allotted stage in the quickest possible time—neither snow, rain, heat, nor darkness. The first, at the end of his stage, passes the dispatch to the second, the second to the third, and so on along the line.[14]

Persian couriers likely looked like the rider depicted in this bronze figurine.

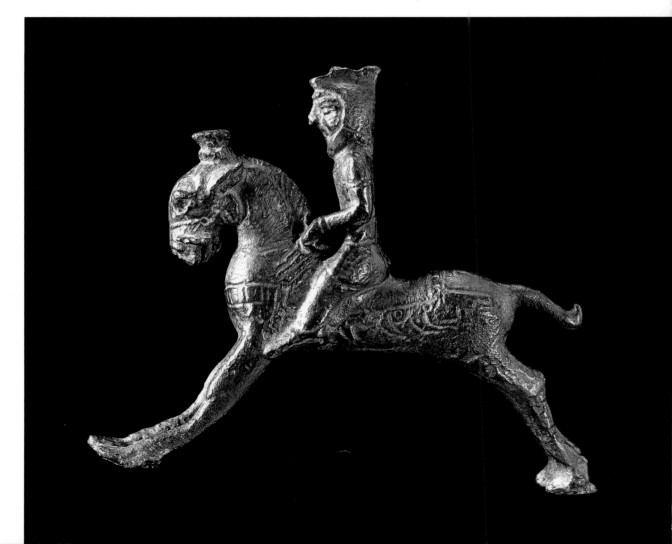

Xerxes's Canal

In his account of the canal constructed by Xerxes through part of the Athos peninsula (in northern Greece), Herodotus wrote:

"Men of the various nations of which the [Persian] army was composed were sent over in shifts to Athos, where they were put to the work of cutting a canal.... I will now describe how the canal was cut. The ground was divided into sections ... on a line taped across the [peninsula]....

When the trench reached a certain depth, the laborers at the bottom carried on with the digging and passed the soil up to the others above them, who stood on terraces

Xerxes ordered his workers to dig a canal through this site in northern Greece.

and passed it on to another lot, still higher up, until it reached the men at the top, who carried it away and dumped it."

Canals and Aqueducts

Another impressive engineering feat completed by Darius was a canal that linked the Mediterranean Sea to the Red Sea and Indian Ocean beyond. It covered a distance of about 125 miles. The canal increased trade and prosperity in Egypt and Palestine, and it remained in use off and on for more than a thousand years. Darius's son, Xerxes, also built a large waterway. Just before he invaded Greece in 480 B.C., Xerxes ordered his engineers and workers to dig a canal through part of the Athos peninsula, in northern Greece. Herodotus claimed that two warships traveling side-by-side could pass through at the same time.

These holes in the Iranian desert lead to underground aqueducts.

A different kind of large-scale water project overseen by the Persians was to maintain and improve the underground aqueducts built by earlier Mesopotamian peoples. An aqueduct is an artificial channel that carries water from a lake or other source to distant fields and towns. The Persians called such a channel a *kariz*. (The Arab name, *qan*, is better known.)

To construct a *qan*, the workers dug two vertical shafts. Then they climbed down and dug a horizontal shaft that connected the bottoms of the vertical ones. The water flowed through this horizontal shaft. To lengthen the channel, they sank more vertical shafts and continued to connect them. Some of these waterways were many miles long and supplied badly needed water to irrigate fields in parched areas. Though the Persians did not invent these aqueducts, they introduced them to less developed areas of their huge realm. Their effective use of massive amounts of manpower in large-scale engineering projects remained unmatched until the Romans surpassed them a few centuries later.

Notes

Chapter 1: Society Dominated by a Privileged Few

1. Herodotus, *The Histories*, trans. Aubrey de Selincourt. New York: Penguin, 1972, p. 97.
2. Athenaeus, *Authorities on Banquets*, quoted in J.M. Cook, *The Persian Empire*. London: Dent, 1983, p. 139.
3. Herodotus, *Histories*, p. 97.
4. Herodotus, *Histories*, p. 97.
5. Herodotus, *Histories*, pp. 97–98.

Chapter 2: Lifestyles of the Rich and Poor

6. Quoted in A.T. Olmstead, *History of the Persian Empire*. Chicago: University of Chicago Press, 1948, p. 175.
7. Quoted in Samuel N. Kramer, *Cradle of Civilization*. New York: Time-Life, 1967, p. 84.

Chapter 3: Religious Beliefs and Practices

8. Quoted in Olmstead, *History of the Persian Empire*, p. 97.
9. Herodotus, *Histories*, p. 96.
10. Herodotus, *Histories*, p. 99.
11. Herodotus, *Histories*, p. 99.
12. Quoted in Olmstead, *History of the Persian Empire*, p. 229.

Chapter 4: Large-Scale Engineering Projects

13. Herodotus, *Histories*, pp. 359–60.
14. Herodotus, *Histories*, p. 556.

Glossary

apadana: The audience hall of an ancient Persian or Mesopotamian palace.

aqueduct: A channel that carries water from a lake or other water source to distant cities and fields. The Persians called such a channel a *kariz*; the Arabs called it a *qan*.

ashavans: In the Zoroastrian faith, followers of truth.

ceramics: Objects made of baked clay.

couriers: Message or mail carriers.

daevas: Early Iranian gods; in the Zoroastrian faith, evil demons and spirits.

drugvans: In the Zoroastrian faith, followers of "the lie."

dynasty: A family line of rulers.

inscription: One or more words carved into a durable material, such as stone or metal.

monotheist: Someone who worships a single god.

orthodox: In the religious sense, strict and conservative.

pantheon: A group of gods worshipped by a people.

polytheist: Someone who worships multiple gods.

posting station: On a road, a facility that offers services such as fresh horses, wagon repairs, and food and water for people and animals.

sacrifice: An offering made to appease a god or gods.

serf: A person who lived and worked on a small plot of land in exchange for turning over a share of the harvest to the landlord.

For More Information

Books

Michael W. Davison, ed., *Everyday Life Through the Ages*. London: Reader's Digest Association, 1992.

Samuel N. Kramer, *Cradle of Civilization*. New York: Time-Life, 1967.

Harold Lamb, *Cyrus the Great*. Garden City, NY: Doubleday, 1960.

Hazel M. Martell, *The Ancient World: From the Ice Age to the Fall of Rome*. New York: Kingfisher, 1995.

Don Nardo, *The Persian Empire*. San Diego: Lucent Books, 1997.

Websites

The Persians, History for Kids (www.historyforkids.org/learn/westasia/history/persians.htm). This Worthwhile site has a brief summary of Persian history, supplemented by several color photos of Persian ruins and several links to related topics.

Persia, the International History Project (http://ragz-international.com/persians.htm). A brief but informative overview of Persian history, with numerous links to related topics.

The Qanats of Iran, Scientific American (http://users.bart.nl/ ~ leenders/txt/qanats.html). A detailed look at the underground water channels constructed in Mesopotamia by the Persians and others. The reading level is challenging.

Index

Picture Credits

About the Author

Historian Don Nardo has published many volumes about the ancient world, including The Ancient Greeks, The Roman Empire, Greek and Roman Sport, and histories of the Persian and Assyrian Empires. He lives in Massachusetts with his wife, Christine.